I will not be pushed, filed, stamped, indexed, briefed, debriefed or numbered, my life is my own.

The Prisoner, 1967

... when you have only a very few cubic meters to yourself and your innermost feelings, that private space must be subjected to the severest discipline if it is to withstand the dissolution, destruction, and pressure to yield coming from all sides.

Peter Hoeg's *Miss Smilla's Feeling for Snow*

SHOWMEN

The Voice of Travelling Fair People

Sally Festing

SHAUN TYAS
DONINGTON
2012

.

Published by

SHAUN TYAS
1 High Street
Donington
Lincolnshire
PE11 4TA

ISBN
978-1-907730-18-4

Quotation from Peter Hoeg's *Miss Smilla's Feeling for Snow*,
published Harvill Secker, reprinted by permission of the
Random House Group Ltd.

Printed in Great Britain by the Lavenham Press,
Lavenham, Suffolk

CONTENTS

FOR BERNARD AND CARLA

FOREWORD

Everyone has been to a fair. Showmen as they call themselves – men, women and children, are part of many people's lives, yet few know much about *theirs*. They are, as it were, a hidden society. Until thirty years ago, the Community was almost closed to outsiders except for inter-marriage, usually by showmen to girls met in the course of business. Roots went deep, sons and daughters didn't often leave. There was a solidarity about the group born out of mutual striving that instilled such a fierce sense of identity, that even the settled component – known in their telltale idiom as 'sandscratchers', 'sandsneakers' or sometimes, 'sanddancers' – tended to behave as if they still belonged: "They don't travel any more they just dance on the sands" (attributed to Fred Warren in Vanessa Toulmin's 'Fun without Vulgarity: Community, Women and Language in Showland Society', unpublished Ph.D thesis at Sheffield University's National Fairground Archive, 1977). Much of this remains true. Sandscratchers can retain a trailer on the showmen's quarters, or a ride and its fairground rights. They can even hold a position in the Showmen's Guild, a body that protects the interests of its members. Offered such freedoms, successive generations are often lured back to the fairground.

My quest began at Wells-next-the-Sea where a few showmen moved into houses in the 1960s after annual visits with their fairs. I enquired in the Library and contacted the Local History Society; no one, it seemed, knew much about the former travellers who owned shops and amusement arcades along the west end of the harbour. But a friend knew one of them. This man was very industrious, she said. Shy to outsiders, he might none-the-less be persuaded to speak to me about his early life. From then on there was a natural progression; the settled fair people passed me to the travelling contingent, so that when I produced a voice-recorder those who spoke with me were not obviously wary.

Showmen are instinctively sensitive about the way they are presented in the media. A series of programmes on 'Five' television in the autumn of 2011 showed some aspects of their ways, but colourful coverage of three affluent families can't be said to represent the hundreds of showmen with smaller attractions, some of whom were embarrassed by the portrayal made in their name. What I learned from my interviewees was full of surprises. Recordings are perhaps the best means of reconstructing a person's mental maps, their enthusiasms, their spirit. It became my mission to learn how the bonds among fairpeople are shaped and retained. I don't want to make of them something they are not. Bertoldt Brecht

1

observed cryptically that 'The People has no wish to be Folk'. It's a tendency I'd like to think I have avoided by making their words the foundation of this work.

Fair people slip in and out of society with their own rules and rituals, it is at least debatable that they have survived as long as they have by being private and having their own methods of communicating which are not much shared with the rest of us. As always, their relationship with the public is crucial, and maintaining it is a tentative game, one that needs juggling faster every year as changes in society speed up and historic fairs continue to be closed down. Only after protracted consultation with the Guild did Cambridge County Council agree to the Midsummer fair being held in 2010, the year before its 800th anniversary.

* * *

Transience undoubtedly contributes to the sense of wonder fairs inspire. You don't associate them with the avant-garde although Angela Carter drew stories from them, John Burnside has written poems, and the Whitechapel Gallery celebrated fairground architecture. It may not be without relevance that composer Maurice Ravel's father was a designer among other things, of fairground rides. There are plenty of well-illustrated, densely written books about showmen's apparatus, and no shortage of posters, family histories, photographs and, latterly, oral tapes about them. These have a market in people already interested in fairs, often for genealogical reasons. But renewed interest in authenticity, markets and leisure has not brought showmen the same attention as other travelling communities.

Vanessa Toulmin's *Pleasurelands* (National Fairground Archive, University of Sheffield, 2003) supports history with oral recordings in an invaluable factual account of showmen that supported an exhibition, although nothing has fully updated Duncan Dallas' study *The Travelling People* (Macmillan, 1971) in the last forty years. Dallas was a producer, chiefly of documentary films. It was his work on a film about the fairground which led to the book, yet even his work tends to see the present in terms of the past. Tradition and ceremony are hugely important, especially among showmen from families long established in the business. At the same time, I have sought to uncover what it is like for them to live from day to day, bringing in the past only as it manifests itself in the present; in a thought, a motion, a desire, a reaction to an external event.

Yorkshire's travelling fair people may feel they are the cream. The Midlander might reckon that even fourteen acres of fun at Hull in early October don't compare with Nottingham Goose Fair. Notwithstanding, I have stuck loosely to East Anglia because it is where I live and know best. Showmen's strong affinity with one another throughout the UK suggests the pattern is repeated in varying shades. I have spoken at length with 35 present or one-time showmen and show-women, a chief borough planning officer and the General Secretary of

2

the Showman's Guild, and called upon the expertise of many others.

The assistance of fairground historian Graham Downie has been invaluable. Not only has he looked through the whole manuscript, he supplied some of the reference notes, contributed a large proportion of the glossary and answered continual requests for information and contacts. Clive Brown of the Showmen's Guild's Eastern section let me copy parts of his Thurston family tree; he and Jane have also extended contacts for me. Vanessa Toulmin of Sheffield University's National Fairground Archive checked an early version of chapter 2, and alive to the interest of the work, Nick Sign printed a long excerpt from the manuscript in the *Suffolk Review* (Autumn 2010, Suffolk Local History Council, pp. 19–35). I would like to thank Tessa Newcomb for her vibrant cover painting, worked up from drawings at Beccles late-night shopping centre, and publisher Shaun Tyas for dogged support when there were far more lucrative ways in which he could have spent his time. Most of all my thanks go to the showmen who have talked with me in their trailers over cups of tea, sometimes with the flurry of business fast around them. Every year brings changes in the Community, individual and personal as well as overarching ones. Two of the shops in Wells-next-the-Sea have been sold out of showmen's families and the troublesome Arcade has been demolished. David Smith and Josie Gray won't see themselves in print. Josie Gray knew that she wouldn't be alive to read this book. I would like to remember a big-hearted show-woman who died before her time.

CHAPTER ONE – THE COMMUNITY

they've set the fair up at the harbour's edge ...
The rides look pale and quiet in the grey
of four o'clock, and most are stalled, or vacant,
waiting for the night and mystery.[1]

John Burnside

You could spend your whole life in Leiston without realising there's a field full of showpeople living at the top of Victory Road. Everyone in the town knows this road; it is fairly central, home to local schools and various club headquarters as well as a playpark. Neighbours, of course, are aware of the funfair vehicles that slide in and out of their quarters, returning in the small hours. Residents with children might know that a smattering of fairground youngsters attend the same schools, not that showpeople's children generally mix much with outsiders, at least not out of school time. For the most part, showmen keep themselves to themselves. Still touched with the mystery that attends their presence on the fairground, they are to some extent what they have always been: the family who appear from nowhere with rides and stalls before they bundle everything into pantechnicons and, like the fair itself, they disappear. This first chapter sets showmen in the context of other travellers, the second picks out salient features of their history. Chapters 3–5 reflect my initial contact with the group. Each of the remaining chapters focuses on one or more individuals, using their words to illustrate a particular area of their lives.

The secluded nature of the yards is universal. How many of Norwich's population know that a nucleus of 60-odd families occupy a single site within a mile of the city centre? How many negotiating the M25 know that the biggest nucleus of showmen in Europe lies just north-east of the Dartford Crossing? The glint of metal is visible if you know where to look, but unless you were heading for Grangewater Country Park it is not a route you would often take. From Plymouth to Shettleston, Hetton-le-Hole to Llanelli, and another large base at Selston, showmen's yards or 'winter quarters' scatter the UK. Most are tucked away, acres of rough land on the outskirts of towns and villages where two or three generations of a family nestle among a large number of vehicles, their

---

[1] 'The Singer from The Asylum Dance', John Burnside, Jonathan Cape. Reprinted by permission of The Random House Group Ltd.

occupants safe from unwelcome guests and free to live as they please.

King's Lynn, Chelmsford, Peterborough, Wilburton, Wyton, Clacton, Claydon, Leiston, Bardwell and Bradfield St George all have their showmen. Groups of Thurstons, Buggs, and Grays overwinter in Norfolk from where they can reach the big Midland fairs as well as local ones. In comparatively rural Suffolk all the yards are associated with villages. Chance contributes to their location, anywhere a small piece of land was available and came cheap might have been snapped up. A relatively recent change is that showmen now tend to live behind a gate, often an iron paling gate, instead of homing in on a spare bit of land outside the local pub. What the sites have in common is access to fairgrounds. Selston is just off the M1, the Essex conurbation mushroomed because it is close to London's circular motorways. Like most travellers' yards it is not signposted and not on an established route. The big hidden agenda is, of course, survival. Showmen have long been wary of outsiders and there's a logic behind this since contact with society can result in depletion of the group. Survival underlies much of their strongly indoctrinated ethos, which is responsible, in turn, for the contradictions they encounter.

So who are travelling fair people? It is something they often find themselves called upon to explain, and understandably, since they are travellers by definition, yet they disown the term. 'We was proud to be travellers but then when you got the 'New Age' people calling theirselves travellers, we didn't like the way they went on in farms and fields. So we changed ourselves from travellers to showmen.'[2] To confuse the question further, they appear to outsiders to have quite a lot in common with other travelling groups. This means circus people, Irish travellers, New Age travellers, and Gypsies (Roma).[3] But one of the hallmarks of a group is that, homogeneous as it looks from the outside, to its members, it is the differences that are conspicuous: moreover differences between themselves and other travelling groups seem greater from within.

A show-woman had said I should talk to Robert Thurston; he was youngish, he had been to places. She'd alerted him and I'd rung his mobile; we had arranged to meet. I was waiting for him in a garden centre close to the yard where he lives with his wife and in-laws on the Cambridge side of Huntingdon. Which of the men milling round with cups of tea would he be? None of them, as it happened. I knew that he lived close by. It was his definite walk through the mazelike furnishings that offered a clue; the hint of being at home seen in a medium-built, brown-haired, clean-faced man.

---

[2]   David Remblance, chapter 13.

[3]   In the Afterword to the second (2009) edition of Isobel Fonseca's *Bury Me Standing*, Chatto, 1995, the author writes of disagreement about the term 'Roma' which I use, as she occasionally does, interchangeably with 'Gypsy'. The terms are now commonly used together, as considered less discriminatory than 'Gypsy' on its own.

Come Christmas, the Robert Thurstons dress up as 'elves' to play host in the garden centre. It is the sort of activity showmen have always taken on in wintertime, more refined perhaps than traditional alternatives. At any rate, Robert was familiar with the place and felt relaxed there. Outside a fairground, it wouldn't be easy to pick him out by his trade but he *is* 'every inch a showman': practical, businesslike, versatile and easy with people. From time to time he attends fairs with his Matterhorn, mostly in East Anglia. Twice he drove *en famille*, four up, with a member of staff, right across France to try his luck in what is known as Gibraltar Week. The rest of the time his trailer is parked some 50 feet from his father-in-law's chalet in a 35-acre yard.

Robert Thurston's identity is extremely important to him. He is indignant that people don't distinguish showmen from other types of traveller, indignant because the Thurston clan, relatively young, started in the mid-nineteenth century, making four generations of showpeople behind him. Proud of this, he doesn't want to be associated with people who denigrate the esteem he reckons his group deserves:

> I'm a Mason in a lodge at Sandy. I'm the only travelling showman and it's quite surprising, you go in there and you have to educate them. I say I'm a showman. They say what's that? I say fairgrounds, and they look me up and down, and think hold on a minute ... People don't realise we're mobile businessmen. I say what do *you* do?

The showman gets on with things. Everybody works from the moment they have the strength to fit a shoulder beneath a piece of equipment to the day they virtually fall under it. Nobody could reasonably argue for the preservation of traditional ways. To do so would be to forget that showmen led lives in which the burden of physical work was oppressive but the job means who they are, what they are worth, entitlement to that modicum of respect, of self-esteem, of legitimacy in a culture where they don't really have a secure place. You might get a circus person or one of the more trendy Roma calling themselves mobile businessman. The only group Robert's definition eliminates with certainty would be New Age travellers, which is why we need to consider travellers in general before looking at showmen more or less as they might see themselves.

'Traveller is a generic term defining diverse cultural and ethnic communities who have a similar, essentially mobile way of life', a website informs. 'They have in common, strong social networks, whether in housing or in trailers. They live within close-knit communities with distinct traditions around cleanliness and gender, and often travel, but each has its own patterns of movement, history and aspirations for the future.'[4]

[4]   www.plymouth.gov.uk/gypsy_and_traveller_culture.pdf

CHAPTER ONE – THE COMMUNITY

Needless to say, nomadic people fare badly in the face of conformity, colonization and constraint, especially legislation that directly or indirectly enforces a more sedentary life. Thanks to robust endurance and family ethos, showpeople have not lost their identity, access to their past, or their children. But even if they work from a single base, the balance of lives depending on the freedom to move is easily upset. Such legislation has had an enormous effect on the Roma, imposing throughout Europe, the dependency documented by Isobel Fonseca in her remarkable book about Gypsy culture.[5] Similarly, a Norfolk showman built himself a house, *only*, he asserted vigorously, when new laws against stopping[6] made it impossible to maintain the family run of fairs.[7] In general it is convenient to live on wheels, and a home on wheels is bound to be restricted in size.

A host of contingents follow, because where people live in a confined space, a culture of prohibitions evolves around sanitation which makes outsiders' habits seem unwholesome. Groups tend to adopt some values as sacred – rites and rituals make them stronger and more assertive. Moreover, taboos against the possibility of contamination have a metaphorical parallel in the risk of being invaded by strangers. Like showmen, most travellers live on the margins of cities and towns – away from public view, and resistant to assimilation. The outsider is referred to in private words – showmen say *Joskin* or *Flattie*, the Roma say *gadge* – best avoided except for dealings in business. The trouble is that communities who have less to do with other kinds of people find it harder to trust them, and fruitful dialogue with outsiders is hampered by lack of trust.[8]

Travelling people's livelihood is obtained from the rest of society, giving them as it were, a foot in each camp. It is their dilemma to be trapped between different risks; on the one hand, of assimilation, on the other, of mistrust. The situation changes if children cross boundaries, go to college and return to the group, as is happening among showmen. But this breaches another utilitarian principle of minority groups, that solidarity of the Community should take priority over the emancipation of the individual. Once again, progress and tradition tug in different directions. The mind says compete, revitalize the Community; the emotions sublimate fear of loss in disapproval shown towards high flyers who muddy time-honoured codes of behaviour in pursuit of personal development.

---

[5]   Isobel Fonseca, *Bury Me Standing*, Chatto, 1995, 2009.
[6]   *Environment, Transport and Regional Affairs Committee, House of Commons Ninth Report on Travelling Fairs*, 2000, I:xvi, 32 (hereafter ETR).
[7]   David Smith.
[8]   Richard Wilkinson and Kate Pickett, *The Spirit Level*, Penguin, 2009, pp. 56–8.

Who, then, are showmen? We could say they are in the region of 17,000[9] men, women and children whose families have been running fairs for hundreds of years, and they are proud of it. Most can recite their genealogy for at least three or four generations, some further back, to days when stalls, shows and wooden, hand-turned or steam-driven rides were trundled across the country, travelling to wherever there was a public to engage. Being a showman is not just a job, it is a way of life, they insist, reinforcing how much of their identity is tied into the world of fairground. Showmen are not an 'ethnic' group, rather they are defined by their lifestyle. But among them there is a range of lifestyles which means they don't fit any tidy category. Wholly bound up with the tools of their trade, their lives revolve round the concept of themselves as businesspeople earning their living as entrepreneurs and entertainers.

Showmen share common goals. All conduct the same business; they perceive themselves as a group, and are interdependent, so events affecting one of them, affect them all. They, socialize together; they intermarry. And they are defensive about their image, understandably perhaps. But they live quite differently. Nipper Appleton's living wagon is in a residential part of King's Lynn, surrounded by rows of semis with corner shops. One of his sons has a substantial chalet in the yard, the rest of the family have stuck to trailers. Since Nipper's mother died, none of them is around for much of the year but they meet up at different fairs from time to time. John Bugg owns a house and an ice rink in Peterborough, and a yard adjacent to a string of others in the Cambridgeshire village of Wilburton. This makes him well-off by average standards; only a fraction of the Community own houses. Furthermore he travels all over the world, by road, boat and plane, anywhere there is custom for his rides. This too is unusual though his beginnings were humble enough. The low position Robert Thurston detected in the hierarchy of social status would be painful to most:

> If you had a class system in this country we're bottom of the table.
> Fourth class citizens if you like.

The offense is offset by the solidarity of the group, but pride and sense of belonging have to be set against centuries of stereotyping. Above all, showmen want the public to appreciate what they feel deeply is their unique standing among travellers, and so common is misrepresentation that they regularly define themselves by spelling out what type of traveller they are not.[10] 'The reality is that Showmen's economy and culture is vastly different to that of [other] Traveller

---

9   This figure represents 4 times the number of Guild members, where a Guild member is considered to represent on average a family of 4. Allowance has been made for non-Guild members as well.

10   ETR, I:xviii, 41; ETR II:57, 5.1.

groups'.[11] Such remarks are not necessarily denigratory. 'They are themselves' says a show-woman for whom the comfort of belonging provides an ambience for certain freedoms:

> It's *vastly* different being a showman traveller, to being a Gypsy traveller *but* there are similarities. Of kind of being on the edge. And even though you can live as a Joskin, your core inside of you is still not that. The other side of it, it's very empowering. A lot of people don't know where they come from. Haven't got an identity. The good side of it is that you have an identity. You know where you come from and be proud of where you come from but be whatever you want to be.[12]

At a certain level, stereotyping is little more than a means whereby people protect their relative standing in society, not necessarily inaccurate or wrong. The problem is that stereotyping informs prejudice. That is why failure to distinguish between showmen and less rigorous communities amounts to them to insult.[13] The problem is aggravated by media appearances on screen and in print. The showman is invariably the baddie in TV drama, cartoon copy that whittles away their lives to comic catchphrases or caricatures in which they provide little more than a splash of abrasive local colour. Theatre can be equally dismissive. Jez Butterworth's comedy, *Jerusalem,* first played to West End theatres in 2009 and 2010, offered a remorseless depiction of fair people as drug-taking layabouts in a nanny culture. Even well-meaning reporting can slip into stereotypes. The same show-woman made the discerning comment,

> Whenever we read things about ourselves, it's embarrassing. There was a big write-up in the *Mail on Sunday* a few years ago, obviously the reporter had been and talked to showmen. He'd written the thing faithfully but it made us sound stupid.'[14]

The media are not the only culprits. The 2000 House of Commons investigation revealed something quite unnecessary about the contempt authoritative bodies offer showmen:

> Over the years I have felt ignored, discriminated against and threatened by some councils. Unable to complain because to do so might rock the boat.[15]

[11] John C. Culine, Accommodation Assessment of Northern Section of Showmen's Guild of Great Britain, private corr.
[12] Bernice Stocks.
[13] ETR, II:2, 12.
[14] Bernice Stocks.
[15] ETR, II:18, see also II:4, 5; II:16, and I:xxii.

It is easier to arrest or give showmen hassle as we do not fit the
a norm. There is a stereotype image of us, ie tattoos, scruffy, law
breakers who wear straw hats, stripped shirts and who fleece the
public by dubious means, of their money. None of this is the case.
We are a moral, upright, law abiding group of people. Divorce is
very rare, children born out of wedlock unheard of. I have never
known a showman's child go into care.[16]

Showmen haven't always encouraged publicity. The recognition of possible
benefits that took place at the end of the twentieth century was largely a response
to the realisation that if they got a bad press, Gypsies and New Age travellers got
a worse one. To which end, disassociation from other travellers has a strong
motive. At the same time, they perceive the benefit of forging an image that
distinguishes their unique status through 'greater understanding of their business
and way of life ... to dispel the prejudice and ignorance which in so many cases
prevents travelling showpeople from taking their proper place in modern
society'.[17] The view is held not only by showmen but by others familiar with
their culture. A chartered town planner argues:

In my opinion this is one of the greatest problems that still
continues to face Showpeople. It manifests itself in two forms, one
of who they are and secondly of their need ... They are constantly
mistakenly associated with Gypsies and other (New Age) travellers
and not recognized as fiercely independent and self-sufficient, self
employed business people. Unfortunately this ignorance prevails
not only amongst the general public, who display bias and
resistance to them being located in their communities but all too
often by local planning authorities. It is not unusual ... to have to
explain ... the characteristics of the Showpeople's way of life.'[18]

Prejudice is complicated territory. It's an old chestnut that the more people
feel devalued by those above them in the social hierarchy and the fewer status
resources they have to fall back on, the greater will be the desire to regain
self-worth by asserting superiority over more vulnerable groups. Put more
succinctly, those who receive offence will be offenders. Showmen have a
long-standing record for sensitivity towards children but it is not unusual for the
more conservative among them to harbour anti-immigrant sentiment, to be
homophobic, covertly if not overtly prejudiced against different races, and
intolerant of groups with lower status. Circus people are exempt since there was

---

[16]   ETR, II:20, The Police.
[17]   ETR, I:xxii.
[18]   ETR, II:57, 5.1.

in the past, more intermingling between them and showmen.[19] Billy Smart and self-made Victorian 'Lord' George Sanger are conspicuous among those who switched allegiance from the fairground, moving sideways to create famous circuses. Occasionally members of the two groups intermarried, and both reserve entitlement to call themselves 'showmen'. But where groups compete for scarce resources, each nourishes its pride, despises the other and boasts superiority.

The rivalry between showmen and Gypsies is an old one; George Sanger did not miss an opportunity to emphasize the showman's pre-eminence or to stress Gypsy unruliness, though he himself was handy with his fists and revelled in deceiving the public in the old fairground manner he described as 'hanky-panky'.[20] Denying he ever saw 'genuine' Gypsies involved in showmen's business, Sanger made a point of publicising how they camped in different areas on the showground:

> I want to correct here a very popular error – namely ... that Gypsies were showmen, and most of the showmen Gypsies. Nothing could be farther from the truth. Gipsies, it is true, went from fair to fair, but it was as horse-dealers, hawkers of baskets and tinware, workers of the lucky-bag swindle, fortune-tellers, and owners of

[19] Traditional circus people, (as opposed to contemporary conservatory-trained artists) live in winter quarters, they still have much in common. Three circus yards lie side by side outside Oundle, each of which revolves round a particular circus with its artists and east European employees. Each circus has its businessmen too, though they tend to live in houses. But the main difference between the fair and circus communities lies in circus people being less family orientated, and today they interact less. A few proprietors, such as those in the Roberts family have ancestors in the business, while others, vigorous, self-made men, are new to the work. The two circus proprietors in the Showmen's Guild (Bobby Roberts and David Jolly) are not a representative number since most choose to belong to the Association of Circus Proprietors (APC). Notwithstanding, numbers in the 'tenting' circus community have shrunk to hundreds rather than thousands, grouped round twenty circuses. Animal behaviorists such as Marthe Kiley-Worthington assert that dogs and horses, even non-indigenous species like elephants can positively enjoy performing (Marthe Kiley-Worthington, *Animals in Circuses and Zoos: Chiron's World*, Aadvark Publishing, 1990.) yet the circus has suffered from concerted pressure by animal rights groups. Needless to say, proper husbandry has long been obligatory. The Guild has stern rulings concerning exercise, caging and the length of time animals may be kept for circus use. Only goldfish may be used as prizes on the fairground and they too are subject to RSPCA strictures. (*Showmen's Guild of Great Britain Year Book 2010–11*, p. 125)

[20] Sanger, 'Lord' George, *Seventy Years a Showman*, MacGibbon & Kee, 1966. Sanger was president of the Van Dwellers Association 1900-08. He was one of the first showmen to write his unreliable if imaginative memoirs in 1856. They were first published by Dent in 1926.

knife and snuffbox shies ... they had the trick of making money, and were very fond of displaying their wealth on their persons in the shape of finery and trinkets. Showmen proper always kept themselves apart and, indeed, rather looked down on them.[21]

Showmen continue to assert their separateness from Gypsies and New Age travellers. For instance by distinguishing their own movements – for economic reasons, from the Roma's – for cultural motives, adding thereby one more stick of ammunition to evidence that differentiates the cultures. Individual reactions vary. One showmen expresses pride in his Gypsy inheritance,[22] but even for a child, to be called Gypsy is considered provocative. In fact the association is particularly sensitive as an overlap between the cultures makes the groups less obvious for outsiders to distinguish. On the showmen's side, a good deal of denial is going on. More families have Gypsy blood than care to reveal the fact, and older showmen use insider words, most of them Roma in origin, especially for activities they want to conceal from the wider world. Thus the thief who spots danger knows he should nip away when warned to *scarp* or *geldy*. Some even refer to their private language as 'rokker Romany'.[23] Moreover the Roma have self-styled 'Gypsy Kings' in much the same way that George Sanger dubbed himself 'Lord', and Nipper Appleton's father called himself Lord Lawrence Maxwell Appleton in the early twentieth century. Royal or aristocratic titles adopted to sustain precarious prestige in the same way that 'Punch and Judy' men have their own tradition of calling themselves professors. Are showmen rejecting the part they most disown in themselves?

In today's less flamboyant times, showland's respect favours society's honours for public service – mayorships and MBEs,[24] or their own boardroom hierarchies of presidents, vice-presidents and officers in the Guild.

The Showmen's Guild developed from the UK Showmen and Van Dwellers' Association set up in 1889 in response to scurrilous right-wing criticism of all travelling groups by a Member of Parliament. Eleven years later, the UKSVDA was reconstituted as the far more influential body under its present name. Subdivision followed into ten geographical sections.[25] Some think the Showmen's Guild is responsible for travelling fair people's continuance. That at the very least it merits the accolade of being 'the most decisive and important event in the

---

[21] Sanger, pp. 67–8.
[22] David Remblance, chapter 13.
[23] Shirley Stocks, December, 2010.
[24] At present three showpeople, John Culine, Valerie Moody and William J. Wilson have been awarded MBEs.
[25] Eastern; Midland; Norwich and Eastern Counties; South Wales and Northern Ireland; London and Home Counties; Scottish; Northern; Derby, Notts., Mid and South Lincs.; Yorkshire; Lancashire, Cheshire and North Wales.

history of travelling show people as a community'.[26] The first rules were little more than suggestions, documented without penalties imposed for neglect:

> To promote the interests of the Association, it is incumbent on all members who may be lessees of ground, or others who may have the letting thereof, to give preference in letting and sub-letting to Members of the Association.[27]

Social change has aided and abetted the establishment of law and order that the Guild endorses. It would be far from true to say that every showman became respectable at the tail end of the nineteenth century, yet the Guild's self-administered regulation made members responsible for their conduct. If they didn't adopt new ways, they were aware of what was required of them, and it was a turning point. Modulated, at any rate, was the anarchy that was once an accepted part of showmen's lifestyle. Strengthening cohesiveness made the Community more attractive to its members, and the aura of establishment modified public opinion. The Guild's function lay, as it continues to lie, between that of a modern trade union and a Medieval Craft Guild. That is, as a pressure group that simultaneously supports and furthers the interests of its members in an avuncular way. On its own reckoning, the current membership of 4,230 represents 95% of showmen in one or other of its regional sections, allocation being a matter of choice rather than habitation.

A side effect of the Guild's division into sections was to reinforce members' sense of place. So important is it today to be a Yorkshire section or an Eastern Counties section showman that such a reference may accompany identification. This is the reverse of the Roma, who almost by definition have no home apart from the long road – an attribute that bestows advantage. If you can't say where you come from, you can't be pinned down, can not be blamed.[28]

---

[26] Toulmin, *Pleasurelands*, p. 72.
[27] Toulmin, *Pleasurelands*, p. 73.
[28] Fonseca, p. 85.

CHAPTER TWO – SWINGS OF FORTUNE

'Very good times, very bad times.' A member of the Eastern Counties Section,[1] was giving me an overview. Fluctuation is what he expected and what he got, and this, for showmen, has always been the case. The early history of the fairground has so often been repeated in books about the English fair, it hardly requires re-telling. Instead, we are going to skim through the long-established troughs and fortunes of the last 800 years, trends determined by people's movements and by fashion as well as by national events.

Four thousand eight hundred and sixty fairs were chartered – that is, granted legal status by the sovereign in the British Isles between 1200 and 1400. One after the other, they became harnessed to religious festivals or to working contracts. In rural areas, early fairs provided one of the few opportunities to buy and sell, while on city fairgrounds, trade and pleasure yo-yo-ed for priority. Commerce undoubtedly came first when Samuel Pepys made the journey from London specifically to visit Cambridge's Stourbridge fair in the 1660s.[2] The fair was serving the entire country in a wholesale mart for hops and woolens many days before revellers were allowed on to the banks of the River Cam. 'Where there's money, there's people' said Kenny Gray, meaning, conversely, that where people are present, there's money too; something the showman knows in his bones. But by the end of the seventeenth century, canals and better roads had robbed rivers of transport, and this included the River Cam. The benefits of progress don't necessarily suit everyone. The fair's location on the east of the city became less appealing, and Pepys' favoured venue began to decline.

During the early decades of the eighteenth century, showmen collaborated with classic theatre to entice the crowds. It was then that David Garrick appeared in London to booths of a thousand spectators. High culture wouldn't last. Thanks to agricultural technology, less manpower was required on the land; cities grew apace and in flocked the ordinary folk. Disdainful, the upper classes took their custom elsewhere. You don't get the death of something old without the arrival of something new: Shakespeare disappeared in favour of farce, spectacle and melodrama, while Italian *Commedia del' Arte* was replaced by street shows in the form of acrobats, illusionists and puppet plays. Never again would High Society espouse the fair in quite the same way. But at the same time, show-

---

[1]   Victor Harris, see chapter 20.
[2]   At its peak Stourbridge was the largest fair in Europe, it was enshrined as Vanity Fair in Bunyan's *Pilgrim's Progress*.

men were profiting from a functional shift in the big fairs from trade to merry-making, a move that took place more slowly outside the capital.

Their ranks swelled after the Napoleonic Wars (1799–1815) with hopefuls avoiding the army or a casual life of crime. In reality, what appeared a convenient retreat might prove as unpalatable as its alternatives. Prior to the end of the nineteenth century the fairground was as unequal as the rest of society. Rewards might be enormous but only for a few, and the hazards were considerable. Huge distances were travelled, often on foot, to reach a fairground, battles were fought for the most lucrative site, and living with a horse and chronically crowded wagon was far from easy. Some died of starvation on the road. Besides the inherent hardships of the trade, disruption that was often a fair's accompaniment drew objection in urban venues. Crowds attracted drunks and pickpockets, followed in turn by police, so that showmen became scapegoats for the violence and crime that gathered in their orbit as well as for their own lapses in etiquette. Once alienated officialdom could be relentless. Middle class pressure to close fairs down was gathering force. They were ripe for another trough although paradoxically, some of the most spectacular innovations were about to emerge.

It took the diligence and the expertise of Norfolk agricultural engineer Frederick Savage to realize the practical implications of combining steam – which had filtered through to the fairground some decades after entering the British way of life,[3] and the small, crudely-built, wooden forerunners of fairground rides propelled by gangs of boys[4] that lurk among booths and sideshows in early woodcuts. In 1868 he devised a prototype for the typical merry-go-round. Ever alert to improvisation, the showman was quick to put the extraordinary novelty of Savage's invention to the test. Once again his business would be transformed. Galloping Horses, the Cakewalk and Steam Yachts lay ahead. Before the advent of public cinemas, the showmen exhibited cinematographs and other novelties. All-time records were broken when an estimated 200,000 people visited the Easter Monday fair on Hampstead Heath in 1910.[5] Nor had the boom ended. Never had there been as many showmen as in the two years immediately before the First World War, vying among themselves to make their fortunes with bioscope shows, massive carved organs and gilded baroque rides.

The old state of affairs held true; provided there was money, more was not difficult to make. As always too, the showman's luck wouldn't last. The next challenge was the first World War itself. Duncan Dallas noted the showman's 'imperturbable exercise of initiative in the face of misfortune' that sprang from necessity as much as planning,[6] a proclivity that made him a dependable ally in

---

[3]   1861 or 1863 depending on the source.
[4]   *All the Fun of the Fair*, Graham Downie, Showmen's Guild, 1987.
[5]   The venue had been popular for a good 35 years.
[6]   Duncan Dallas, *The Travelling People*, Macmillan, 1971, p. 16.

a crisis. One notorious example of level-headed cheekiness was said to be the Sanger family's improvised performance in front of a toll bridge to pay for their passage through. This may be apocryphal, but proof of impromptu management lay in a family's standing in for an absent member, or taking an act upon itself if an exhibit failed to turn up. Women and children frequently ran shows and stalls when their husbands were called up.[7] Come what may the show went on, at least until greater forces intervened.

Most fairgrounds closed during the war. When showmen reopened, everything was a struggle; to regain sites, pay for labour, afford new rides or adapt from steam to petrol. Although better times lay ahead, rival entertainment had proliferated, and so had reactionary politics. On the plus side, most new rides would be electrically driven, eliminating the need for a steam engine in the centre, which made space for an organ, lights, and colourful scenic decoration. Old technologies mingling with the new produced a passion for different velocities of movement, and the wholesale installation of electric lights helped to combat crime. The '20s fairground glittered into the '30s. All the major new rides that we think of today, such as the Waltzer, arrived in the period when Billy Butlin made his wealth. Scrolls of Southwold Fair painted during the period[8] suggest how strong and appreciative communication between the showman and his public could be at a charter fair.

Fluctuation was set to continue, for another war was simmering. Its effect on showmen was not, however, predictable. This time round, an increasingly powerful Guild managed to turn events to its advantage despite a welter of restrictions. Fairs were morale boosters the Government decided shortly after the outbreak of the Second World War, a directive the Showmen's guiding body adopted with alacrity. Close links with relevant ministries regulated dispensations made to Guild members, allowing them special rations of strategic materials. Even supplies of sweets, donated for the stalls. Operating at night under a big black tent became one of the stories passed down in the Community. A showman who spent the war in Thetford, claimed,

> We'd sheet the Dodgems all up, play music and put a dance on free
> of charge before they shipped them [soldiers] across the next day.[9]

In 1942 the Government called on its citizens to holiday at home, a move encouraged in larger towns by the instigation of British summertime. Two Norwich showmen mix memory and hearsay in reports of the fair held at the time in Chapelfields Gardens:

[7]   Toulmin, *Pleasurelands*, p. 67.
[8]   By a stockbroker from London, Mr D. Turner, see chapter 14.
[9]   Larry Gray, East Runton.

As soon as the sirens went off, they all went down into the shelters. When it was clear, they opened up the fair and all the people got on again. [10]

People was getting killed everywhere, just thought they was going to die tomorrow anyway, and as it got closer to D-day they didn't care. Forget the troubles, go out and enjoy themselves. That's when the fair done really well. They [German air force] tried to bomb Caleys because the German's knew that underneath the chocolate factory was a big machine shop and they used to make parts for the war machine. But while they was dropping incendiaries, which is small bombs, they [British and US forces] was on the Wheel-em-in. They say it was hit one side and still open on the other. (Laugh at possible tall tale) Where there's money, there's people, aren't there? [11]

Fairground antiques became collectable between the two world wars and by the mid twentieth century, fairground equipment was fast being acquired by museums. Painting had long replaced carving as the principal visual dimension of the rides, a genre to which Edwin Hall, the Howell family and in particular, the celebrated fairground artist, Fred Fowle made major contributions. Fowle's source material was in popular culture. 'Anything that was attractive, I absorbed, the national press, magazines', [12] at the same time he was close to the showmen. When exhibits were being viewed by artistic circles as 'commodities' in isolation from the world of 'fun', it was easy to forget the showmen's participation. The Whitechapel Art Gallery's fairground exhibition of 1977 [13] celebrated Fowles' work while investigating the collaboration.

Businesswise, the 50s stayed briefly golden. Afloat on capital accumulated in more lucrative times, the parents and grandparents of present showmen bought dilapidated buildings or a plot of land, sent their children to boarding school, and invested in increasingly ambitious rides. Until costs and competition cut in, a successful family might own five rides; an exceptional one such as Pat Collins, many times more.

This brings the story to days the older showman remembers with affection. He recalls building up the village fair at the harbour edge in Burnham Overy Staithe, with its rifle range and coconut shies, his sharp-eyed children doling out goldfish for prizes and the machines belting out strains of 'Pretty Little Black-

[10] Arthur Morrison, Norwich.
[11] Kenny Gray, Sheringham.
[12] Fred Fowle, quoted in National Fairground Archive, http://www.nfa.dept.shef. ac.uk/history/art/painting.html.
[13] *The Fairground*, catalogue, ed. Ian Starsmore, Whitechapel Art Gallery, 1977.

eyed Susie' late into the night; or the bigger fair where his Rock and Roll hailed the fair-goer both in music and in artwork. It was unlikely to have been a show-man selling fancy china on Cambridge's Midsummer Common, but his family were there in force, frying onions, minding stalls and keeping an eye on the bumper cars; providing noise and smells rolled into a heady ball by strangeness that still courted a cross-section of the public. Family visits being the social norm, showmen ran a mixture of traditional and contemporary fare.

From scenic to art deco, followed by pop and commercial art; one after the other, the showman drew them into the fairground in the '60s and '70s accom-panied by soul, disco and spin-offs from movies like *Easy Rider*. The identity of each decade was emblazoned on his machines by artists infatuated with 3D let-tering and futuristic design. By this time, the oscillations of the fair were well established. Not for a moment did he expect the post-war boom to last. Sure enough, the last decades of the twentieth century brought enormous cultural as well as technological changes; pressures on land and pressures from a mobile and rapidly changing society in which family pleasure trips became less common. The fair's exoticism was easily lost on the well-travelled, couch-lingering youngster, familiar with a multi-cultural population and the Chinese take-away.

As traditional businesses ceased to be remunerative, showmen restricted the variety they offered to what had proved reliable, this meant concentrating above all on the rides – the scarier the better, with sex and spin aimed at teenagers because they were dependable customers. It does not mean that the 1980s and '90s were static; on the contrary, thrill or 'white knuckle' rides blossomed. Images from major '80s films like *Ghostbusters* and *Terminator* appeared on the fairground in massive high-tech-inspired headboards accompanied by booming electronic music and prominent lighting. Orbiter, Sizzler, Satellite, Tip-Top, the spiral was dizzying, whilst traditional artwork all but disappeared.'[14] Once again, progress brought mixed blessings. With a growing number of his rides made abroad, the showman was no longer involved in the development of his equipment.

Back in 1874, Thomas Frost warned that fairs had ceased to contribute to the national economy.

> What need of fairs and shows? ... as dead as the generations which they have delighted, and the last showman will soon be as great a curiosity as the dodo.'[15]

The subsequent boom among ride-manufacturing companies, Thomas Walker and Savage's of King's Lynn, suggest nevertheless that this was a buoyant

---

[14]   Toulmin, *Pleasurelands*, pp. 21–2.

[15]   Thomas Frost, *The Old Showmen and the Old London Fairs*, London: Tinsley Broth-ers, 1874, p. 276.

period. Frost was premature in sounding the alarm; only *some* of the London fairs were in decline. Fairs continued, and some showmen blossomed for another hundred years. At this juncture, Duncan Dallas confirmed the threat, 'For the last ten or fifteen years the fairground has not been a very attractive proposition for the investor'.[16] Concern was voiced again in the largely positive House of Commons end of the twentieth century report.[17] If undervalued, the fair was still popular, contributors claimed, where the resident locality was sympathetic to the concept and willing to co-operate with showmen. Evidence came from Kirkcaldy Links Market Fair where coach trips from surrounding villages helped to bring in an estimated 40,000 people a day. Liverpool City Council and the London Borough of Newham found that any inconvenience fairs caused was far outweighed by enjoyment they gave.[18] Prime hurdles were put down to cultural prejudice and consequent oversight by authorities.

In 1996 *The Guardian* referred to showmen as 'Britain's last lost tribe'.[19] Tribe was a good word to use, suggesting as it does, a family-centeredness. Commitment to family is not only a binding priority among showmen, it stands as a counterpoint to the fear of effacement that lurks behind the inherent precariousness of the occupation. It is worth reflecting when the next fair comes along, that the small boy, six or maybe seven, passing giant Teddys and Eyeores to his father to hang round the stall, is, like the young woman helping toddlers into her twizzling Teapots, filling a slot seen almost as a birthright. They are doing what generations before them have done – generations who travelled comparatively light, tumbling in and out of wagons and trailers on their circuit. Their heritage is stocked with tents and caravans flowering in streets, town squares and river meadows; smells of cooking and crushed grass, the whinny of penned ponies, the sound of canvas slapping in the wind. There is, of course, a less romantic aspect. The muscle and sweat, the grind and the uncertainty go on. Notwithstanding, they are the flying people, self-propelled, tent pegs barely inserted before they were plucked out again. Fairground life is about impossibilities. The showman is magic, a conjurer; it is something people pay for, an image he can't altogether afford to lose. At a deeper level he invites us into an alternative world without the usual boundaries, restrictions and oppressions, where risk helps us to forget our inhibitions; a world that relates to ritual's yearnings to turn life into celebration. By contrast he lives in a highly structured way. And the real crash came hundreds of years before Thomas Frost.

---

[16] Dallas, p. 38.
[17] ETR, I: xii, 13–19.
[18] ETR, I: xi, 7, 8, 10.
[19] Dea Birkett, 'The Show on the Road', *The Guardian Weekend*, 14 December 1996, pp. 12–13.

The 1792 edition of the 'bible' for traders, *Owen's New Book of Fairs*, lists 121, 126, just over 100, and 23, respectively for Norfolk, Essex, Suffolk and Cambridgeshire. When the Royal Commission's *Report on Markets & Fairs* was compiled in 1888, all counties showed dramatic reductions. In Norfolk there were 43 fairs, Essex had 20 at 15 locations, Cambridgeshire's were down to 18 at 8 locations, and Suffolk's to a mere 14 of which two (in Ipswich), were held in the same place. Two and a quarter centuries after Owen's calculations, Norfolk's historic fairs have dwindled to three (King's Lynn, Norwich, and Yarmouth) Suffolk's to two (Long Melford and Southwold) Cambridgeshire has its Midsummer fair in the county capital and a statute fair in September at Wisbech, and Essex has none.[20] The rest of the UK fared much the same as East Anglia. Doubtless the reasons for this decline in the early part of the nineteenth century take us back to mobility and fashion. As the industrial revolution sucked thousands of country dwellers into the growing towns and cities, denuded villages became less attractive to traders and showmen. This bird's eye view makes it tempting to see prospective closures and the twenty-first-century recession simply as new hurdles among ceaseless ups and downs.

[20] The 1888 list does not include the famous Stourbridge Fair on the edge of Cambridge. This would appear to be a misunderstanding on the part of the compilers. Also missing from these figures are the statute or hiring fairs. As they were not held by charter, Owen tended to ignore them, possibly because they weren't so important for the traders who were Owen's main readers.

CHAPTER THREE
'GETTING A FEW BOB AND MOVING ON'
A SENIOR SHOWMAN

There is an element in David Smith of going his own sweet way and this is something he developed early. Whether exaggeration is part of his complex personality is a moot point. A cousin warned me not to take his stories too literally but David is perfectly able to distinguish between what took place and truth overblown to provide a listener with what he feels the listener wants to hear; he just likes to tease. When he knew what I was after, he was direct.

All his working life he has been a showman, and if it is a label he sometimes tries to lose, he hasn't succeeded. Living more or less as a flattie, he still feels most comfortable in showpeople's company. His occupation wasn't restrictive anyway, periodically he moved in and out of building, and at one point he hired out caravans. Earning a living is something he has never shied away from. He was in his early thirties when he bought 4 acres of land, a shrewd move that has given him a lot more security than he was born to.

I met a tall, gentle man of 74, catering for himself in the detached house he built between 1989 and 1990, together with adjacent cottages. A pleasant brick building set back from the road in rough cut grass on a windy corner outside Tattersett in North Norfolk. The rear is permanently congested with old trailers and fairground equipment in tatty repair, huddles of vehicles that seem to provide a defensive barrier against the world. For the past year a transport trailer has been parked parallel with, almost touching, the side of the house. He calls it an office, and smiles, as if to say, 'make of it what you will'. Relaxed about what he refers to as his 'clutter', he tolerates and enjoys his own mess in his own back yard. It has creative possibilities, makes him feel relaxed. What others find ramshackle could be a productive mess; a mess to be used rather than one that stultifies. By attrition, he won planning permission from the local authority for what was originally intended as a commercial enterprise; later, for the buildings. But the council has refused to extend its consent for further plans. The day I arrived, the scene was eerily reinforced by a wildly banging shed door.

First cousin, Perry Underwood, says;

> It could be a very nice house. He is quite a clever bloke but he doesn't finish things. At first he had the caravan 6 feet from the French doors, I said why d'you put it there David. He really should

clear up, shouldn't he? Lots of people used to have loads of junk, it'd keep on coming handy. Some of stuff is much bigger than what other people keep, so it's more visible. There's several different projects out there, very few come to fruition. But he's never going to get rid of it, is he? A standard joke actually. Old habits die hard, people have got too affluent. When he built the house, he was looking after mother, she was 90 when she died. That's the theory, I think she was really looking after him.

David's mother, Elvina, was an Underwood on her father's side and a Hewitt on her mother's; an inveterate, gutsy show-woman brought up travelling largely among small fairs. Businesswise, the fair family works as a unit. In this case, five of the eight Underwood siblings had shares in the 'firm' – Elvina, her brother, Walter (Perry's father and David's uncle), an older brother and two sisters. Dodgems had been a mainstay among established rides since their arrival in the 1920s, side by side with the mass production of the motor car in the wider world, and for the Underwood clan it was a reliable source of income. Although nominally their set of Dodgems belonged to Walter, all partners reaped the benefits. Brothers and sisters came and went, meeting up and separating with different equipment at different fairs. Sometimes they all inhabited the same winter site in the small town of Wymondham.

David's father, the son of a station master, was a casualty of the First World War, and after being gassed, he was unable to work. Elvina may have welcomed support from her brothers and sisters, for she threw in her lot wholeheartedly with the business. The strain of insecure and stressful schedules was not without side effects on relationships within the family. Perhaps, Walter and his late-married wife had slightly different codes of behaviour from the rest. Perhaps, too, Elvina's early widowhood fell harder on her elder son than on her second son, circumstances which can precipitate a breach between siblings. At all events, not much love is lost between David and his younger brother by thirteen years, who is camped in an even less amenable muddle of cars and caravans on scrubby land, the other side of the road. David says waiting for him to die, so that he can move into the house. But he's not going to get it! About this David is adamant. Love, hate, and competition, mitigated by mutual assistance in the face of threat from outsiders is the general rule for people who maintain among themselves a level of ideological and personal obligation. Life, however, is invariably contradictory.

David is alert, articulate and full of memories. Helping to assemble the Dodgems was one of his first childhood jobs. Another task was to act as an early Satnav, guiding senior showmen drivers on Norfolk's narrow unkept roads. Attitudes were learned. Good showmanship meant constant vigilance with the public and among fellow fairpeople, for instance, in ensuring a good pitch at a fair.

Pitch or position being all-important, competition was and still is intense. But useful as children were, it was easier for adults to concentrate on the essential job of earning a living if their offspring were out of the way in the busy season. This consideration together with problems of attending school while moving from place to place, led to the custom of temporary fostering outside the travelling community that David remembers. Like all showmen's children, he preferred to be with the fairground, but his mother thought differently. He spent many months in an alternative home, rallying to the advantages of the system.

By the time he went to school a certain independence had been established. If academic achievement was scant, after a spell of being bullied, he learned how to fend for himself. It was a fair open fight; he protected his reputation the way he knew. Because David does not pretend to be anything he isn't, he feels no need to justify his reactions, and typically, he bears no self-pity for the rigors of his childhood. Rather than see himself as a victim, he admired his mother's professionalism, providing for her into a good old age. The small world he grew up in was full of pitfalls. He survived by being fine-tuned to them. Life would be tough, native wit told him. Be circumspect, keep a step ahead of those around you. Trust very few but stick by them. Above all, be resourceful. Like freethinking 'outsiders', he remains amused by life's odd comedy, impatient of strictures, and subversive of orthodoxies. Always, he is welcoming. Sometimes, you guess, he is lonely. He is close to his cousin, and friendly with his brother's daughters but a little estranged from his brother.

As a senior, David is familiar with showmen's language, once an important part of identity and cohesion in the Community. From time to time, when speaking with other showmen, he uses esoteric words, especially in conveying messages he doesn't want overheard. Turns of speech that concern money, getting away with things, not getting found out, outwitting outsiders, not necessarily lawless but sailing, as it were, close to the wind. When the Community grew more regulated, the use of covert speech declined.[1] Today it is hardly known by fairground youngsters.

Disrespectful of ostentation, David refers to the flashier showmen photographed in the media as 'dropped darts'; people with inflated egos he has no interest in knowing personally. Here is his story:

> I was going on seven when the war broke out, five when me sister was born, nearly thirteen when me brother was born. My father was in the war and he was gassed. After, he got asthma; he was bent over. We didn't realize how big he was until he died and he was stretched out.

[1] Vanessa Toulmin, *Fun without Vulgarity* contains a detailed section on showmen's language gathered in the 1990s.

The fair's no different really to living in a village, if you can imagine a village as they were years ago. Lord of the Manor; well that was the man who hold the big ride; and a lot of tenants, they are the side stalls. Each showman has a run of fairs. Their parents perhaps had done the same run. My mother and father had a round stall, we call them hooplas. You want to book ground with somebody and you'll say 12ft, 14ft, 16ft hoopla. Sometime they'll say 20ft overall which includes the canopy which is wider than the actual stall. The rides used to be 42ft across, now you get a big ride; that can be 50ft. The main thing, you don't want side ground, you want middle ground.

My mother's family were the last [of the clan] to do [take part in a fair at] Wells-on-Sea. They had a Cock Fair there on January 4th, I suppose that's when they sold the stuff off they hadn't sold at Christmas. My [Hewitt] grandfather used to go there with swinging boats and side stalls. He travelled right up to Norwich Christmas fair. I've heard people who knew him say how the hell did he get there with a horse and cart! But in his time every little town and village had a fair day. Marston and Briston was in March. The fair at Foulsham was May 2nd. The old farmers used to say, we can buy some crabs now the fair's been. Because your crab season used to start in May. You only went 6 or 7 miles to the next village and you got another fair. If you could keep going you were a little bit better off than the farm labourers. Doing as well as a small farmer. We used to say, we want the same weather as you.

Our first winter quarters was Wymondham, that's old Saxon, Vym-mond-ham for vinyard on the hill.[2] Nearly all the pubs had a bit of a field at the back for the cab service, and they kept a few horses and perhaps a cow for the milk, few chickens for the eggs. When you'd finished you'd pull in there. There was no television, very few radios, and most showmen had a tale to tell. When I was about two years old, my father had two hooplas and some side stalls. I can always remember carrying what we called the cock peg. You put this on top of the canvas so the water didn't come down the little hole in the middle, probably had a flag on it. To me that weighed a ton and I'd get me clothes all greased up. Me mother was always swearing at me.

I did the Dodgems when I was 3 or 4. First you laid 40 foot sleepers; the stretchers went across them, wooden, 4ins by 5ins and

[2] It is Old English, but the place-name means 'homestead of a man called Wigmund' (see A. D. Mills, *A Dictionary of English Place-Names* (Oxford, 1991).

you laid the plates on them for the Dodgems to run on. At the end there was a plate we called the coffin, 7ft by 4ft one end, 3ft the other end, and where you turn there was four small triangular plates the shape of the circle 'cos Dodgems was round at the time, now they're square. Well they was heavy things, it was all I could do to lift them and again me mother used to swear at me 'cos I got rust all over. My next job, when you went place to place you'd have somebody come with you who didn't know your run. One of our first fairs was Diss, I'd remember the little back roads, show him [the route].

Right from when I was born me mother used to what was called 'leave you behind' when she was travelling. We arrived at Horning Regatta [NE of Norwich] where my mother had a stall we used to call the Wheel-em-in; you roll pennies down a shoot and if that landed on one of the black lines, you lost. We had an Alsation got into a chicken run; there was a hoo-ha about that and a local woman came up on the fairground, said where's the baby? That was me. Me mother said, he's under the table in the pram. So the woman said, I'll take him round the fair. Mother was packing up that night when the woman appeared again. I'll have him back now. Me mother said, You're too late, I'm taking him home. She said no! So after that she was my second home. Mrs Fraser's husband had an electrical business; she was a typical housewife and me mother was born a business woman. They were both all right. I mean I always wanted to be home, Wroxham was too quiet, but they had a couple of dinghies so I learned to row up the river and ride a bike. I think I was better off there because I was like a slave on the fairground, everybody was. Mrs Fraser used to say that when I went down there I'd sleep for two or three days. I didn't realize I was tired, you were eager to get up the next morning, and all my pals were on the fairground. Me sister came down with me to Wroxham but she cried all the while so they brought her home.

I started going to school at Wymondham, then when I went to Wroxham I said I already started, thinking I was going to get out of it. The little village school at Wroxham was a good school. I wouldn't say I enjoyed it 'cos they didn't know where I come from and some of the older boys used to bully you. One of the men at work was probably sent to pick you up, you'd say, he's being awkward, and he'd [the showman] grab hold of him [the offending pupil.] I don't know how I got in to grammar school in North Walsham 'cos I only went to school six months of the year. Anyway

I got through the entrance exam and that's where I was first called 'Gypsy'. We're nothing to do with Romanies. There's a lot of prejudice against fairground people because we're not there all the while. Some people say what do you do when you leave here? What d'you say to that? We get on a roller and go out with the moon? I should think I fought everyone in the school. I was small then, and I got the name of school bully.

My father was a good carpenter and I used to be. We had a foundry at one time and 'though the foundry actually made steam engines and ploughs before we bought it, we used to make fairground equipment [there]. It was about 1958 when we built our first amusement arcade at Hopton-on-Sea. My father had died. I went into the air force, came out and picked the fairground up again. You mustn't worry what you do. After you get a bit of experience, you say I can do the job efficiently, satisfy people and get a few bob at it. Really that's what fairgrounds are about; getting a few bob, moving on to the next place and repeating the exercise. That used to be a good business because like a farmer gets his harvest once a year, on a fairground you got your harvest every week. I was quite happy travelling but we weren't earning a lot of money and my mother was determined to settle so we found a caravan site by the seaside to settle down. But I hadn't somewhere to keep all the stuff.

In the early '60s when Bullards sold the place at Wymondham, my uncle Walter decided to buy a place in Wells. My mother wanted to be near him and we were looking round when this came up. I bought it for 11,000 quid because it had planning permission to store caravans on. So I bought a Land Rover and carted caravans for 6 or 7 years. Then Lord Leicester took back the caravan site at Holkham from the council and let them [the public] stay there all the year round, so there was no need for one here. Anyway, by then I'd got permission to store fairground equipment. It goes out of fashion so you wait a few years for it come back in. You paint it up and try again. I went abroad, came back and bought a place in Jaywick [Essex]. My brother ran this place, but he made a mess of it and we lost the planning permission. He's been where he is for the best part of 20 years. I think he got permission initially but they want him to move and he won't. He was spoiled. There's him and his wife, two daughters, a son and a grandson. He goes to Sandringham and to the football field at Wells with a bouncy thing. People up on the estate they keep grumbling, I say it's nothing to do with me, I've got rid of him, that's all! I think he's waiting for me to die so he can claim this lot but he won't. I don't feel brotherly one bit. I regained the land, built this house and sold the cottages. Look at the clutter I've got out there.

Some words have two or three meanings depending on how you use them. [like Humpty Dumpty] A lot of Romanies still speak that way. 'Fiddling' isn't something wrong for a showman, it's when he's taking a nice few shillings. 'A burster', that's taking tons of money. 'Rackler', a woman, not a show-women, unless you didn't like them a lot. It's what travellers call a Joskin if they're a bit hoity-toity. 'Wafty' means bad; say you go to hire some ground and the man you're paying is on the take, asking for £50. You'd say he was a wafti omy.[3]

[3] See Addendum for fuller account of language from David Smith.

CHAPTER FOUR
'QUITE A BIT OF STICK'
A SETTLED SHOWMAN'S EARLY LIFE

Perry Underwood does thing quickly; walks like the wind, juggles several jobs simultaneously and speaks an individual brand of Norfolk, running his words together in little spurts. As do the majority of showmen with whom I spoke, he often makes use of the persuasive 'because' as a conjunction, and ends sentences with a tag question 'did it?' or 'you know?' He invariably prefixes the past tense with 'used to', and takes liberties with pronouns. But is he a showman? These days, he says, he probably mixes less with them than he does with outsiders, and he doesn't necessarily identify himself as one of the Community. So it depends with whom he is speaking.

He grew up in Wymondham twenty years after his first cousin, David Smith. Neither married although both have had girl friends and Perry has two daughters of whom he is extremely fond. Of medium height, with dark, centrally parted hair, he is single-minded and every bit a man of the twenty-first century. At the same time, he is shy, wary of publicity and not, for a one raised on the fairground, gregarious. By the time he left school his father had settled, so he stopped travelling. Like a high proportion of settled showmen, he stayed with the amusement industry.

Our rendezvous was a Spartan office leading off the back of his amusement arcade in premises carved out of old warehouses at Wells-next-the-Sea. The door bears *W. Underwood*, on a brass plate. Perry put it up in his father's memory. The room is just big enough for a desk, sideboard and portable fan-blowing heater, its sole adornment a card from one of his daughters pinned to the wall, inscribed, I LOVE YOU. But seldom there, he is notoriously elusive, always at a given time, difficult to catch. I have waited and he never turned up at all. If I was lucky, he'd be deep in one of the machines, the front opened up, tools scattered on the floor. Juggling his various business concerns requires flexibility and he doesn't want to be pinned down by other people's expectations. Asked to with-hold his home address, the staff are appropriately evasive as to his whereabouts. After first agreeing to let me take his photograph, he realized it might be used for a newspaper and quickly retracted the offer. A book was different, but I was too late. A certain anonymity gives him the freedom to set his own agenda. To live closer to the way his father did.

If Perry's office is equivalent to his father's trailer, the arcade also seems haunted by the spirit of fairground. Walter Underwood himself would not have felt out of place in the extensive hall full of shiny slot machines, with fluffy toys, chrome, and the tinkle of fill-space music. At opening time the music starts to jangle, and the odd machine spills out its guts amid orchestrated thumps, coughs, little cries, and squeals from this alternative world. Staff say that Walter's son can spot a cobweb as he walks in the door; if necessary he will get rid of it himself. A boss prepared to perform any job deserves special loyalties, which Perry receives. He is, besides, not only extremely hardworking, he has business acumen that serves him well. One of the building's smaller rooms is a casino, and upstairs is a closely monitored childrens' playroom. 'No smoking', 'No food', prohibitive notices warn. A windowless area is divided into smaller sections, one with slides, another hung with plastic punch-bags, like sacks full of dead bodies. At the entrance end there is a refreshment counter; along the far side, a distribution of child-size chairs and tables. In Norwich he owns another children's recreation room.

But the decade that set the present in motion was what I had come to hear about. As the only child of elderly parents, Perry was humoured by being allowed a cat inside the wagon. This marked his family as unusual. Cats don't travel well, and as a rule travelling people dislike them. That the Walter Underwoods set great store by education was again unusual for showmen of their generation. To help their son with schooling, they tried fostering but he was a clingy youngster. More than once Perry interrupted his account with reasoning that 'memories are very selective' and having exaggerated, he corrected himself. There was no doubt however that before the decade was up, his life was disrupted by an episode he wrestled with and left behind but does not forget. It was not comfortable for him to recall. The event was provoked by the Education Reform Act of 1988[1] imposing a penalty on parents for a child's absence from school. As a result, Perry was sent away to boarding school in Norwich. David Smith reckoned showmen's children got bullied because their school attendance was spasmodic; this made them different to the majority, giving the larger group a pretext to exclude them. In the knowledge that lack of education hasn't, finally, held him back, Perry reasons that his reaction to boarding school was one of an outsider to the pack norms – the tyranny of the group. That his parents had made a sacrifice to send him away made him feel worse, but he learned at a private school the need to be inconspicuous, something he continued to practise. Maybe events which left him sensitive to other people's vulnerabilities have helped him in the end.

Fairground children's reaction to boarding varied. Perry's experience was markedly different from that of youngsters in the prolific Whyatt and Thurston

---

[1] The Act stated that school attendance in the nearest establishment to the fair should be as regular as the business permitted, otherwise a fine would be imposed for non-attendance.

clans among whom three cousins were once at Rushmore School in Bedford. Four years there didn't make a scholar of Theodore Whyatt, nor alter his uncertainty about the benefit of learning to showmen, but he had shared the experience with relations, and natural aptitudes were allowed to blossom. Theodore says:

> There was 3 of us there at once, all in the cricket team, the rugby team, the swimming team, everybody wanted us in their team. Obviously you don't like being left behind, sun shining especially but I used to come home each weekend. I did think at the time, why am I taking Latin lessons. When I left school I came straight into the business, it's all I ever wanted to do. I never went that way with my children [boarding], perhaps I should have done.

When Walter Underwood moved to Wells, his son was able to go to the local school. The family were moving into a new era anyway.

In the network of small town and village events that covered the country, change had been slow and entertainment rare. Until the advent of the ride, a gingerbread stall and a peepshow might supplement sporting displays that ranged from all-in wrestling to bear-baiting. This made Walter Underwood's Dodgems a welcome diversion. Like *his* father before him, Walter was known as 'Rhubarb', a nickname that arose inconsequently and stuck. Travelling rural Norfolk and Suffolk with his wife and six sisters, he would arrive annually with the fair, its side stalls and rides emblazoned 'Rhubarb Underwood'. Until the '60s, it was still normal for people in rural and urban areas not to have travelled much beyond the boundaries of their immediate city or village community. Married brothers and sisters, parents and grandparents tended to remain living nearby so the community consisted of people who had known each other for much of their lives, and their sense of identity was embedded in that community to which they belonged. Walter Underwood knew that the colourful presence resonating with the residents of Wymondham was all part of the business. His relationship with those he entertained was dictated far more by tradition than is that of his son, yet the stamp of Perry's formative years is never far away. *His* first memories date from the late fifties.

> Father travelled from village to village on pub fronts with a Coconut Shy, a Dodgems and a couple of side shows. Local people would know them and he saw the same people every year. The ironmongers was called Clarks and they'd take phone messages for him. We used to spend the winter at Wymondham, 'cos father had done it for years and years and years so he was quite well thought of in the area. The King's Head Meadow was a football field used

to belong to the pub, which is no longer there.[2] They had a bowling green and a large empty space where we'd winter. Father was on very cheap rent with sufficient room, when I was younger, to keep the Dodgems. Once it was built up, he was able to do some [winter] work. Build up the sides, keep the cold winds out, do things on the track ... it does require maintenance and fair life afforded full employment six days a week. Wymondham was a reasonable sized town. Unless the weather was incredibly bad he used to open on the Friday and the Saturday night to get a few local people. Even Christmas. I think my grandmother's actually buried in Wymondham churchyard. Grandad might be too.

There was no communication and transport, no electric light, so when you went from Burnham Market to Wells, you'd get a completely different set of people. Year in and year out, you'd move in just short hops. It'd be a big novelty. There was a captive population. In those days the fair was a regular major social event so you'd know them from one summer to the next. You went back every year. Fifty or sixty might turn up from a tiny village. Things never seemed to change. Very few people would move away, they only died. Father had this big flat truck he'd put the Dodgems on. He'd put the music on. I remember seeing people dance on this trailer. Loads of people used to say, I met my wife there 50 years ago. Some of these places you went to to get drinking water from the houses on a regular basis. Unfortunately people started to get cars and they moved out. You had to go further and further. Plus people with bits of spare land had been prepared to let the fairs move into them. As time went on those fields got developed, and as the 60s, 70s moved in, even places to hold fairs became hard to find. We used to have a coal fire stove one end [of the living wagon] and a coal-fired range the other. Had coal scuttles and my mother'd cook on this coal-fired range; there was the grate, the fire and the rings on top. She'd cook for the men who worked for us as well. They'd eat in their own space or outside unless they was one of the more chosen ones (Laugh). But some of the old boys weren't the best, it was difficult to get employees – there wasn't plenty of money, it was a bit boring perhaps. It's probably even harder now.

It was exciting, it was different. You could run freer than children do now. I used to help mind the dart stall when I was three or four; it was a big family thing. You take the money and give the darts.

2 The site was built on by Woolworths but the store, in turn, has been demolished.

You'd put little brooches on card, down on the floor. Got to hit the card with the dart. There's a choice of the bottom shelf or the top shelf. The joke was you couldn't get a dart in cleanly because that was impossible. You soon got over shyness 'cos kids don't know their own embarrassment. You're probably very good at it and look quite cute. It was dark, there was music, there were other stalls and probably lots of people around. Some of the places were nice we went to: one was Wells. I used to mind the stalls, set them up, take them down; Dodgems, Coconut Shy and a hoopla. Mother used to mind the Coconut Shy. I have minded it but the wooden balls used to fly around quite a bit. Men were much stronger than they are now, and they were keener to play. You can get coconuts anywhere now for 30p at a supermarket but then you never saw them unless the fair come round. Used to get a sack of them. On the hooplas too, you used to have goldfish. That's something else you wouldn't find. We'd go to Needham Market, Whit Monday they had a big carnival. The gold fish used to come down by train in boxes with a plastic liner half-full of water. My godfather put the goldfish out in tin baths. But I had a cat went round on Sunday afternoon, must have eaten about 200 goldfish. There weren't too many cats and mine wasn't *strictly* kept outside. I mean sometimes ... Most of them had dogs.

The Primary School in Wymondham was very nice. The big problem came during the summer times 'cos obviously you used to travel round. Every time you move, you're supposed to go to the next school which I did have a little go at but that is dire because you're a new boy every time you turn up and the teacher says, There's no point you know. You're only here for a week. Two weeks. You didn't want to go. That was all right when I was younger. But eventually they noticed and Father got into trouble. One time I stayed behind in Wymondham with a lady who Mother was friendly with and went to school there. It was all right for a time but I didn't like being left. Then I went to Stowmarket, stayed with someone there for a summer. Eventually they had a brainstorm and sent me to a private boarding school in Norwich [Cawston College] which, with the benefit of hindsight, wasn't a good idea because you were so different from the other kids. Not being used to finding my way among people because I hadn't found it before, particularly at Wymondham where they knew you.

Two and a half years at the private school ... I was eight when I went; the youngest boarder. Must have been in the region of 150, all boys. There was boys there probably 16–17-year-olds weren't there? In the dormitory of an evening I was fair game. There's nothing worse than kids you see. When they got you on the run as well, they don't leave you alone. It was a shame but unfortunately it's human nature if you get someone from a different social background as well as being quite naïf. At one time, particularly in smaller communities, people didn't like outsiders; even if you came from a village down the road you were frowned upon. If you had a completely different background to what they did, people were suspicious like they are now with immigrants. I was very uncomfortable I tell you. It was the children rather than the teachers. At the end they found someone else to bully, but for quite a long while I used to loathe it. I did walk out a couple of times which probably wasn't the best thing. Everyone wants to conform, particularly when you're a child you crave normality. Poor old Dad was illiterate so he had a strange fascination with education; he thought that was the way forward. At the end he decided perhaps it wasn't the be- and end-all of creation, which it's not. But I got quite a bit of stick because you like to conform at that age. Later on, when you went to a social function you didn't want to have that happen [to be humiliated].

CHAPTER FIVE
'THE RIGHT PLACE AT THE RIGHT TIME'
COLONISATION AT WELLS-NEXT-THE-SEA

There are those who regret the conversion of the old quayside buildings at Wells-next-the-Sea. But already it is more than half a century since the small businesses at the west end of the harbour – amusement arcades, café, rock-shop, and corner bucket 'n spade shop – all prominent premises, began to cater for summer visitors swarming in to enjoy traditional amenities.

The little town with its dignified Georgian square and narrow high street dipping down to the harbour was somewhere the showmen looked forward to in the annual itinerary. A place where floods thrilled the children by rising high beneath their wagons and trailers, parked on reclaimed marshland down Freeman Street. How would Wells suit as a home? It is important to realize what a big venture it was for family-based people to forfeit the support and pleasure of the clan, even for a relatively close alternative base. Yet travelling was tougher in the 60s than it is today. Some of the showmen were weary, others were in poor health. In Wells, they may have spied out the land with an entertainer's eye, reckoning the port had little to attract the day tripper. At all events, the territory looked sufficiently propitious for Donald Gray to envisage moving there; so when a building came up for sale at a bargain price, he went for it. Along with Bugg and Thurston, the Gray clan, with their complicated family interconnections, are prominent among the East Anglian show community.

Walter Underwood was the next showmen to arrive on Wells waterfront, followed by John Gizzi. Like Perry Underwood who took over his father's business in one of the amusement arcades, Donald Gray's daughters, Kay and Jacqueline, now work in the premises their father converted: second-generation sandscratchers whose allegiance to the travelling community is unwavering.

Jackie hasn't married, she is current treasurer of the Eastern Counties section of the Guild. Kay married Tommy Gelder, a showman who sometimes travelled with her father as a tenant. They produced a daughter but no more babies came, something she attributes to years of physical labour on the fairground. After a spell with her husband's family, who owned of a Bingo hall and an arcade in Skegness, the couple returned to Wells. Here Tommy died after 36 years of marriage. Here he chose to be buried, among friends the couple had made in the town.

Today, in wintertime, K's Burger Bar is a snug place to drop in out of the wind. The counter lies at right angles to the entrance, from behind it, handsome

Kay Gelder spots people even before the door tinkles and is immediately at their service. A sense of pride for her family is infused with fierce loyalties towards the extensive clan, her daughter and granddaughter, the forbears who laced her own young life with a sense of purpose, and relations who continue to travel. She had told me about her father's Dodgems and an Octopus, so I was surprised when Jackie escorted me to his gravestone in Norwich's Earlham Road cemetery, to find it inscribed with Gallopers and a Gavioli organ – a barrel organ converted to paper music he inherited from his grandfather. Before being filmed with it by the BBC in the '70s, he took it back to its manufacturers in Belgium for its workings to be restored. He died soon after he had finished painting it, and Kay still keeps it in Wells.

The number and scope of his machines suggest that Donald Gray had won a certain prowess in the entertainment industry. In his case it was a shaky heart that led him to seek a less rigorous lifestyle in the first year of the 1960s. At 48, not without qualms, he and his wife, Emily, eldest child of fair people still travelling in the Midlands, left the family yard in Norwich for premises that became one of three arcades in Wells.[1] With them were 22-year old Donald Jr., Kay, fifteen; her elder sister 21; and Jackie,[2] ten. In the course of about seven years, Donald proceeded to buy a small place to the west of it, Don's Snack Bar, now K's Burger Bar; Quality Stores on the corner of the High Street; and Jacqueline's Jewelers adjacent to Quality Stores.

There is among the Grays a reputation for fieriness. Short-tempered and volatile, their rages are phenomenal, but over in a flash. They laugh and cry easily, are not introspective, nor prone to intellectual analysis. They get by on their wits and rich sentimentality. In theory, the family transcends internal rivalries, in practice this can't always be the case. The evidence is Donald Gray's first acquisition in a prime position on Wells' sea front. Following a fire in 1998, the arcade was boarded up because of a disparity over what Donald and Emily (who died 22 years later than her husband) wanted for their children. Kay has a disarming way of contradicting the main drift of her argument in a final statement; suggesting for instance, that the family have their own rules, regulations and prohibition, she acknowledges that they may not be quite those of others. At one point she agreed with a comment I had heard; they are a 'law unto themselves'.

> There's an arcade down the bottom which unfortunately has had
> a fire. That was called Festival Amusements, the first thing Mum

---

[1] In Armes Street, where Carl and Jonathan Gray's extended family still occupy the yard.

[2] Jacqueline Gray became an Associate of the National Teachers of Dance, in which capacity she taught Ballroom and Latin American dancing for many years after a day's work in the shop. She was the first woman on the Committee of the Eastern Counties Section of the Guild.

and Dad bought. Each piece of property, they got a flat put above so if anything happened, we all had a business and a home. My brother stopped here with Dad to get ready for the following season, while my sister, Pamela, and I had to find a job in the winter but we still travelled with Mum and the Dodgems. My Mother was 86 and she was working until she broke her hip. They was very clever people, they worked morning and night and we just continued on the same. I was 14 when I worked in Clark's shoe factory. But we had to have somewhere to live, so they then bought this place known as Don's Snack Bar off Tom Grange – he had all the lorries in Wells at the time. The council said that had to be pulled down but because they [showmen] had knowledge of putting things together, they made it safe – my dad, his brother – Uncle Clifford, whoever would help, and we lived above. Then, next door to the arcade was Sam Abel's property, Dad bought that. Then a little shop at the side what sold Calor gas and petrol became available. You could say we broke the chain [by settling down] but Dad got to think of his girls and I know I've only got to pick the phone up to any of my cousins or vice versa. If they needed help I'd be over there. We had our fall-outs, don't get me wrong. It's a known thing that Grays have big mouths and we do tend to have your say whether that offends you or not. We was brought up to be independent but we're still there for each other. We got to live here, Mum and Dad said, when we settled down. You *do not* get a bad name in this town. I know Tommy was liked. I think we're well liked. I find it very difficult not to work, hence I'm still here after 47 years.

For four years Donald spread his little empire. The Grays' initiative would have been watched closely by other showmen, but there was almost no competition in Wells until Walter Underwood's cautious arrival four years later. The town's travelling community increased again in the last year of the decade when John Gizzi moved in to manage one of his Uncle Donald's businesses. That is not to say that relocation was appreciated by the younger generation. Like Kay, young John loathed an upheaval that meant losing the familiar buzz of extended family in Norwich's vibrant subculture based around Earlham Road. It was a shock for which Wells' economic advantages never completely compensated.

Largely because his winter quarters were no longer available, Walter Underwood moved to Wells in a caravan. No longer would the Grays have sole sway over the town's early days of tripperdom, but Walter's beginnings were stealthy and the styles of the two ex-showmen was recognisably different. Two of Donald's siblings were killed when still toddlers in a fire caused by an oil lamp at Norwich Fair: something he never forgot, something that affected the lifelong sense of responsibility of the elder boy in a reduced family. While Donald Gray had authority, Walter was known among contemporaries for what his son called the common touch. It was a surprise to him that, one after the other, his settled ventures began to flourish. A very small building he converted to a café was followed by an arcade, and then the quayside warehouse next to it. In his later years, Walter collected paintings, he liked an audience, and his audiences felt comfortable in his presence. Long after he had died, people who had known him in Wymondham paid their respects by visiting Perry.

The two men's differing personalities extended to their roles as fathers. Showmen's sons are traditionally guided by the male head of family, girls by the women; for both, discipline is strict. Walter Underwood was an older parent with a single child and this had a bearing on his relationship with Perry. The son's adaptation to Wells was clouded by intense dislike for work in his father's cafe, but mature for his age, he observed the task objectively, rolled up his sleeves. For his father's sake, he carried on.

We came to Wells after the Harvest Fair in Dereham '65 when father was 55. 'Course he had been here before for the regatta but if they hadn't built the Community Centre [on the pub field where he'd wintered] in Wymondham, I suspect he never would have bought this place. I think he would have struggled on. He could still put the caravan there but there wasn't room to build up and open any more, so there was a long winter period. It is a good life but it was changing all the while, and it wasn't getting any easier. Father was worn out and I wasn't going to be much use for some time. There was a big garage at the top of the [Wells] car park they called Warham Garage, we pulled in the caravan and lived in that for a while. The first year or two Father went out again with the Dodgems while my Mother stayed here with the Pop-in Café – it took a while to get planning permission for it, and I went to the school here. I started doing things with my father before I left school but I used to hate the cafe. It used to craze me. It was very busy there and there's no end to it. Your social standing from the fair, in those days there can be a bit of glamour, particularly the age I was, 'n you end up washing up! It's not a thing a young boy want to do. It almost broke poor old Father's heart. Poor old Dad loved the cafe. He said, Oh dear. I said, Yea, ok I'll do it! I had it 'til five years ago. Should have got rid of it years and years before but it was a bit of nostalgia. We had the cafe, a very small amusement arcade, then the fellow next door decided he wanted to sell. It was on sort of personal loan – we was very hard up 1968, '69. But every action has a reaction, Father thought there was going to be something here and there was.

It is said that among showmen, everyone is related to everyone else. No surprise then that John Gizzi of the eponymous Rock Shop is Kay's first cousin. Their mutual grandfather, Kenzer Gray, a Norwich wheelwright, married Henrietta Cheesman,[3] and one of their children, Bertha, married an outsider whose father had arrived from Italy after the first World War. John is their son. To young John, his uncle was an inspiring leader. As an adult he is no less reverential, remembering Donald with respect bordering on worship. Indeed, this uncle and grandmother Henrietta were the two great influences in his life. As a young woman, Bertha asserted her initiative by earning money outside the family business. Her independence, however, was not approved and in the end, John reckoned, his mother accepted the lore of the clan. Such tales shed light on the Gray family.

John is a big balding sentimental man, moved almost to tears by memories of annual Christmas gatherings in the old Norwich Cattle Market. Video footage taken by his mother, shows him as a youngster on the Earlham milk float, a small, scampering child with a recognizable thatch of dark hair who skips and runs everywhere for the pleasure of being alive. There is one shot of Blakeney sea front with trailers and wagons deep in water, rising up to the steps as it did at Overy Staithe. Another is of young John riding on a merry-go-round at Yarmouth, the traditional first fair of the year he enjoyed as a Sunday visitor. With childhood a paradise, it is understandable that any present might seem lacklustre.

In the mid '80s John Gizzi married a Wells girl and purchased his pink and white palace, stocking it with all the things you should only allow yourself at the seaside. Rows of sweets in jars behind a counter stocked with fudge, rock, nougat, humbugs and coconut ice – the last two still made on the premises, as did his mother before him. Showmen sometimes use the word 'normal' as others say 'usual', to emphasize the mundane quality of their own life; at other times to discriminate between their lives and those of others who are, in turn called 'normal'. Here John uses it the first way.

> They all had a very hard life. Before Mum was married, my Grandmother used to make her walk round the Larkman estate, that's a very rough area of Norwich, to knock on the door and

---

[3] Henrietta Cheesman had two brothers, one of whom had a wet fish shop in Wroxham, Norfolk. Of her six sisters, Eadie, Omie, Kate, Pansy, Maggie and Violet, three married showmen, linking her with the Thurstons, Barkers and Summers. Omie's fish shop was no. 88 Benedict Street.

hawk the rock. This particular year she said, I don't want to do it. I'll get a job down the brewery. My grandmother said, You're not going down there. Anyway she went down there [the brewery] for ten shillings a week. But when she come home she said, I never got no dinner because they didn't agree with it. After so long I had to go back to taking the rock. Where[as] she got ten shillings a week at the brewery, she might earn that a day. That's what Granny was trying to tell her. But the things what she'd see on the estate ... I can't tell you things what ladies done, it would be unbelievable. But she got her first pram for Auntie Emily, a second-hand one, and coats and that for the kids. They'd say, You don't want that. She'd say, Yes, that'll do fer one of my nieces. My grandparents had a yard in Norwich where we used to all live, Donald, Ethel, Bertha, Clifford in this one yard before the war.[4] It was just normal life; all business people in it together. Kenzer had a bit of a drink problem as they did in them days. One of Grandmother's [Henrietta Gray] sisters used to have the Dial Pub on the Dereham Road. Another had a cockle and whelk shop in Benedict Street. So all the sisters had something and my Granny went on the Dial with the rock stall in the war time. There was a garrige at the back of the pub was Perry's uncle's store place.

When the war come my mother had to move out of Armes Street because the city was getting bombed, so my mother moved to Costessy, 5 or 6 miles out of Norwich, and ended up buying a yard there. I'd go to school in Costessy and we'd go to Norwich Christmas fair on the old cattle market which is now gone because its all been developed. We'd all go round to my Uncle Clifford Christmas morning. He had a big family. That was a thing to look forward to. See all your friends what you'd met over the years and who you grew up with and all the kids. Grandad died early in the war and Uncle Donald took over, so he was like our father. He looked after us all and what he said went: you didn't mess with him or nothing. But you didn't have to because what he said was always right in the end. And coming to Wells, he was in the right place at the right time. I think I was twelve when we come here. Kay and Pamela and them were already here. There was nothing here at all. You'd come from Norwich where you'd step out your door, there was all your friends and cousins to play with. That was the first time they'd [his parents] lived in a house, having water, toilets and everything all in. I hated it, I was very lonely. I cried for

4 Refers to the same yard in Armes Street mentioned in footnote 1.

six months. I said to Mum let's go back to Norwich. But they [his parents] must have had a talk with Uncle Donald, my mother idolised him. Absolutely. She loved them all but 'Shaggy' she used to call him because he used to smoke shaggy in his pipe ... if Uncle Donald said something, that was it! He had these girls but he was definitely the father figure and the man's man.

My Father had a set of Dodgems then they sold them. We had a Coconut Shy and a Roll-up. We used to rolls balls down, they'd be like different numbers on the bottom and you'd try to get the highest numbers. He had a few slot machines and a rock stall to make home-made sweets like we still do. My mother'd worked with her mother. Mum would buy in sugar and boil it up with all the flavourings. Chuck it over the hook, swinging it on the hook how it should be until it changed from grey to white. She used to make these wonderful white cough sweets and cough medicine for the winter. They used to work but she never told what she did and they never did write them [recipes] down. I wish I had done. I'd help her make them but you didn't take no interest. When we was at Castle [Meadow], we had a great big shed and my job was to feed the rope through the machine and make the humbugs. A little hand machine with a handle, all brass. We still got it. You had to feed it through quick cos the time you was getting to the last one that was cold and that would set so you couldn't get it through. I used to hate doing it. That was so boring when you was young and my grandmother used to be a bit costy with us. So when I come out of school it was, What's it Granny, d'you want an icecream? If Granny wanted an ice cream I used to have to walk right back because the shops was quite a long walk from the yard. Then Mum and Dad would be in there, arguing as usual like they used to do. That was very hard but that was good. When she died at 62, Mum was worn out. Never had a holiday in her life. Never went anywhere. Never done nothing. She loved what she done and she didn't have the money to know the difference. You got to remember, no one had nothing.

Until the 1990s Wells fair opened on the quay, a custom brought to an end by health and safety regulations. Wells resident Bernard Phillips, offered indelible memories of watching the rides and stalls being dismantled after the final night there. Working in near silence to the music of lapping water below, a small lit unit was almost swallowed up by the dark. The fair people moved as if in a dream, each economical motion learned through years of experience.

CHAPTER SIX
'THE FINEST LIFE FOR CHILDREN'

There are times when showmen appear to retain their culture almost as a defence against the modern world. Nowhere is this more apparent than in rearing their children. Interaction within a group starts from the day a child is born; and this was constantly brought home to me. Nipper Appleton, for instance, stepped out of his living wagon, a muscular man in a singlet clasping his youngest grandchild with one hand and a mobile in the other. 'She's had a really bad night again. She's restless and it's been raining', he was speaking, not, as it transpired, about the child but his 93-year-old mother in the next trailer. The little girl had been to a circus with her grandpa the previous evening, she confided from a sleeping bag on the floor. Another time, at Alexandra Palace, two youngsters minded by a 7-year old girl darted out of John Manning's wagon as we walked in. While John's wife managed a Juvenile[1] on the fairground, he had been sitting at a computer, poring over VAT with grandchildren playing in the background. For a showman, Cilla Morrison confirmed, neither scene was unusual. Their lives demand a high level of teamwork. Sooner or later the young will take their part, so it makes sense that they should be brought up to respect its disciplines.

In a twist of fate almost beyond bearing, Arthur and Cilla Morrison's four children died one after the other of cystic fibrosis. The parents might have grown embittered but they haven't, and totting up more than fifty years of the firmly-based marriage you often find in showland, they have made a significant contribution to the community that lives in seven and a half acres north east of Norwich city centre.

The land that comprises Hooper Lane yard was bought in the '50s by the Showmen's Guild and laid out like a chessboard. About 60 homes and a club-house are packed into two levels, of which the wooded upper one was still being developed 15 years ago. Lasting relationships have developed among the inhabitants in this hive of dwellings where older people who do not own yards can retire to tend gardens with yuccas in pots and bedding plants in containers.[2] Where youngsters can lodge while getting established. The Morrisons, have a cool daisyless stretch of lawn and a rose arch in an end-of-row site. In the summer, out comes a table with a central sunshade. On the table rest two indispen-

---

[1]   A children's ride.
[2]   In practice older people tend to outnumber the young, a trend that grew over 3 years from 2007 when I first visited.

sable mobile phones. Cilla tells how child rearing becomes a shared responsibility, making the yards and fairgrounds extended playgrounds. From the start, social conditioning is designed to encourage bonding. Attitudes are deliberately induced, and directly or indirectly what adults set store by gets instilled.

> In our business we've got the children with us all the time. If I want to go out, put the baby in the pram, along she came and sat there with us. Soon as the babies are old enough to toddle they come along, playing around whilst we were there. If we meet people, we say how are you, and I think the children do the same. My grandson lives in a house; his father is not a fairground person. He loves to mix with the fair children because they've got so much freedom. They can ride bikes, they can play football in our own little community park. We don't have to worry about them because everybody knows everybody's child where [as] my grandson, when they close the house door, they don't know the people live round them unless it was a schoolchild came to visit. I know every child on here, so if a stranger comes on, he could come to me and I'd know where to take him back.

Josie and Larry Gray are another couple solidly entrenched in showland. After 46 years together they have four children, all married, all travelling, frequently on the same site. Confidence in the quality of their nurturing is something about which showpeople are virtually united. Josie hopes that she has managed to establish what to her is worth passing on:

> They're with us 24 hours a day. Quite often they sleep with us. Just crawl into Mum and Dad. We squash up and you wake with the child in the middle. I think it brings your children closer. The family work as a team, don't wait till 6 o'clock for Dad to come home, and we're together still. We have our arguments, what they call sibling rivalry, but we manage to make it work because we're brought up with this family orientation. You put your differences aside and get on with the job. I think it's a good philosophy for life. They [her children] bring their children up with the same ideas so it's not something that's going to die out.

'The old values', as young mother Kim Thurston called the expectation of respect and discipline, are passed down from times when family law presided absolutely. Showland reflects general trends towards licence and informality, but respect remains a word that is often used. It might mean not being cheeky to parents or wearing a hat in church. Kim says:

I [too] was strict; the way I was brought up. The old values we usually call them, still come down through the generations. Not everyone have them. Some aren't quite a strict as others.

Notionally Church of England, showmen's convention has been one of observance for the form rather than participation in religion's spiritual dimension. Kay Gelder spoke about a certain awe reserved for worship among the Grays that was part of the firm hand employed in her young home. It was an authority that evidently left room to encapsulate the family flair for individuality:

We was lucky I think you realize, though they was strict. Because you hate them when they won't let you do something. No you do not walk the street. No, you're not going in a public house unless you go in with your husband or boyfriend. Ladies don't smoke in the street. Ladies don't eat in the street. Never let me hear you swear. We was ladies as far as our parents was concerned. The only word I heard, my Mum would say blooming, and sometimes she'd say bloody. She'd say, Bloody's in the Bible. Bloody's in the Book. If you don't bloody believe me, go and bloody look. I'd say, *Mum*! Because they all very much believed in God. They'd do a Christmas service and an Easter service on Norwich fairground. I've got pictures of that, me as a little girl, standing on Dad's Dodgems' steps. And some of the Ladies we got to know, they'd say, do you want to come to Sunday School? I remember putting stickers in the books. We wouldn't enter a church without putting something on your head. And you don't go to a funeral unless your head, hands and legs are covered. We knew what we was, we might be big mouthed but we knew our place and we're not big-headed. I'm not saying we were angels because kids are kids. We scrumped and done all the things but nothing *really* wrong.

In the past, discipline was administered physically to boys at school and at home, said octogenarian Victor Gray. The youngest of 12 born in 24 years and reared in 14 foot caravans, he grew up in a world that required him to treat others with suspicion, be on the alert and ready to fight for what he could get. This called for very different skills from those needed for dependence on empathy, reciprocity and co-operation. Early life in effect provided a taster of the quality of social relations he was likely to have to cope with in adulthood. It's an expectancy that time has altered. Besides, showmen have an accepting view of their nurture; for along with a stern line taken in obedience, the child receives strong messages about belonging and worth, and they leave an impression.

Evidence lies in Victor's own fatherhood. Far from being a heavy-handed disciplinarian, he was a loving parent. Victor's eldest son says that his father made sure his three children did not take liberties, but wasn't especially authoritarian. Here are Victor Senior's words:

> It's a wonderful life for children to be born into the travelling fraternity, they've always got plenty of company, they're always told how to behave. It's amazing how good they were brought up considering, because we moved about every week. But they didn't get any bad influence because they weren't in one place very long. We had a schoolmaster with a big stick, You singing, Gray? because I wasn't singing loud enough. If I came home, said to my father, I got the cane, he would hit me again. You must have deserved it so how's that! You never got any pity in that respect.

A sense of community in which children are fully involved was conveyed to me unforgettably, by the Elliott family based in South Ockendon, in a chalet bursting with mixed ages. It was the day before Halloween, a busy time of year, and around mid-morning Swales Elliott Senior and Junior were manipulating a transport lorry out of a yard so packed with dwellings and vehicles that there was little room to manoeuvre it on to the unmade road. Elliott Junior was heading for a Showmen's Guild site in Strood. It would be ten o'clock that night before he arrived. Two teenagers were late-breakfasting after a sleepover, and a ten-year old niece, Alice, had walked across the yard to investigate her aunt's cosmetics. Eleven-year old Grace, another neice, cleared the table, washed up and tidied before she and Alice were absorbed into an adult debate. The Elliott's staple day would be spent going and coming together, making a small world inside the big one so interwoven that everything is seen from the same angle. The bustle is, on one hand, comforting; the commitment to work sets a pace that can seem stressful. Bev Elliott smokes continually in a home she described as a communal hall. Swales explained how the extended family lives as a unit even after marriage:

> The family's very important to Showpeople because not only is it family, we all work together. You could see up here this morning me cousins, friends, nephews. They'd all be up here eating breakfast 6.00 am. 7.00, 8.00. There's no such thing as 'On yer bike'. We don't say you're 18 now or you're 21 now and you got to go and find somewhere else to live. They either go with that side of the family or they go with that side of the family. My son's out there, 25, he ain't going nowhere till he gets married then he'll probably come back here anyway. He's very interested in the business. He's

just bought hisself another ride. We never ever chuck anybody out no matter how old or how awful they are. (Laugh) It's the other way round. When the children get married, the grandchildren come, the great grandchildren.

Until the end of the 1950s, fostering was the first episode that interfered with fair-children's puppyish play in the family yard. How does it fit into the pattern of vehement togetherness? The answer is uneasily, though the parents of David Smith, Perry Underwood, and John Gizzi accepted what was generally considered a mutually beneficial custom, despite some heart-ache on both sides. A girl might be withdrawn from a substitute family if she didn't settle in but boys were expected to tolerate temporary sojourns for the greater benefit of the Community. In practice, the move could be upsetting for a child used to spending time in the company of grandparents, aunties, uncles and cousins. On the other hand, fair-children were used to alternative parents, so it could be seen as part of social conditioning that would aid their independence. If the trauma of school was hardly reduced by continuity that fostering provided, sometimes the human interplay worked. John Gizzi was left with happy memories about his foster home:

> The parents left me with some people at Norwich. Mr Parks was a lovely man. He only died last summer; we kept in touch right to the end. He lived right near; he'd look after our yard for us. Cut the grass. He had rabbits and used to grow everything himself because there was no supermarkets then. On Sunday we would eat a rabbit. We was all organic then. (Laugh) They had rabbits and guineapigs for sale at Dereham Fair and I used to be a cheeky young boy. They never saw I was trying to get one for nothing. I got two rabbits actually, and had them on a lead. We went away and Mum said you got to leave them with Mr Parks, so I said all right then. When we come back he said, They was lovely. (Laughter) Mr Parks had 3 or 4 children. I'd go to school with Janice, they tried to give us an education you see, and church and all that on a Sunday. We [showmen] were religious, believe in it and all that, but not *strongly* religious. A couple of days I'd be all right but I used to always miss them. I always wanted to be with me Mum and Dad.

It was a source of pride to Kay Gray that she wasn't fostered, although she regrets the shortfall in regular schooling:

> At New Buckingham there was a farmer and his wife, Mr and Mrs Brown, wanted to adopt me. My father'd shoot a lot so he most probably got to know Mr Brown through clay-pigeon shooting.

They didn't have any children. Little fat, red-cheeked person which perhaps a farmer thought was a healthy looking child – they'd spoil me and they'd take me on the Broads on a Saturday so that was a special treat but when they wanted to adopt me, Please don't let me go Dad. He said, certainly not. We haven't had children to give away. I always remember that but I wish now I'd stopped and had schooling say for the summer.

Showman Frank Sedgewick made the point that the conditioning their children receive makes them 'streetwise', a quality he enlarged upon as being able without hesitation to climb on to Dobbies or into Teapot rides. Other youngsters, by comparison, need parental assistance. Setting aside the show-children's familiarity with the apparatus, it is evident that initiative was and is highly valued. A spunky girl and a tomboy, Kay Gray was certainly encouraged to use her enterprise on the fairground.

My Mum used to do what we called *mind* the Dodgems; sit in the pay box, take the money. She used to drive lorries, and she would help erecting things. We can't do the heavy work as much as a man, though I did. I used to do everything. From 8 years old I can remember building Dodgems up. So did my sister Pamela. I was quite a strong girl, taught how to do this, how not to do that. My dad showed me. Marvellous parents. They had so much common sense. My Uncle Clifford had the Noah's Ark which people in Norfolk call the Royal Hunt. They was positioned first and built up, with me helping Dad. My brother, young Donald, used to look after the Coconut Shy. My late sister Pamela had a Dart Stall, and I had what was called a Pick-a-straw.

Showman John Manning affirmed his faith in the system:

Our children are out on the road and learning life. Bit loud. [But] it's the finest life there is for children. They know all the values and finally, the value of staying out on your own. They see all life, it's a great character-building. I've got 4 children, they're all in the business. The only drawback is the [scholastic] education; that's your hardest part.

CHAPTER SEVEN
'HE ISN'T INTERESTED'
EDUCATION

By referring to education as 'the *hardest* part', John Manning meant the most difficult area to integrate into the travelling life. It is something others acknowledge. The culture is good at nurture, good at sharing; but is still catching up on the balance between home and school. It is not as if measures haven't been taken inside and outside the Community to help the 2,000–2,200 school age children;[1] rather that the problem poses a special challenge.

An article in *The Guardian* by a traveller in 1996 posits the traditional view:

> In Showland, education is seen as a flattie indulgence. A child's education is on the fair – at the gaff handling money, mending machines, and on the road learning the directions and distances between towns. A six year old child can change a £20 note but may never be able to read or write … illiteracy is regarded as an attraction to the fairground, and showpeople turn mistakes to their advantage.[2]

Fifteen years on, the message sounds dated. A growing number of showmen's sons and daughters are pursuing secondary education, a few at university;[3] at the same time, schooling remains a headache for the average showman's son. There is doubt about how much education matters but it is clear

---

[1] Personal correspondence from Ken Marks, The School of Education, Sheffield University.

[2] Dea Birkett, 'The Show on the Road', *The Guardian Weekend* (14 December 1996), p. 16.

[3] Personal communications with Kirk Mulhearn and Valerie Moody, education officers for the Showmen's Guild. Valerie Moody has been awarded an MBE for her contribution to supporting and promoting the education of showmen's children through collaboration with NATT and the Traveller Education Support Services (TES). The president of the Showmen's Guild appointed her as National Education Liaison Officer for the Guild and she was their representative to the European Federation for the Children of Occupational Travellers (EFECOT). Following the loss of EU funding five years ago, this body became ENTE-European Network for Traveller Education. Valerie took part in several European-funded projects including one where she was supported in the preparation and printing of six 'early reader' booklets, based on her memories of growing up in a showman's family (note compiled with the assistance of Pat Holmes, Vice-President of EFECOT).

that some bewilderment and a great deal of sensitivity surround the subject.

Given the lifestyle youngsters plan to pursue, it is hard to make the case for investing time and energy learning something they find a trial and may never, at least directly, use. Then there is fear of the unfamiliar – people, places, fear of being snubbed, and genuine fear of being unable to accomplish the work itself. Boys' antipathy to bookwork is not specific to fair people, but fairground sons are not often given the pressure or encouragement to make the essential effort. What is more, everyone is aware that generation after generation of showmen have found traditional education irrelevant to a lifestyle that, as children, they could hardly wait to embark upon. In effect, this allows boys to consider the long-established platitude that what is known as 'fairground' education, together with modest home-tutoring can substitute for the conventional alternative. Changing attitudes means persuading parents that it doesn't do in the modern world to be illiterate. That the effort *is* worthwhile.

One or two 'educationist' members from the Midland Section have made stalwart contributions on showpeople's behalf. Most statistics gathered by educational bodies, class showmen with other travelers, so their figures may not be reliable,[4] but there is less under-achievement, they say; attitudes *are* changing. The situation is improving all the time. Some of the showpeople's daughters have worked hard and flourished all round, especially as boarders, but when middle-aged men are barely able to speak for emotion, you know you've touched something significant. So it was with some of the showmen who spoke with me about their experiences at school. Lack of understanding from staff as well as from peers, together with social defensiveness made them feel inadequate. John Gizzi reflects:

> I was only young but the teachers used to look down on you. It was in near enough all the schools. Put you at the back of the class, exclude you. We was respectful which you were at that time. People said what you had to do, you never questioned it. But Granny Gray was a clever, clever woman. She was king pin to all. Used to make Mum read the paper, Mum could read and write. I used to learn bits and bobs like that.

---

4 Personal correspondence from Natika Brown, Northamptonshire County Council, Race Equality Team: 'Unfortunately some years ago we, the Regional Group for Traveller Services including Norfolk stopped collecting and analysing regional figures as it was no longer seen as beneficial as the DFES did not request specific data from services ... unfortunately when trying to get the data for Show/Fairground families it is quite difficult as many will ascribe their ethnicity as White British and they then become lost in the figures as there is not a category for them as theirs is a lifestyle and not an ethnicity'.

For Kay Gelder too, most schools were a trial and a perplexity though her willingness to learn was recognized by one memorably good-natured teacher. Like John she fell back on her family:

> Mum made us go to school every place we went to, so every week this was different. You was given so much knowledge from your parents that you could cope, but you was bullied, not only by the children, by the teachers more than anything. We just ignored ignorance, that's the only way. I went to Burnham Market School and the teacher there was horrible to me because I couldn't spell. My Granny Gray said, think how you can get round a word, some people call that a *road*, some say a *highway*. Or perhaps where we'd say, lorry, they'd call it a vehicle. That's a hard word anyway, I still can't spell vehicle though I can read it now. We had to write a story about going down this road on our bicycles, so remembering what my Granny said I wrote *I rode down on my bike*. When that was read out, the teacher said I got it wrong. But I can't spell bicycle, Mrs Clatton, that's why I put bike. It's the same thing, that's what Granny says. For the rest of the week I had to stand on that stool in the corner of the room and recite *bicycle*. I can spell it now because of that, but I never did like going to Burnham Market school after. All I could think of was bicycle. Teachers perhaps couldn't cope with us. But I can remember New Buckingham School, Mrs Honeysuckle the headmistress was lovely. She said if you want, you can stay after school, we will help you with the spelling. Uncle Clifford and Dad used to make me read the newspaper to them. If I come across a word I didn't know, they would make me read it over and over and over again. As you get older you realize how important education is.

A show-woman thought the old complacency had altered for the good:

> Showmen didn't really class education as necessary when I first got married because they thought they knew it all. I shouldn't say that. (Laugh) But they didn't think it was necessary to their business. I remember one of Jimmy's uncles saying when we left Lesley behind at school, you don't love your baby like I love mine. That stuck in my mind.[5]

One showman has not made up his mind about what sometimes seem the dubious benefits of education. For him the problem continues anyway.

[5]   Pat Bugg.

> My boy hates school, most young boys do don't they? I think showmen anyway are brought up with quite a lot of maths dealing with the money and English goes with the job.[6]

Another recounted similar difficulties,

> With our son we really tried. We had tutors. They said to me, Listen, your son is not interested. He's working with us at the moment, he's not interested in doing anything else.[7]

The topic was raised both in jocular and in a despairing vein by parents who felt deeply the impossibility of teaching children what they don't require to know, or intuit as necessary to them. Over and again, they said, 'He isn't' or 'wasn't interested'; a dilemma to which their solution was, in the past, to resort to family lore. The disadvantage of curricula taught at home is that it doesn't encourage critical thinking or creativity. Instead of shaking the status quo it serves to buttress it. On the other hand, some showmen's children benefit from their parent's willingness to extend boundaries, and might legitimately find outsiders' views limited. Perhaps the important question is how much youngsters' antipathy for schoolwork is a reflection of their elders' deep-held instinct about the sufficiency of fairground education with its macho image.

All sections of the Guild have education officers who liaise directly between showmen and the local education authority. In this capacity officers receive a stream of literature from various bodies such as the National Association of Travellers' Teachers (NATT) and the Gypsy Council. NATT[8] takes a wide view of their function, focusing their work not only on individuals but on encouraging integration and informing society about the structure of showmen's lives. At the same time they work with a network of Traveller Education Services (TES) based with local authorities. Perhaps the most visible work of the TES has been the provision of distance learning packs.[9] Using such packs, youngsters benefit from an uninterrupted curriculum instead of attending a series of new schools

---

6   Theodore Whyatt.

7   John Bugg.

8   NATT established in 1980 to support the teachers of Traveller children (Gypsy, Irish Travellers, Showmen's [both Fairground and Circus] children, New Age Travellers and, later, Eastern Roma). NATT was renamed NATT+ in 2008 to reflect the change in Government requirements for Local Authorities to generally restructure for more 'joined-up' services for children and families under a single Director of Children's Services. In practice this often means multi-disciplinary teams drawn from education, social services, health and sometimes the voluntary sector working on an area basis.

9   Personal communication with Chris Derrington, 'We started putting together distance learning packs for Showmen children in about 1992 and this [i.e., the group she worked with in 1992] was the first group of Travellers to access this type of provision in a big way'. See also chapter 14.

during the travelling season – a process acknowledged to be disruptive. Results have been impressive, especially when a family is supportive. The disadvantage is that the onus of study lies with the child and her or his family over a period when earning a living is a pressing priority.

Computers help showchildren maintain contact with winter-based schools when the family is touring. Moreover, the internet provides two-way communication, so a child can receive feedback. Following research sponsored by the Nuffield Foundation in 2003-4, various projects have explored the use of internet technology among travellers. Leicestershire ran a computer-based programme for its travelling communities, as did South Ockendon, towards the end of 2009, when the local branch of the TES arranged for computer equipment to be driven up to the showmen's yards by an instructor. Results of these projects tend to parcel travellers into a single group, but one referred to as ELAMP (E-Learning and Mobility Project) kept some results separate. From the early days, they found computer work developed much more quickly with 'occupational travellers', ie showmen and circus people.[10] Ken Marks, who collated a mass of data from the initiative, believes the project acted as a catalyst in other localities. In general, fairground families were encouraged to purchase laptops, a move they rose to themselves once they realized the computer's potential for their businesses.[11]

As education officer for the London and Home Counties section of the Guild, Swales Elliott communicates both with the showmen at South Ockendon and Thurrock's education authority. Although his own educational background is not unusual and his view of its purpose is largely pragmatic, he has influence because his badge of office is respected, and can sometimes resolve quite quickly problems that seemed to have reached a stalemate:

> All the business is done through the computer. For using a laptop you need to be able to read and write. I didn't do too bad. I got through secondary [school], barely, but I still got through. We do our work on the floor. But the best education showman's children have got is life. A lot of the boys, it's the practical side they do, driving, welding, cutting.

. Niece Grace knows that she drops behind her class when she uses a pack. Being what they call a 'good learner' she is able to catch up. But it is difficult for her to rate schoolwork as highly as fairground work.

Everything we've learned about showmen all our uncles have

---

[10] www.natt.org.uk/elamp-initiatives.
[11] Personal communication with Ken Marks.

learned us. Like my uncle learned me how to drive and all that.

Grace can drive a car, off the highway, of course; as can her ten-year old cousin, Alice. Swales Junior could drive at 7, and the Elliott's grandson took on a lorry when he was 6. Books don't lie around a trailer for the obvious reason that the less you have, the easier it is to travel, so the last thing a showman wants are bulky possessions. Magazines are in evidence, and most showmen families receive weekly installments of *World's Fair* but those who read use libraries whereas, naturally, vehicles are always parked around them. Fairground education is *part* of life, rather than peripheral to it.

It is a paradox that the universally expressed wish to do the best for their children should clash with the view still commonly expressed by male showmen that young men learn what they need to know on the fairground. Nor does the older generation's regret at wasted opportunity seem to make the cycle easier for their sons. Indignant about the quality of education her son received, Swales' sister-in-law was anxious for her granddaughter to attend a school of her choice:

> My son never learnt nothing at his school, only to smoke and fight.
> I went to see the head, I was told he got *forgotten*. Can you
> imagine! It was a terrible school, that's now been closed.

At the heart of the matter is perhaps a further dilemma. A smattering of fair children went to university in the 1970s and moved away from the old life. Education may mean losing members: a small community has to be sufficiently bold and generous towards them to take the risk.

CHAPTER EIGHT
WOMEN'S SPACE

Living in a confined space is an art in itself, there isn't much room for extravagance or originality, yet individuality does surface. Margaret and Pat Bugg are ready company for one another, sisters-in-law and both widowed early, in neighbouring sites in Hooper Lane yard. Two Buggs, they say, laughing at an old joke. Their dwellings display an invitation of outside chairs, and in the narrow strip of grass between them, a long swing seat with a canopy. Pat's corner garden is full of pot plants.

It goes without saying that the chalets are impeccable. What might surprise the uninitiated is just how house-proud the show-woman is with her eye for the bright and shiny, harmonizing colours and matching woodwork. The standard of hygiene expected by custom and tradition competes with that of the most obsessive housewife. This was so even when domestic arrangements were fairly basic. Margaret tirelessly re-arranges her furniture to suit her mood, revealing her love of order. At 82, Pat confesses, she likes a little luxury, a partiality rewarded by presents from her family of decoration and furnishings. Her home is elegant in artistic modern décor rather than the usual browns and beige. Otherwise, there is little else to suggest that she was born an outsider while Margaret comes from showland. Pat says:

> Our first trailer was ten foot which is very small. I'd come from a
> house, we had a living room, front room, kitchen, hot and cold
> water, bathroom. Our bathroom was as big as the whole trailer.
> You got used to everything.

Showpeople reckon the size and lack of storage in their dwellings is the aspect of their lives that outsiders who marry-in have had most difficulty adapting to.[1] This didn't happen with Pat who adjusted instinctively. She was working at a photographer's and going out with the proprietor's son when her gaze caught Jimmy Bugg's at King's Lynn Mart. Time passed, the fair returned, and they met for the second time. Romance hooked her; a pawn to circumstance, her future was sealed. Admitting disappointment, her parents reckoned their ravishingly beautiful daughter's life had taken a dangerous turn. She married knowing that her living area was not going to have the conventional house-dweller's division between living and working areas. Labour-saving gadgets would be limited,

---

[1]   Toulmin, *Pleasurelands*, NFA, Sheffield University, 2003, p. 71.

and everything comparatively cramped. But the bonds of community would reside in space used for everything. There is more to homemaking than smartness, something that time has confirmed. Pat's son was immersed in the fairground until he, like her husband, died young. Looking back on a long fairground life, she finds there are no palliatives to compare with a supportive community. Even mod cons have their disadvantages:

> When I first came up here you had to go to the tap to get water and you'd stand and have a chat. You'd empty your bucket down the drain and you'd have another chat. You'd have one telephone, whoever was near would come and tell you. Now everybody's got everything inside. Water on, deep freezes, the washing machine, the mobile. You don't stand outside and rub on the rubbing board, you just dump it [dirty clothes] in [the machine]. You have to make an effort to get around. I've known everyone up here for 60 years, the nice and the nasty. Though I'm on my own, I don't feel alone. I can go to anyone, d'you want a cup of tea?

Showground historian Vanessa Toulmin finds the first contemporary reference to van-dwellers appears in Charles Dickens' *The Old Curiosity Shop*, published between 1840 and 1841. The house on wheels he describes came fully equipped with a stove, a chest of drawers and a bed. By the 1880s the more prosperous showpeople had begun to use the living wagon as a form of transport as well as a domestic vehicle. The custom spread, and manufacturers sprang up to cater for clients' requirements.[2] The elaborately decorated wagon from 1900 illustrated in David Kerr Cameron's book on fairs is a potent expression of individuality and standing.[3] The front face is framed by carved wood supporting a narrow carved roof. The door has shiny brass accessories, frilly curtain and painted panels in classic design. Side panels are further decorated with carved scrolls and inlaid mouldings, and centrally placed in large letters is the family name. Until quite recently annual visits to the appropriate section of London's Ideal Home Exhibition were an important part of a showpeople's agenda, their homes tasteful evidence that small can be beautiful. Modern living vans as long as 30–40 feet, with pullout walls, bedrooms, bathrooms and fitted kitchens, have only the basics in common with their predecessors. Much ingenuity has gone into domestic amenities and there are plenty of them, as showpeople feel bound to mention. Retired showmen may move into chalets, some of which are brick-based and very solid, but theoretically they can be lifted up and removed from a site, so they pass as mobile homes with planning authorities. Their benefits are noted by a 19-year old whose mother opted for extra room:

2   Toulmin, p. 71.
3   David Kerr Cameron, *The English Fair*, Sutton, 1998, p. 183.

It's been nice to have more space and free-standing furniture, because in a trailer, everything's bolted. Nice to have a full length bath and know when you turn the tap on water's always going to come.[4]

Spaces inevitably influence behaviour. Shirley Stocks remembered her mother's reaction to a hoard of coins that threatened the standard of hygiene in her first home. The coins had been received in payment for selling the Irvin's wagon. She remembered too, the canvas kitchens in which all their food was prepared and eaten when they were travelling from 1935 throughout the '40s. The stove in the living wagon, polished to reflective sheen, was considered sacrosanct:

> Mum had a Hostess stove in the wagon, it was all chrome. But she didn't want to use that one to cook with. Had to have another Hostess stove in the tilt kitchen. It was built with a pole in like the stalls, the canvas went round and on the top so it was almost like a stall. Dad built it up wherever we was, had a big table and chairs and you washed up and did all your cooking there. After a while we had a built-up toilet with an Elsan, I won't tell you what we did before that.
>
> We sold the wagon 'cos Dad was ill, it was a bit hefty for him to drive around and he wouldn't let Mum drive it. Dad delivered the wagon to someone in Oxfordshire and when he came back the money smelled. He said she got it out of a tin from underneath her bed. He said this woman was so scruffy he wouldn't even had a cup a tea, and Mum said we got to wash this money. By then we'd got a bungalow, so we washed all this money in the bath. (Laugh). It would only be £300, it was a lot then. And Mum kept saying, oh my poor wagon! Oh my God, what are they going to do with my wagon. 'Cos Mum was so *clean* you see.

Previous sanitary services were explained by another showman:

> Caravans now have got water tanks built in and sewage tanks so you've got a flush toilet. You've got a shower and a bath and you just fill the tank up, 4 or 500 gallons with a hose. When I was a boy you had what they called a water can. A lot of people still like to have them for the emergency water supply. Four gallon water cans with a neck to fill them up and a spout. Just before the war the Government brought in a law that you had to have a toilet. Most

[4] Zoah Hedges-Stocks, see chapter 14.

of the showmen all their lives dug a hole on the edge of the field and just bury it four or five feet down. In those days that was acceptable. They used to call it the bucket and chuck it.[5]

Hardship is relative, and conditions have eased since Nipper Appleton and his wife, Sandra, lived in a bus. It wasn't all hardship anyway. The scope for improvisation was considerable, a quality that excelled among the Appletons:

Not long after the war we never had a wagon. All me Dad's brothers would buy discontinued buses, I lived in a variety, they was public service vehicles and always well maintained. My dad would fit it up inside with the bunk beds. Wardrobes. Put the back up to make a bit of a kitchen. We never had gas or electric, no central heating. No gas cooker or nothing. We'd have what was called a Hostess stove which was designed particularly for showmen. They had a metal stainless steel frame round the top, with a round lid you lifted for the coal, a little grill and a very small oven at the side. You used to keep them alight when we was on the road. You'd travel in the bus with the family so mum could do cooking on the way to the next place. You packed the shows on the top, some in the front. You'd have that bus 4 or 5 years, then buy another one and start again; they became universal vehicles. We carried on like that until things got better and then we got trailers. We built this ourselves, mostly me brother. Other showmen used to order them and he'd make them in the winter.

Like any group, showpeople embody a range of characteristics, as often as not in the same person. Openness may hide reflectiveness, and extroversion, the desire sometimes to be private. Kim Thurston thinks she needs to be able to retreat because her father, an Eastern Counties showman, stopped travelling a year or two after she was born. Growing up in relative seclusion in Cambridgeshire's Wyton, she had to adapt when she married back into the travelling sector of the Community. On fairgrounds she missed her personal space.

The only thing I have qualms with, is the privacy. I'm a bit of a home bird, 'n when you go on a fairground you got other caravans there, there, and there! That's not your patch. You've got your garden in a house, you got fences round you and that's your domain. This is my domain up here, but not out on the fairground. I find it more difficult than what Robert does, I think it's because

---

[5]   David Smith.

I've been out of the business, I notice the difference between me and him.

While the men have their thoughts fixed in some external object, the trucks and rides, the future; women are more concerned with intimate territory. Together with perceived flirtatiousness, privacy can lie at the very core of feelings about sex. As a child Bernice Stocks saw sex as something that happened between people who love one another, that belonged to them and was their secret:

Before I had this chalet sited, I used to come down and see which way the sun was shining to make sure I got the maximum. I woke the other morning, my bedroom is just the other side of that kitchen. I never shut my bedroom window, nobody can see in and I like to be able to see the sun and the moon. I face those trees; there was a full moon the other side of the tree and it was so beautiful... and if the sun is shining on the winter solstice at noon, it shines straight in my back door and that's important to me. I always think I'm a very basic person and where there's the favours of the solar system, it does definitely effect my mood. People say do I suffer from SAD. I say no, I get angry when it gets dark at 5 o'clock. By the 10 of February it'll be daylight then again and I'll feel like I've come through the winter. I'll feel more alive. I walk quite a lot out the fields with my dog and it's lovely the sunsets and things.

In the site where Pat Bugg's on, the basic space for a caravan is 20 foot width, that's for your caravan and your car. This is something you only realise when you come out of that environment; that we *do* respect one another's privacy. Or maybe you get used to *not* having privacy. We don't live as openly as perhaps people think – we are quite open but when you're in your own home, that's your own home and you make your own privacy. Even though people can hear you arguing next door, you don't get involved. You know *when* to get involved but you don't need to do that very often. How do we make love? *Quietly*, I suppose is the answer. No swinging from chandeliers. I think when you done it all your life ... but basically you have to wait until the children are asleep. (Laugh) I thought my parents' love life was lovely, it made me feel safe. I can remember once or twice some sort of mumbling going on late at night and thinking my mum and dad love one another. That was at the big wagon which we had when I was 12 or 14, Mum would have talked to me about things then so I had an idea what the mumbling was about. It made me feel warm and cosy. That's probably down to how my mum brought us up. I hope to do the same with Zoah.

In children lies the future of the business and security for old age, the 'bread and butter', so to speak, of the parents. But along with national trends, the size of showpeople's families has fallen steeply. This has an obvious bearing when travelling in a confined space. A prime example lies with the Grays, where families of ten, eight and twelve have become reduced to two or three in three generations. Older showpeople can remember times when privation was taxing. Victor Gray, eighty-two in 2008, was full of sympathy for the burdens his mother bore through her fertility, constant moving and lack of space:

> My mother died at 52 because she had a child every other year for 24 year. It was quite a normal thing to do, Queen Victoria had all those children but they didn't have the trouble of them. Mum had 9 girls and 3 boys and I was the youngest. Unfortunately, in those days the caravans were only about 14 ft long. When I come along we had two very long ones, one parted off for boys and [one for] girls. But it was very hard for the women with one or two children, 12 must have been terrible strain. I was 7 when Mum died and I can quite understand it [her death] because in those days there was no aftercare or before care. Wherever you was in the village, you had to find the local midwife. Came down on the bike, ripped the baby out, that was it! Any complications, they had to do theirself.

Mrs Lawrence Appleton II was made of tougher stuff: 10 sons, 4 daughters, and notwithstanding she lived to be 93. Her eldest son, Nipper, had a round-up in 2010, shortly before her death the following year:

> We did have a head count last year. Mum had around 112 or 115 grandchildren and great grandchildren but there's been some more increases since then. She worries at Christmas time or at times of birthdays. She says to me, Oh God, I'd need to borrow from the National Debt to give them all presents.

Strong family codes of ethics preclude aberrant behaviour. A Cambridgeshire showman told of a grandmother who could knock a man down with her fists, and a Suffolk show-woman complained of one family in which children suffered undue corporal punishment. It's impossible to speak for the whole Community but self regulation is the norm where domestic violence is concerned. As Robert Thurston says, if it occurred, fellow travellers would know about it:

You'd see it wouldn't you? We walk down our steps, there'll be another caravan right beside us. You couldn't walk through with a black eye. (Disbelieving laugh). They'd say straight away, what you been up to? Because most of them on the same fair as you is family.

CHAPTER NINE
WOMEN'S SHARE

> It's a blooming hard life, especially for women; you do the cooking,
> the paperwork, the washing, the cleaning and then you have to go
> out and open. You help to build up. Pull down. Pack up the stuff.
> Didn't *have* to, we just did it.

Margaret Bugg's human stoicism shows through, tinctured with humour. Her
emphasis on work and the indoctrinated need to work goes for most show-
women, although many live to a ripe age, reactive and companionable, as was
her mother whom she nursed in an adjacent trailer until she was 95. The married show-woman, invariably more literate than her husband, has often been economic facilitator as well as housewife, child nurturer and stall-holder, moving
seamlessly from the ironing board to the paybox, from the Juvenile to feeding
the family at any hour food is required, from writing letters to totting up
finances. Patently, the acceptance of women's activity on the fairground has not
offered the reverse scope to their men whose gender roles have remained far more
fixed. This goes back to boy's slower intellectual development. By and large, girls
are more adept at the three Rs, so boys were let off the hook. That 'women are
the brains of it, men are the brawn' remains to some degree an apt comment.[1]
Show-women have been queens of what we now call multitasking with its continual small achievements.

Constant moving can be stressful, even if packing a trailer involves the same
procedure each time. You need a ready supply of tea towels to fold between items
of crockery and to block a cupboard's contents. Televisions are laid on a bed,
ornaments wrapped and placed somewhere safe before the sides of the trailer are
pulled in ready to leave the yard. Things do occasionally get broken. It's all, as
showpeople say, 'part and parcel' when plates fly from a dresser. One of the big
questions of modern times is how to combine work and family with a full time
job, something the show-woman has been doing for a hundred years. Her ver-
satility is noted by Vanessa Toulmin:

> One of the striking aspects of fairground society is ... how the
> structure of the society allowed and encouraged women to perform
> whichever role they were good at. This could include all the

[1] See http://www.bbc.co.uk/radio2/radioballads/2006/fairgrounds/index.shtml for an
archived Radio Voices programme.

traditional male jobs such as driving vehicles and doing manual work ..[2]

'Wives in showland are part and parcel of the business and they know that as soon as they get married.' 'Girls do everything they learn the business same as Mum'. The people who made these comments never spoke truer words.[3] Newly married Pat Bugg was prepared for her downsized dwelling when she moved to the fairground, but initiation to her part in the daily round took greater courage.

> We went down to the hoopla. Jimmy said you have to get in there, you got to talk to people, walk round. Don't just stand because everybody will look at you and think you're a fool, and they'll think of you like that for ever. I just wished the ground would open up.

Some division of labour was acknowledged by a senior showman.

> The men usually do the driving the building and the pulling down, the maintaining of whatever. The women even now mostly do all the cooking, send letters and get the *Worlds Fair,* look what's on and where.[4]

If this reflection makes women's work sound subordinate to men's, it belies the fact that women are expected to understand the fairground as thoroughly as fathers, husbands or brothers. The large number of girls and women involved in the shows goes back to mid-Victorian times when they paraded in front of wild beasts, and war brought their powers of leadership to the forefront. An editorial from *The Worlds Fair* of 1916 stressed how they 'rose nobly to keep the business going'[5] to become pioneering rôle models for heroines like Mrs Cohen from Ireland who travelled alone in her living carriage and built up her photography booth when she was 74.[6] Right up to the present day, there have been stalwarts like Laura Manning (1900–80 or 81) who held the family business together for some thirty years after her husband died.

Patently it takes a certain kind of personality to respond to the energetic camaraderie and demands of the Community. Fiona Gray was another 'incomer'; 18 when she met Kenny, 21 when they married, and married now for as many years again. One of the first things Kenny said on the telephone was 'I'm

---

[2] Vanessa Toulmin, *Pleasurelands*, NFA, University of Sheffield, 2003, p. 67.
[3] Arthur and Cilla Morrison.
[4] Nipper Appleton.
[5] Toulmin, p. 67.
[6] *World's Fair*, August 15, 1908.

a very lucky man' for being married to Fiona, so the match worked more than just notionally. Like Pat Bugg's parents, Fiona's had misgivings about losing a pretty daughter to what they supposed were less congenial ways, but her father, a quantity surveyor, was a communicative man; and his wife was open-minded. Fiona grew up in a big house and garden, landing herself a 'good' i.e. *well-paid* job in the accounts department of Norwich Union, a skill she put to good use in her married life. Kenny describes her parental home as 'extremely posh', a comment with which she agreed.

> I didn't like being enclosed [in an office] and often when I was younger, I moaned about work. Now I think well, that did come in handy [training in accountancy]. People see you on a sunny day and think you've opted out. They forget there's Saturday night and Sunday you've got to get it all down. Pack up the trailer and move on. They don't realise all the things that come with it. But it's the freedom. Whilst you've got these things, you've [also] got the freedom.

Women have tolerated a good deal for companionship and what they refer to as freedom. This is partly physical. The freedom to inhabit a sphere that has few doors and no edges, a knitting of inside and outside that a lot of Westerners may seldom experience unless they are camping. To bring in money during the winter, Shirley Stocks' father, Tom Irvin, went logging on a contract for pit props at a small place near Sandy. When they were permitted, she and her mother accompanied him. It was the great outside that Violet Irvin hankered for, said Shirley, in whom something of the mother's exuberance surfaces:

> He didn't let me go very often but I used to like to do it. Used to get on the back of the lorry with me scarf and gloves on when we took them round. Mum used to love to be out if she could be in the yard working that saw, therefore I had to learn to do the inside work days I wasn't at school. Soon learned how to cook. Grandad used to do scrapping and one of her jobs used to be breaking up batteries. She loved it. Sorting the iron and stuff like that. Used to have a bus to pull the wagon. Mum said 'I can drive that bus'. No she weren't allowed to do that while Dad was alive. He wouldn't let Mum drive the wagon [either]. But it was a bit hefty for him cos Dad was ill. He died when he was 43, Mum drove the bus for a while with a small trailer behind .. We jogged along. If something happened like that, I mean we lost Dad early, you picked yourself up by your britches and get on with it.

CHAPTER NINE – WOMEN'S SHARE

No one denies that women have played an active part in showland society. During the Second World War they represented their husbands on the Guild Committee, and Jacquie Gray now holds office in her own right. Despite their ability, the only females to fracture the male monopoly and serve on the Showmen's Guild's Central Council are Margaret Deakin-Studt, treasurer for eleven years from 1938, followed by Sandra Wright who became area representative for the Yorkshire Section in 1996. Had show-women feminist sympathies, they might have objected to their outdated subordination, starting with the debatable word 'showmen'. To have remained uncompetitive with their husbands could be the greater strength. They appreciate that the man is adept in the physical world, his credentials proclaimed by the diameter of his calves and biceps. He has remained conservative and they defer to his protectiveness.

Margaret Bugg looks back on her life with astonishment at how much she accomplished. She might, she owns in retrospect, have been wary of such engagement had she realized the extent of its commitment to tough multiple duties. The reward is a sense of achievement for half a partnership in which shared responsibility has always been basic. It is a paradox seen in Asian cultures where women may take a lead role in domestic and economic affairs but appear subservient in public. While the men have nominal authority, women retain the power.

CHAPTER TEN
'THE GLUE THAT BINDS SHOWMEN TOGETHER'
THE SHOWMEN'S GUILD

There is no shortage of praise for the Showmen's Guild; no other travelling community has a presiding body with the same authority or overarching functions. In 1957 *The Times* roundly approved its solidarity, ranking it as 'one of the best governed and most co-operative' professional bodies and Employer's Trade Unions in the kingdom.[1] At the end of the millennium its prestige was still recognized in official circles even if its power had diminished, due largely it was reckoned internally, to the weight of functions it was required to perform.[2] Whatever it's shortcomings, the Guild's democratic principles have excelled. There is no division between members and management, and although there is a recognized command structure, the only paid officers are the secretaries of each region and the staff of a small central unit in Staines. Its sole source of income is subscriptions calibrated according to the equipment a family possesses, but as each member receives a single vote, the weaker are better represented than the strong. There is, of course, no obligation to belong. Alternative groups[3] have been set up, a number of which operate independently. But until recently it was difficult to function outside and difficult for someone who was not born into the travelling community to join.

Founded in 1889 as the Van Dwellers' Association, the Guild was reconstituted under its present flag in 1902, and ratified into sections by 1907. Since then it has had to fight on many fronts, against government legislation, local authorities and property developers as well as prejudice. After the Second World War with a significantly increased membership, it helped to defeat 268 Private Bills, and exemption clauses in more than a thousand Bills over sixty years.[4] First concerns have been running fairs, liaising with local councils and lobbying Parliament. On top of this, an extensive agenda includes regulating rents; inspecting equipment; running charity events, a composite calendar of social gatherings; and organizing an internal disciplinary system. This last governed by rules that have evolved over the years. Victories have been and continue to be offset by difficulties, as longtime General Secretary, Thomas Murphy, understood: 'As fast as we overcome one set ... others arise, and so it

1   *The Times*, 5 August, 1957.
2   ETR, Fairs I: xx, 47.
3   See chapter 16.
4   Vanessa Toulmin, *Pleasurelands*, p. 73.

will go on ...'[5]

The slick green cover of a *Guild Year Book* belies the comprehensive nature of its contents. 'Issued for the use of members only' informs a line beneath the title, followed by the year, and fairground emblem. Lest any fail to recognize what the body is all about, photographs of the central office in London and the boardroom with its long table come next. Page 2 gives a map of how to reach the office; which direction, which motorway, at which junction you leave the M25. Private, modest and eminently practical it may be, but the *Year Book* bulges with names and faces. For a people who respect the trappings of office, the 2010–11 edition allots 40 of more than 200 pages to photographs of its committees and past presidents, complete, since 1932, with chains and pennants. Another 50 pages go to lists of members and officers in regional sections, leaving roughly half its close-written text to rules under headings such as 'membership', 'procedure at meetings' and 'rights and privileges held on the fairground'. Notice of meetings and reports from the Central Council are published in the independent weekly paper, *World's Fair*. The Guild might appear neatly presented with regulations, names and annual subscriptions; the truth is that changes in ruling have to be approved with a two third majority in all ten sections, and abiding by collective decision can be unwieldy. Not surprisingly, the organization seems on occasion to be a slave to its complicated constitution.

Perhaps the most basic of the Guild's rules was introduced in the 1920s to protect weaker members against internal rivalry. In effect it has governed proceedings ever since. The Two-Year Rule as it is called, maintains that any showman who occupies a site on a fairground for two years has 'an established right of tenure'[6] in the next one. The effect was immediate. Instead of a fairground dominated by riding masters (ride owners) as they had been since the Guild's inception, causing a markedly unequal distribution of wealth; showmen who possessed favourable positions held on to them. Subsequently, these positions got passed to their heirs, ensuring the stability of the family business unit. Democracy had its downside. Sites vary conspicuously, and continuity of site meant continuity of equipment to fit its size and shape. This took place at the expense of development and innovation. Indeed, conservatism and protectionism are criticisms the industry has had to negotiate. On the other hand, the new rule helped to serve community spirit in more than one way. There is evidence that social problems are related to inequality of income rather than average living standards.[7] Inequality is likely to be accompanied both by more status competition and more anxiety. So what matters is people's standing in

---

[5] Thomas Murphy, *History of the Showmen's Guild of Great Britain 1889–1948*, quoted in *Pleasurelands*, p. 74.

[6] *Showmen's Year Book*, 2010–11, p. 105.

[7] Wilkinson and Pickett, pp. 20, 25, 27, 29, 44.

relation to others in their own community. If promoting equality is the best way of improving the social environment, the Two-year Rule was a masterly piece of social engineering.

Keith Miller, the Guild's General Secretary since 1986, was a banker by training,[8] born in Wales where he knew its fairs from childhood. He might not have daily contact with individual showmen, but he is a good communicator, and well aware of the impact a single person can make. An example he cites is the high status offered German showmen, something he puts down to his opposite number in that country. One of his own first projects was to take on European legislation, his aim being to comply with its broader regulations. This forced them to adopt human rights legislations, and opened membership to people from outside the UK. In practice the move made little difference to numbers in the Community which continues to draw largely from British showmen's families. Other aspects of Guild policy have been profoundly influenced by European law, especially rules on safety – something else he sees as absolutely basic to the business.

> Rule 29 [in the *Year Book*] tells you basically what my duties are. My number one priority is always to look after the interests of all my members. But though I am administrative head of the Guild, there are 10 sections and they look after their members in that locality. Number two is financial – this maybe is why I got the job 'cos there were about 10 people downstairs, Wing Commanders retiring early from the RAF; they [the selection committee] might have been impressed I was a bank manager. The last one includes legislation that may affect the members. Planning, safety, that sort of thing. Our parliamentary agents, Bircham, Dyce and Bell, send me a copy of any Hansard reports on legislation that's going to affect this industry. If I see something that's worth looking at, I'll speak to the all-party chairman or co-chairman and say I want a meeting with this department before they make a green paper law. We do have a group of parliamentarians in the house to look after our interests, it's called the All-Party Parliamentary Fairs and Showgrounds Group[9] The membership of MPs and Lords is about 80 so we're the biggest group in the country after the CIU [Working Men's Clubs & Institutes Union] who look after working men's clubs. They are a great help.

[8] With associate membership of the Chartered Institute of Bankers.
[9] An unofficial group of MPs who are interested in a specific subject who help the group convene meetings with the Government. The Register of All-Party Groups for April 2010 gives 6 officers and 20 qualifying members.

After I joined, I pointed out to the Central Council of the Guild that the Treaty of Rome 1982 led the member states on matters like safety. I said you should also open membership to the EU states as well as people domiciled in this country. They thought I was mad! but I persuaded them to change the rules and open the membership. I'm sure you're aware what power – in certain matters – European directives have. They have a very very keen safety union, and anyone who comes to a fair is guarded by these directives. I was amazed coming into the industry and doing research on their safety record which wasn't good. I said look, you are a ride-selling industry, and the majority of ride-occupiers are children, why are you so lax? Didn't go down very well but I persisted and it's a lot better. In 2000 we had 3 bad fatalities, two in London and one in Redruth, the worst we've ever had in one year. By then our safety record had begun to improve, it was because someone from an inspection body we were using wasn't doing his job properly. He was prosecuted and went to gaol. I had one of the civil servants from the Ministry of Works and Pensions phone up and say Mr Miller, if you have another bad accident the PM is going to close it. Thank God, nothing happened and it's improved again over the last 2 years. Now other Guilds in Europe are envious of the record we have. But the General Secretary of the ESU [European Showmen's Union] was a German chap called Ulrich Rust. He was 6ft 6, a very persuasive man, very good at his job, and he made sure the facilities the Germen showmen were offered made ours pale to insignificance.

The Guild's basic democracy means a lot to Arthur Morrison. After three years on the Norwich and Eastern Counties section, he moved to Central Council. Since then he has been given life membership in token of respect for his contribution and he is proud of it. Moreover the relationship is reciprocal because dry humour, courage, and a longing to be understood make him a good advocate for the Community. Incensed by false perceptions of showmen, he doesn't miss a chance to instruct and educate. At meetings with councilors, for instance, he will ask to be seated next to the most influential man in order to put the showmen's case. Official honour and decoration are significant to him; and a penchant for official language suggests his way of trying to beat bureaucracy is to emulate bureaucracy at its own game. To Morrison's mind image is all-important. I met him cleaning his car in respectfully creased greys outside his chalet in Hooper Lane yard. His shiny briefcase was carefully stocked with items selected to inform our talk. Known among friends as 'the Norfolk terrier', he has campaigned doggedly to improve the fair people's lot.

Until you make friends with people you're not accepted. We got an awful lot of friends, but I've known someone here for 30 years and he said, they're trying to do away with your fair in Norwich's Chapelfield Gardens. They're worried about the damage to the roots of the trees underneath the trucks. You can understand it because you don't pay no rent. I said, excuse me, we pay £5000 for one week and another £5000 in case we *do* any damage in the park. That will never be published in the local paper, they don't seem to be interested in putting our point. And when there's a debate, you get all the people what's totally against fairground but nobody that likes fairground say anything. In the year 2008, it's amazing how some people think you're still in the dark ages. People don't think we're organized. They think we all live together and share our babies. *Honestly*! Where d'you all bunk? We don't 'bunk' anywhere, we've got proper homes with all the facilities! What we've grown up with, certainly me and my family, is trying to convince people we're not Gypsies. It's another community who for generations have done what they want to do. Good luck to 'em; they're quite proud that they're Gypsies. But meet anybody for the first time, say showmen' s caravan site, they say, Oh, Gypsy camp. I say no, the Gypsy camp is in another part of Norwich, that's run by the City Council, the Gypsies pay rent, presumably, to them. This is our own freehold property, which is in another part of Norwich completely, bought by the Showmen's Guild 60 years ago and showmen have developed it ever since. You get the New Age travellers, that's a completely different thing, educated people who drop out of that society and go back. Circus people are a small community who tend to have their own yards, and in the summer when they're tenting, they employ trapeze artists and horse riders. As soon as the circus season finishes they [artists] go home to Spain, Italy, wherever they live.

The Showmen's Guild of Great Britain is recognized in Government. There's no pecking order, if you've got all the big rides or only a kiddies' roundabout, you're equal in rights, and we've got our own MPs watching how legislation effects us. We've got several showmen are MBE, I think they was in last week's *World's Fair*. We elect a chairman every 3 years. I've done my 3 and was only last month elected to the Central Council which meet for 3 days in January. Then we have an MP's luncheon in London where we invite all the MPs in our own areas. The President of the Showmen's Guild is Jimmy Williams, he's a born and bred showman as [is] his grandfather but he was born and travels in the Midland area. We have our own chaplain and when President Whitelegg was president, we got our own stamps. Each section's got its own football team. They have the Challenge Cups and afterwards dances. One thousand people sat down to the Lancashire Ladies' Evening, about 12 people went from here. So you know everybody, you meet everybody and later on you get invitations to weddings.

Both Morrison's grandfathers were showmen from further north. He was born just outside Bedford, like them, in a caravan. Small, and highly strung, he is not an obvious sportsman yet he played football for the Eastern Counties Showmen when he was single, since when he has totted up more than fifty years of a firmly based marriage with Cilla. He looks after the Club House in Hooper Lane yard and they share the Guild's life membership:

My [maternal] grandfather was named Hood, and he travelled extensively in Northamptonshire. They had the same type of vehicles but not so heavy, which was drawn by a horse. My father's father was a Scottish showman, he must have come down when he got married. My father was born at Birmingham Onion Fair in 1901, and my wife is a Norfolk showperson. Cilla's father was the secretary for this [Eastern] branch [of the Guild] when I was courting. He used to travel all round here with the firm of Thurstons which are a big name in Norwich. We've had children's roundabouts, stalls and various games, food kiosks – hot dogs and hamburgers, and old-fashioned sweets. Cilla and I used to travel all over the place, Sussex, Kent. As we got older, we stayed here for the winter, because Cilla's parents was here. But Easter, we still went off on our travels. I'm 72, I travelled until I was 65. I'd really had enough of moving vehicles up and down the country. You apply to the Showman's Guild for a permanent site.

It was clear from the start that the Guild would have to assert control among its members in order to protect their interests, a jurisdiction that made significant advances after the Second War with respect to fairs. Rule Number 21 in the *Year Book*[10] deals inclusively with fairs, feasts, wakes and winter

[10] *Showmen's Year Book*, 2010–11, p. 93.

quarters, a clause with a prominent subdivision labeled 'Undesirable Activities'. Here prohibited is any method of working that strikes the appeals committee as 'dishonest', 'indecent' or 'in breach of ... the Betting and Gaming Act of 1963' etc. This ruling saw the end of seemingly harmless practices such as palmistry, fortune-telling and selling hydrogen-filled balloons, along with the use of live ammunition in shooting stalls, impenetrable dart-boards and other tricks that took advantage of the narrow margin between gamesmanship and deception. Conjuring and dealing in 'spurious currency' were decried in George Sanger's youth though he was not averse to 'cunning tricks and artifices' in his early years.[11] Warnings to showmen were supported by blanket measures to clamp down on itinerant tradesmen from outside the Community. 'Run out merchants' as they were called because they travelled light so as to make off quickly when challenged, sold useless trickeries on the sidelines. 'They would come with a balloon as big as that ... on a string and there'd be the rest on a tray and nobody could blow... if you could blow 'em at all they'd be about as big as a penny by the time you'd get 'em up'. Showmen sometimes took the matter upon themselves. 'If the write ups didn't stop them, in the *World's Fair* and that – then a punch in the earhole from a Showman usually did. And they had quite a few before they got the message ...'[12]

Regulation for infringement of complaints between showmen has been dealt with, by contrast, in a way that commends itself both inside and outside the Community. This is a self-regulating system of peer-group judgment that moves through a series of stages, and works so well, the law courts are seldom involved. A retired showman says:

> We got the Showmen's Guild Book of do's and don'ts. If you're naughty you come up before the committee. It's a good system, if it wasn't for that, showmen're like any other people, they'd go willy-nilly here and willy-nilly there.[13]

Thanks to showmen's irrepressible humour, proceedings at appeals committee meetings are not necessarily as dry as they might sound. Arthur Morrison explained the system his own way.

> If my roundabout was on a particular site and next year Tommy took it, I would have the right to lay a complaint under whatever rule it was, 23A(c). Then it would be heard by the Eastern Section committee. Whoever lost, if we [I] wasn't satisfied, we would then

[11] 'Lord' George Sanger, *Seventy Years a Showman* (MacGibbon & Kee, 1966), Introduction.
[12] *The Fairground*, Whitechapel Gallery Exhibition Catalogue, 1977, p. 32.
[13] Victor Harris.

go to the appeals committee in Central Office which I sit on. There, you get one person from each of the ten sections so there'd be no relations. If the loser still wasn't satisfied, he'd go to Tribunal which is the Queen's Councillor, and two partners. That's as far as it goes. If it was a big thing you could go to law. We never do; if you lose to three committees, you could reckon you're guilty.

Here the practice receives an overview:

There's a whole system for disputes which operates very well. The first stage is within the community, and after all, we don't have that outside. If you've got a grudge or something against your neighbour, you've got to think where you go. Whereas on a [fair] ground, you can have this thing worked out among a group of peers. But if, you're arriving at a town at whatever time of night, and you've come anywhere between 20 and 200 miles. You've got to get your caravan set up. The loos set up. The water collected. The rides pulled in the right place. Then you've got to build up all the rides. You can't afford to be disagreeing with people at too deep a level.[14]

Whatever its merits, internal criticism will be leveled at the Guild. One showman noted that in serving on the committee, you make enemies. Another owned that under duress from the claims of business, he would prefer to serve well or not at all. A third became disenchanted with the procedure. This could reflect the caliber demanded for leadership in reconciling the views of strongly voiced members:

When I was 21 I was on the Central Council, vice-chair for the section but I got very frustrated with the members. It started out to protect the business from outside and it spends 90% of its time arguing showmen between showmen which is not what my grandfather started the Van Dwellers Association for. Told them when I see some new blood coming on ... I h'ant seen any yet.[15]

It is not only showmen who lack volunteers for public office. Difficulty recruiting officers from people with so many calls on their time means that the burden is apt to be left to those with the strongest social conscience. As a result, the same people show up where circulation would be more representative. Notwithstanding, most showmen appreciate the tireless exertions made by the

[14] Ian Starsmore.
[15] Frank Sedgewick.

Guild on their behalf. Donald Gray and Walter Underwood belonged to it in their time. Nipper Appleton served for ten years during which he was a safety officer among other commitments; John Bugg, Jacquie Gray, Swales Elliott, Frank Sedgewick, Ian Starsmore and John Thurston have each done a stint on committees and John Manning was the London Counties Section chairman of the body described as the glue that binds showland society together.[16] Victor Harris, Chairman of the Eastern Counties Section for a dozen consecutive years and a strong proponent for cultivating relationships with his local community, is back on the committee in his retirement while undergoing chemotherapy for cancer. Harris recognizes the problems and the gains inherent to service:

> Normally you do it for three years, but nobody don't want the job.
> It's a little bit time-consuming. When we were travelling full time
> it's hard work. You can't neglect your business. It's easier for me
> nowadays. Matter of fact, I've got a committee meeting tomorrow.
> The Guild has its drawbacks but it looks after us and keeps us
> together.

16   Toulmin, *Pleasurelands*, p. 74.

CHAPTER ELEVEN
'A LOT OF SOCIAL EVENTS'

Everyone knows almost everyone by name, business and heritage in showland's tight intermarried world, an aspect of the culture particularly pronounced in bigger congregations. On Hooper Lane yard, for instance, where nearly all the Eastern Counties showmen have relations, Cilla Morrison knows the showmen's ages, what businesses they possess, how many children they have, their present run of fairs and how long each is likely to last. Her information will be factual, making a compendium of statistics that slot together like pieces of jigsaw but for another fair person, listening, emotional content is there too. Belonging to a social network establishes and confirms identity, and this sense of belonging leads showmen to interact in extroverted ways. John Manning says:

> It's the way they're brought up, they go to social functions. But they don't all marry into the business, it's not so close as it was.

An invaluable aid to networking is the weekly *World's Fair*, an independent trading paper in which virtually every household follows events. Because the paper tends not to find room for stories that feature independent activities, it perpetuates the image of the group as melded and uniform. De Francis Mellor, the founder, first published in 1904; and present editors, Paul and Lynne Whatmore are related to him, making the tabloid family-orientated.[1] The staff is small, the circulation up to 20,000, the size of the paper varies with the time of year. The language is simple, the coverage, now, fairly predictable; the bulk of space going to detailed reports of recent fairs. Then there are correspondence columns, genial birthday recognitions and photographs of ever more elaborate weddings. The *In Memoriam* columns are as deep-felt as the nuptials are ostentatious. Each highly illustrated issue is rich in personal sentiments. Josie

[1] The Mellor family founded *World's Fair*, editing and presiding over the paper until 2005, since when the Whatmore family has owned the business. Paul Whatmore is the great-nephew of the founder, de Francis Mellor whose sister, Rosalie, was involved with her brother in the business and sold the first copies of *World's Fair* at Belle Vue in Manchester. She married travelling showman Thomas Whatmore, from a prominent Lancashire showland family. De Francis did not have children. Paul's father, Mark Whatmore (de Francis's nephew) became Chairman for many years until his retirement. Paul has worked in the business since 1988. His wife, Lynne joined the firm in 1994. *World's Fair* allots two pages to the smaller circus community and its fantastical shows.

Gray explains how the paper fills a combination of business and social needs:

> If we've got a fair that we need extra equipment at, we can
> advertise there's some ground to let, then if somebody's got a spare
> week they can ring up. We fill in with each other like that. And if
> you've got something to sell or you're looking to buy something,
> you look in the sales column. But it's increasingly more expensive
> to buy and sometimes it's quicker just to ring up and say, where're
> you going the week after next? I read the things that interest me, it
> might be the birthdays or the letters, and Larry reads the reports on
> the different fairs, see if everybody's getting a living or not.

The desire to amuse is a sociable instinct; showmen are all for pleasure and
they know how to mourn, their first reaction to the big events in human lives
being to get together. An oblique view of their sociability comes from someone
who married into and travelled with the community, serving as chairman of the
Guild's Eastern section for a chunk of his life. Ian Starsmore marks how
responsibility and respect for the elderly are features of collective living; patently
something from which all parties benefit. His perspective is that of an outsider
from a small town background.

> I came from a family in Lincolnshire ... how typical are these
> things? English families, who don't talk to their relatives, who
> barely talk to their neighbours, and I entered this world of almost
> an un-English gregariousness and physical strength and joy and
> energy, which was overwhelming. Which I adored and learnt a lot
> from. We met at Brighton because I was at Sussex doing
> post-graduate and Lesley was doing a degree at the Education
> College. We married in 1970 and between 500 and a thousand
> people appeared. This is very common at weddings and funerals.
> The first year James was born, I worked at Leeds Polytechnic and
> we'd spend the whole summer, Christmas and Easter, travelling
> round East Anglia with the Grays and the Bugg families on the fair.
> Sometimes I built up the rides, mostly the stalls, and worked on
> them. It was a wonderful education.
>
> The people I knew best were my in-laws, Pat and Jimmy Bugg. I
> don't like these people being thought of as 'characters', as though
> they're finished, quaint, nothing-to-do-with-us. Jimmy Bugg was a
> great guy. He had a wonderful baritone voice, would sing at the
> dances or weddings. A very outgoing chap. And my former
> brother-in-law, James, was a great favourite with everybody, funny,
> amusing, as many of them are. The sort of person who can go into

a pub and make the whole place come alive. James died of cancer a few years ago. While he was with the fair he redesigned and rebuilt the Waltzer. He was divorced[2] which is unusual on the fairground. We come to this paradox, because it is quite an old-fashioned society where people marry and that's what you do, and don't get divorced. But James remarried and took a pub on, and made a lot of money from nothing, it was all his energy and work. He and his dad and the Grays would go to Norwich and drink and party with everybody. They knew shop keepers, traders, publicans, councilors, lots of local lads. After all, fairground people are business people, that's what it's about really, getting a living. There's this style to it which is more outgoing, much more physical; partly to do with entertaining people. I think it rubs off because they know so many people. They're able to maintain a kind of ease and at the same time be aware of what's going on underneath. Very quick because they have to watch carefully what's happening behind them, to the side of them, in front of them. They're good at reading people. Good at telling stories – wonderful stories that are shared across generations.

A different thing – again it's not an English thing – you hear so much about generations being split. Well, small children, teenagers, middle aged and elderly people will all talk to each other. They learn this. Strong young men would address senior women with respect. How you gettin on my darling? How's it going? Lovely to see you. And a great sense of that kind of dynamic community which I thought was beautiful and impressive, and was the only thing that could sustain a life of such hard physical work. Of course there were rogues, there are in any community, but the people I knew were absolutely straight, honest, hard-working, great to be with, very generous in themselves and with their time. I remember James once on the grounds at Norwich when there was a group of teenage lads being very dangerous. He lost his temper, ran across and dived into the middle of them, knocked out about five lads and the rest ran away. (Laugh) Great physical strength and good humour as well. They have a characteristic which is, I want to say more Latin, so that people are not afraid to touch each other. We live in a country where nobody must touch a child. What they do is grab a child, squeeze as hard as you can and say, are you all right, my love? That's the proper way to deal with people. And you put

---

[2]   See ETR, II: 20, 'Divorce is very rare'.

your arm round the old person. Look after them. At James' funeral there were a thousand people I think. That's not uncommon, meanwhile I heard someone at the college say they weren't going to go to a funeral because it was five miles away. Showpeople do all the things that other people do, lose money, travel 200 miles, take care of the kids, whatever it is, *together*. Big talks afterwards about James, his life. About each other. Exchanging of stories. This intensity must be quite rare in England. I've seen a similar thing in a hospital in Peterborough, where a large group of Muslim people came through together, visibly showing grief. I don't want to paint too sentimental a picture but certainly there was this strong sense of this community and togetherness, and if you were in trouble, you wouldn't be on your own. That's what I learned from them, this way of behaving which was the opposite of what I'd known in a small shop in Stamford where you'd lock the doors and not get involved in other people's lives. Don't speak to your aunt in the doctors – she doesn't know who the hell you are anyway, and people barely shake hands. Sometimes they don't look at each other.

Another incomer, one who has remained in the Community since her marriage, says:

It's a different lifestyle. They're more close-knit and a more outgoing because they're always meeting and dealing with the public, it gives them a slightly different outlook to someone who has a job and works within that job[3]

It was thanks to the Guild's dances that Kim Thurston remained in touch with travelling showmen after a settled childhood near Biggleswade. Kim's father, Tom Irvin, withdrew from the fairground around 1970, sending his three children to the local school. After a while, he started breeding wild boar in a large yard with moorings on the river off Wyton's Huntingdon Road. His son became a marine engineer, one daughter married outside the Community and if his younger daughter, Kim didn't 'parade'[4] as their mother had done in her

---

[3]   Fiona Gray.

[4]   A term used by senior showmen for taking part in dancing or charade shows once popular on the fairground. Martha Irvin was in a show called *The Half-bodied Lady* for which she blamed her arthritis, and another show known as *Second Sight* in which she held a skull blindfolded. Kim still owns the costume she wore, a leotard and gentleman's jacket on which she hand-sewed thousands of beads and sequins.

travelling years, her good looks won Sandy's vote as Carnival Queen.[5] The honour brought her a prize of £100 and a ride on a float. Although Tom Irvin left the business, he continued to maintain close ties with show people and returned increasingly to showmen's ways. Eventually he sold his house to set up home in a chalet he called *The Wagon* after the memory of showmen's dwellings. Today his land contains a boat as well as fairground apparatus. Kim duly met and married Robert Thurston, saying:

> It was just comfortable to go back in [with the travelling community]. It's quite nice because everywhere you go there are people you know. Robert knows friends out of the business and there's all my school friends scattered all over the place. Some are abroad. You try and meet up with them but their holiday time is our busy time. Mum and Dad have got a lot of friends from when they settled down so we keep in touch and socialise with them too.

Robert and Kim's trailer is pulled up not far from *The Wagon* on Tom Irvin's land. The yard is approached through a remote-controlled gate set in a high hedge opposite Huntingdon Garden Centre where the couple take on seasonal work when they're not travelling. Conviviality is natural to both partners, Robert said:

> Me and Kim about 5 years after we was married, went into the amusement park at Billing Aquadrome on the outskirts of Northampton for 7 or 8 years. We stayed in one place all the time. We had several rides in there, a Burger Bar, a big Astroglide [a slide]. When my son was about 12 we decided to come back on the road so we bought a Super-Bob from Belgium and improved it. We tend to speak to everybody. We speak to the manager and the lady that cleans the toilets, speak to farmers who are millionaires. We do have a lot of [Guild-run] social events. We have dances at Cambridge fair, then Peterborough, Nottingham, Hull. Most of the big fairs have 2 or 3 dances as they call them. They hire a big night club. The Easter dance will be in the middle of London somewhere and then we got a load of football clubs as well. That's where you meet people from different sections.

The whole dynamic of the Community encourages internal marriage, dynastic matches between powerful clans based on business and social criteria. That is not to say that romance doesn't feature. Fairground weddings are less

---

[5]   In 1983.

distinctive in the twenty-first century than they were before society at large developed a fashion for the big splash, but just as 500 will attend the Cathedral funeral of a showman of relatively modest standing;[6] two or three-day gatherings are not uncommon at weddings. Weddings mark the initiation of a routine in which spouses work closely together, firmly under each other's eye. The rewards are manifest; as an institution, marriage is valued highly. Kim and Robert's, relatively simple, took place in Northill church where Kim had worshipped as a child. To judge from the experience of three older showmen, they could receive some of their most sustained delight from their matrimonial partnership.

Tall at 82, with film-star looks, Victor Gray might have been ten years younger; he was nevertheless, depressed, for marriage had been a flame without which his life seemed hardly worth living. This made it difficult for me to regret his escape within a year of our meeting:

> I think the main blessing in my life was meeting my wife, I was 36 and she was 23. I loved her for a long time before we got married, but I don't think her mother ... you know they were a very big concern, their name was Thurston, and that particular time I just had a couple of stalls, so I wasn't good enough. (Laugh) We made it in the end and we had 3, I think they're marvellous, my kids. I couldn't ask for better children. When my wife was alive we still carried on with the business but since she's been gone there's no point. She was only 66 when she died. After you lost the one you love you find yourself looking out the window all the time. There were places like the Cambridge Fair, you'd think how lovely, next week we're at Cambridge and all your mates are there. That and King's Lynn Mart was my highlights, there again there was dances and parties. It was what you looked forward to all the year.

Divorce remained rare in showland until the twenty-first century. This is reflected in the willing rectitude of a show-woman:

> In my day nobody ever got divorced 'cos quite simply you just had to make it work. (Laugh). But nowadays they work on the principle that we've only got one life and they're not going to be unhappy. Divorce is still quite rare and infidelity is very rare. Probably because we haven't got the time to spare. (Big laugh). Basically we're just very boring. I love it though, wouldn't change it for the world.[7]

---

[6] Tommy Bond's funeral was held in Peterborough Cathedral in January 2011.
[7] Josie Gray.

Showland can not be wholly resistant to national social swings. Changes are apparent in each generation, and seniors invariably rued their married children's restlessness. Unmarried couples live together on the fairground, yet this has been the case outside the Community since the end of the first World War when clumsy contraceptive devices became available.

With formality being eroded at all levels of society, even mid-life showpeople have a nostalgia for their fading rituals. Bernice Stocks remembers the big winter Guild meetings of the mid '60s when her family stayed at the Regent Palace Hotel, making expeditions to London sights, the Ideal Home Exhibition and a pantomime. A highlight for women was the Ladies Night at the Grosvenor, and as always, business combining with fraternization meant that bars were packed all day. Alf the Lamp Man would be in the hotel foyer selling 110-watt light bulbs of different colours made especially for showmen. (He also went to the Cambridge Midsummer Fair.) For 3 days there was an exhibition of equipment at Alexandra Palace where, tempted by the quality of bright saucepans, buckets, water cans, equipment for kiosks, and better wearing chimneys for their trailers, virtually every showman purchased something from the big transit van of Nigel the Stainless Steel Man. These things continued until the early 1990s.

The pleasure that companionship brings the showman ripples out from Kenny Gray, who seemed always to be on the verge of participation, as if he was undergoing the story he tells.

> There was quite a few of us, we was lucky to be not bad looking people and we had lots of friends everywhere we went. My 2 sisters are quite handsome, then there was Lesley, James and Jonathan, me, Carl, Roger – all young people. I had a little car called Clare, a Morris Minor with a top off. I think I had that at 17 or 18. We used to go out in it, there'd be 10 or 12 people. We were *always out*, socialising, swimming. We had a very nice life just going about round here. Blakeney and Wells are lovely places. Briston, Burnham Overy, lovely places. Beautiful, and you're there for a week. Swimming when we was young was absolutely marvelous, that's all summertime when it's hot. Burnham Market we'd go to; my brother still go there.[8] In Burnham Overy, Dad and Uncle Jimmy let off some fireworks. All the people called, go on Clifford, get them up. Get them up. Then it hit a boat. You could hear them swearing because the sound echo across the water. In the '60s the fair open right on the quay. Can you remember that song, If ever a devil was born, *Jezebel* was it called? The tide would come up and wash

---

8   Jonathan Gray.

underneath [the trailers] just like it do at Blakeney. They used to have concrete blocks all the way up the quay at Burnham Overy, 6ft by 6ft squares to stop an invasion, stop ships coming in. We used to run on them when the water come up and we got washed away. The place was full of people, there was groups of families in the villages, that judge got tried for Christine Keeler, he was there; but a lot of it now is holiday homes. It's not the same.

Few showmen admit to making money though its trappings are evident in flamboyant funerals, weddings, and luxury cars, and large donations are still made by them to charity. Be they rich, poor, or somewhere between the two, opportunity to celebrate is seldom missed. Christmas at Number 7 Victoria Way, South Ockendon is an occasion for generous celebration, Bev Elliott says:

Christmas morning my brother-in-law cooked for 26 like breakfast. Dinnertime I cook for ten, my sister cooks for 16. Christmas night I cook for 26. We lay the table out and have friends come over. And if they want to stay, we just make beds anywhere. Every day my children are away from me, they ring me every single night and before they ring off they say Good night, God bless, I love you Mum. We do have rows but we're not people who hold a grudge. We're really loud with it (Laugh). There's never a dull moment here. You should come Christmas, see me tree and see how we do the chalets up.

CHAPTER TWELVE
'HELLUVA JOB TO GET PLANNING'

Isobel Fonseca reasoned that the need for a home must be most acute in those whose right to belong anywhere at all has been most stridently questioned.[1] Because showpeople's working life is separate from the demands of institutions or offices they are intrinsically insecure, outsiders reliant on political decisions made by town councillors and city planners who do not necessarily take account of their needs. Planners may, for instance, interpret evasively, legislation designed to assist the showmen, and make blanket rulings that cramp their ways. Regulations affecting transport, health and safety, and planning are all vital to the success of fairs.[2] Fairs themselves can be banned on the slightest whim, but in showmen's minds, the reluctance of public bodies to provide suitable space for their yards or winter quarters is an insult that threatens their very existence.[3] Defensiveness, ever present, can give way to a burning sense of resentment. Three showmen vent their disgust; Swales Elliotts feels excluded, David Remblance is fiery, Arthur Morrison, disputatious:

> We find it extremely hard to get places to stop. They had a site in Cranleigh like what we're doing here [South Ockendon] and had to pick everything up. They was in the middle of nowhere, in the middle of a field. An injunction, and that was it! We try to keep from everybody else because that way it's easier. They don't like us too close. Nobody really knows us until you know us, all they perceive is itinerants. Gypsies. We're on the fringes but we don't like to be that. We don't like to be on the outside looking in, we'd like to be part of where we are, on the inside with everybody else. Because we been here a while we're accepted.
>
> Who wants Showmen's lorries? eyesore; no one. They want the fair; after the fair, good night, nurse. Go! All over the country. Some of them [councils] was good. Some of them gave permission to stop but when I fought for the rights for these people here, I fought for [showmen in] the whole country. We've never been

---

[1]   Isobel Fonseca, *Bury me Standing* (Chatto & Windas, 1995), p. 85.
[2]   ETR, II: 10, 12, 11.
[3]   ETR, II: 16, memorandum by Sue Peak, 'showman representative', a member of the Showman's Guild.

classed anything in Thurrock, uneconomical, insufficient funds, the council kept telling us. We been here thirty-odd year' an' it's only the last two year' they put a speed limit up. Could you imagine 300 houses in a street with no street lighting and no 30 mph speed limit? There'd be an outcry!

Even if we find a piece of land that's for sale, there's problems. The younger people are buying property and developing to whatever council standards are, but they're still getting up against a brick wall when they own it and can't move on. They say where shall we go? The council say that isn't our concern; once you go into Suffolk, that's their problem. If there's not a site in an area you have to prove a *need*.

Shortage of space in a congested country affects everyone, the most obvious sequels being a rise in the price of land and increased regulation. Showmen are overly susceptible because they are less equipped to argue, and because their travelling heritage allowed them informal access to the land they needed, especially from publicans, to plots around their pubs. Besides, recent ways of managing their business have sharpened their requirement. Modern technology with trailer-mounted rides and stalls that can be opened up in hours allow an extended season. Dispersing throughout the country to fairs and fêtes, car boot sales and Sunday markets – known as gaff-catching, brings in money, but when an Act of 1960 made it a punishable offence for travellers to stop overnight in motorway lay-bys, planning journeys became more difficult.[4] Old people live longer and want to remain in the community, and parents want regular tuition for their children. All these factors contribute to the same end. To meet the demands of the twenty-first century, fair people ask for permanent residential quarters with transit sites in which to store and adapt their equipment. Despite Government stipulation to provide such accommodation, recognized by the Department of the Environment in 1991,[5] and reiterated vehemently in the ETR House of Commons report on travelling fairs at the end of the century, very few authorities heed the relevant circular 22/91 in their development plans.[6]

One way in which showmen can influence local councils is to join local politics; this is what Victor Harris has been doing in Cambridgeshire's Wilburton. Victor was born in Baldock where his mother presided over a small stall at the charter fair on Market Square, in the knowledge that once appropriated, the space would be reserved for her in future years. The

[4]   Fonseca, p. 8.
[5]   DOE, 1991, Circular 22/91.
[6]   ETR, I: xvii, 36.

importance of occupancy was instilled in her son. Sixty-five, and semi-retired, his hands are pink from chemotherapy. Unfazed by his health, he is level-headed and spry in mind. The straight tarmacked road running north from the village centre where he lives with his wife is old orchard land, thickly hedged, full of birds and very peaceful except for weekday mornings when cars pass by ferrying children to school. The yard next door was the first to be occupied. Harris began by talking about his neighbour:

> He took on a task coming here on his own. It's a quiet lane at night time, it's a bit dark – but this particular bit of land was three quarters full of plum trees. When the grandchildren get a bit older, they'll [trees] have to go because there'll be more vehicles coming in. We've been here ten yearish, might be 12. In this little area there's 5 yards and one without planning which they're trying to get now. Hel'uver job to get planning here because when we first moved in there was all Gypsies on these sites, which was very untidy. We done the job for them. We offered them money, bit more than the land's worth, they took it but the council wouldn't give us planning. They did say when we moved on there was nothing at all like this [The land had not housed showmen's vehicles in the past]. We hadn't got a sewer. We had a proper tank put in and permission to pump water from the ditch. Everything they want, we do it, which you got to. They [other people] have to do it so why shouldn't we? We did get planning after 4 or 5 year which cost a lot of money, back and forwards, fighting the council. Now, lo and behold, I'm a member of the Parish Council. I wanted them to know that we are human, we can sit at a table like they do and get to know them a bit better. There's 8 on the PC, they're pretty friendly. There's a couple of ladies and they talk to us good. The council meetings are boring but afterwards they go to the pub which I never do. Perhaps I should because then you're talking out of office hours. Recently I saw another friend of ours, who's on the planning committee. He want to know would I go on the District Council. I don't know, that's a bit more time-consuming with the PC and the Showmen's Guild and the Social Club. I said I'll think about it, but it's nice to know they think of you. A showman's site, to be fair, can't be lovely because when you got all your vehicles in, even if they're lined up, you got one painted red, one painted yellow. You might have a canvas over one and it's windy it's flapping about. They may think it's unsightly, but that is us. You're showmen and that's what you do. Years ago you could phone up

a farmer you knew, Can we come with the fair next week, we're stuck? Yes. No problem. Well today it's mostly council ground, recreation ground, car parks and you can't do that because the council have got to sit and talk about it, which takes months. We used to wait for the pubs to turn out because they was our kind of people, and we would be open with the fair til 12.00, 1 o'clock in the morning. But now the music has changed and you can't play so late, and you can't have it so loud.

If the need for living space is a matter to which showmen have in measure contributed, retaining spaces in which to operate lies wholly outside their control. Of two hundred and fifty fairs held each summer week in the 1930s, the number had dropped to about two hundred in 1970, since then it has dropped again.[7] Village fairs are rarely profitable in gross terms, being more or less fillers between larger towns and cities. It is the loss of urban fairs that really matters. Even a charter fair enjoys no protection against an authority that plucks it from a historic site when a city centre is redeveloped. This is precisely what happened in Norwich, where a historic fair of obscure Medieval origin was held throughout most of the twentieth century outside the Cathedral at Christmas and Easter. In the late '80s it was transferred to the Cattle Market on Hall Road because of the Castle Mall development, but poor attendance led to another move, back to Castle Meadow in the city centre in 1991. Six years later, the Easter fair was scrapped because of disruption to the bus company's timetables. Successive shufflings from one location to another, have been accompanied by growing irritation on both sides. The unpalatable belief among showpeople is that there is a motivation for authorities to shake off what are otherwise binding commitments.

A lot of negotiation needs to precede the fairs; loud speakers can be a problem for those who live close, lighting, health, safety, traffic, access to water and electricity must all be considered, a workload that an unsympathetic council is happy to abandon. In such cases, a fairground may be moved to an inferior alternative offered at the same rent in order to create what is then seen as natural decline. Where sites are moved from central squares to the outskirts of a town, a struggle invariably follows but the council has the ultimate power of decision.[8] Such moves are less likely if councillors and civic officials are alert to the benefits of urban renaissance or where proactive relations have been cultivated between them and the showmen.[9] Norwich City's continued reluctance to accommodate Eastern Counties showpeople has been a disappointment in recent years. Arthur

[7]   ETR, II: 11.
[8]   ETR, I: xiv, 22.
[9]   ETR, I: xv, 27.

Morrison feels the city council show an intransigent lack of interest:

> King's Lynn's relationship with the Showmen's Guild is excellent.
> The same again in Yarmouth; fair in the street the first week after
> Easter Monday. In the middle lies Norwich which will give you
> absolutely nothing. When I was chair, [of the Eastern Counties
> Section] I asked the mayor of King's Lynn whether I could possibly
> sit next to the Mayor of Norwich at the luncheon and I put it to
> him, why don't we have a proper opening? The charter goes back
> to 10 something and it's called Tombland Fair which is
> immediately in front of the Cathedral. He was very interested. He
> would come but he couldn't wear the chain or the robes. We always
> have difficulty negotiating for the event in Norwich. We had a
> deputation with a leading showman on it. He said of all the fairs
> he goes to which is Nottingham, Newcastle, Hull – and when he
> got to that point the chairman banged his fist on the table, said 'Mr
> Thurston, we're talking Norwich'. Which I didn't think was very
> respectful. Since then they've changed each year, mayors and all
> that but they don't seem to be any more to our way of thinking.

The view is seconded by Kenny and Fiona Gray who travelled for
twenty-five years before settling in Sheringham to run an amusement arcade.
Norwich City has more than once played host to the Barcelona-based Sarruga's
giant glowing mobile sculptures during its summer festival. Perhaps these
fabulous monsters inspired by insects and mythical creatures could be integrated
with scenes from the fairground to show how one evolved from the other.

> The last few years, they've been very anti-fair. Their reasoning is
> anything they can think up. They want Norwich to be the cultural
> centre of Europe. They want arts and literature; the fair ground
> isn't considered part of it.[10] When the Mall was built on the
> Cattlemarket, they promised showmen a space but the Council
> never did that so for a couple of years they put them in the town
> centre, Castle Meadow. Then they said you can't be there any
> more, you've got to go in Chapelfields Gardens but in December
> the ground was very soft. At first the rent was low because the site
> was unsuitable but after a couple of years they put the rent back up.
> If they have their events, the Lord Mayor processions in Chapelfield
> Gardens, they allow the cars parking but when the fair's there, they
> make all these new rules that no cars are to be parked beside your

---

[10]   ETR, I: xi, 7.

equipment. They make it really really difficult to carry on trading. It shouldn't be so. There are a few councillors who want the fair there but I think one person can complain and the fair's off. I said show me the evidence. They said, We've got one complaint. When you call them to book, they don't answer. They've got no reason to. We said, could you tell us, so we can tell our children why you're doing this? We've written quite a lot of letters and tried to get things changed so that showmen get more rights but that is very hard. We've absolutely no rights. Do you understand the power they've got? When a decision's made, it's like the council have got the final say.

As profitable fairs have closed and competition has increased, showmen look with envy at their European counterparts, notably in German Strasbourg, where central areas of the city have been laid out with moveable planters containing quite large trees so that fairs can be accommodated.[11]

European showmen are more respected. In Germany, Holland or France you'd be a first class citizen. Their showmen get a lot more prime positions, a lot more grants. In Germany they're the only industry with their own VAT bracket. You're in the middle of a town on tarmac and half of them don't need generators, they tap on the electric to run their rides. We've been to Dusseldorf, Tilburg, Hamburg just to see how the other half live. In Strasburg they knocked a disused factory down, levelled it and turned it into a car park to make the showmen a site when the old street fair was turned into a one way system. Nearly everywhere you go there's showmen but they don't go back as far as us because they persecuted them in the war, same as the Gypsies and Jews. It wasn't until after the wars, when there was no entertainment, they got into fairs.[12]

Transport is bound to be a major consideration for the traveller. Showmen receive special allowances in using white diesel fuel but for someone doing between 1,500 and 6,000 miles a year and earning erratically, the price seems astronomical. Since the first decades of the twentieth century they have been subject to rulings that fall hard on them. George Cushing tells how showpeople's steam vehicles with their insistent requirement for water, travelling often by night, and regularly crossing county boundaries, were hampered by demands

---

[11] ETR, I: xiii, 22.
[12] Robert Thurston.

that some of these counties made for special licenses. How they were targeted by complaints that the engines frightened horses on the road, and that the coal or ash they used burnt the greens.[13] Three showmen give personal takes on an aspect of the business that merely changes in its detail:

> Our prices on the funfair have been around the same the past 5 years although the charge for red diesel we use for generators, has overdoubled and the charge for white diesel roadfill has doubled.[14]

> We've got a restricted license because we only move once a week and don't do as many miles as a haulier. Showmen and circuses have got our own special tax band which the Guild organized quite a few years ago. Used to be called the Showmen's Special but they've altered the words in Brussels or somewhere, and now it's called a Special Vehicle. We've got a very good secretary, Keith Miller, who worked and worked on that. And certain vehicles of ours are exempt from tests. But if you get stopped by a VOSA [Vehicle and Operator Services Agency] you still come under all their restrictions. They used to be called the Ministry of Transport, it's a Government body that run all the test inspections. We've got an exemption with low emission for about 2 years, until we get up to Euro 3. Most London showmen have to change their transport [vehicles] within that 2 years to get within the LEC [Low Emission Cetificate], which is like low carbon emissions. You apply for this exemption and they come to check you are what you say you are.[15]

> Transport is a nightmare with the restrictions, diesel, a license for this, license for that. You got to be registered if you want to move on a weekend from London or whatever. You got to plan and there's cameras everywhere so you got to be up to scratch. Got to conform. A lot of effort and in the end there's isn't the money out there.[16]

Stringent health and safety standards are endorsed by the Guild, showpeople know that they protect their reputation. At the same time, regulations do need to have a practical basis, and some feel it would be pure bureaucracy to implement the rumoured ban on standing on a Waltzer.[17]

---

[13]   George Cushing with Ian Starsmore, *Steam at Thursford* (David & Charles, 1982), pp. 148 and 152.
[14]   John Bugg.
[15]   Robert Thurston.
[16]   John Manning.
[17]   Theodore Whyatt.

Restrictions made as a result of intervention by various rights groups are also questioned. Photographic exhibitions of giants, dwarves and midgets are fêted in an art gallery, while abnormality, real or inventively perceived in live humans or animals, is prohibited on the fairground. It is a moot point whether what is condoned as representation but denied in the flesh, doesn't reveal hypocritical standards.[18] Nipper Appleton believes the public would still queue up to view entertainments that were regarded as harmless in his youth:

> The Show Row as it was known with all this live entertainment out
> on the front, you'd have the fat lady and the giant from Scotland,
> today people are still interested but to put them on exhibition you
> get opposition groups. Same as the freak animals group. Years ago
> you got the Chadwicks and all the exhibitions was five legs instead
> of four, this type. Micky Mouse circuses, Flea circuses. Every fair
> in Great Britain had to leave 10% room for the side-shows because
> there was that many of them.

The net effect of over-regulation is debilitating for everyone, but especially for the showman. He can not easily buy land even if he has money, because he has no fixed assets; can not easily borrow money because he is self-employed. He can not sleep overnight in a lay-by because there are rules to stop Gypsies occupying half-way homes. With all the prohibitions against travelling, fair people find themselves increasingly hedged in.

---

[18]   American photographer Diana Arbus. Her work is exhibited all over the world. I first saw it in the US, but noticed the same work in London recently.

CHAPTER THIRTEEN
'A BUSY BOY'

'Bottled Gas' reads a huge corner swag where the B186 turns east into Buckles Lane at South Ockendon.[1] Until 30 years ago the surrounding country was flattish greenbelt scrub and grass – empty, and consequently an invitation to travellers. But much of the land round Thurrock was rich in minerals, they were extracted before there was proper planning control, and the Buckles Lane area was poorly restored. The lane might be fringed at the end of October with buddleas and teasels but even for grazing the soil was contaminated and therefore of little value. If price is all-important, showpeople's sites become self-selecting; the downside being that greenbelt exists primarily to prevent settlements coalescing and is governed by strict regulations,[2] so they buy land before being granted permission to occupy it. In this instance the regulations were gradually, stealthily, circumvented, until suddenly, it seemed, the mass of dots Google now makes of the region had become home and refuge to some seven hundred families in a compact neighbourhood.

All the unmade roads that fishbone off Buckles Lane are named after showmen, and each one contains rows of gated yards. There is a first, westerly set of four or five in which most of the vehicles, dwellings and wheelie bins are regimented behind high fences with ostentatious wrought iron gates; and a second set in which the yards are less well kept. Between the two lies Harry's Road commemorating the Norfolk traveller who ended up circling London with his Dodgems and an Octopus, gradually accumulating enough money to buy on speculation a large slab of land to the north of the lane. The purchase took place in 1978, and the following year, Harry Remblance, a well-known Thurrock Showman, died, aged 60 on a bomb site in nearby Tilbury for want of somewhere to live.

After his father's death, David Remblance stayed at Tilbury until he was evicted. After being evicted a second time, he stayed briefly in Chertsey before returning to Buckles Lane for a long battle to secure his father's land. The first intention was to split the site with his brothers but argument over payment left David sole owner. This could be seen as the initial step in what became a Titanic struggle.

A big fellow, and not intimidated by people who have power, David is on one hand, combative, a rougher-up; on the other, shrewd and domestically

---

[1]   Ockendon is invariably referred to by showmen as Ockingdon or Ockingham.
[2]   ETR, I: xviii, 40.

amenable. Last year he was 29 stone; gastric bypass surgery brought his weight down, whereupon two daughters, his sister and a brother followed suit. At first, David wasn't convinced he wanted to speak with me. I didn't have an intermediary at the time, though I discovered later that he has relations in Hooper Lane yard. So I sent my book on Fishermen to a communal post box. Eventually he picked it up, and the gesture did the trick. He'd pay for it, he said, and he did. Later he tried to give it back because he couldn't or wouldn't read it. When this one is finished, I told him, he can have a copy free. I enjoyed his flamboyance, and a contrariness informed by a twisted logic that was, from his view, a matter of principle.

Commercial instinct developed early. Self-employment is one of the attractions of being a showman, but aged 25 he abandoned the fairground for bigger risks; setting up a tanning shop, wheeling and dealing in concrete goods, and with foresight, in the purchase of land. Despite the uncertain status of his land, he saw a future in the need for showmen's accommodation. To this end, he continued to buy piecemeal from a local farmer until he had some 27 acres to the south west of the strip he had inherited, a new area named Clarry Wheatley after another showman. Allegiance to the group has always underpinned a personal agenda to better himself and his immediate family. The middle child of five siblings, he is surrounded by relatives. Sites for various family members are specified with definiteness, and although divorced, he and his wife live a stone's throw from one another. He could scarcely be more steeped in showmen's ways. Today he sees himself as a leader in a community from which he has diverged only in the nature of his work.

Hygiene has an almost 'moral' status, a term David used to describe behaviour as well as points of ethics. Despite the usual spotlessness in his trailer – and this is what matters to him – the yard immediate to his chalet is littered with various pieces of sodden carpet, bags of trash and other undelectables. Whilst the communal outer yard, deeply pitted and puddled after rain, contains heaps of old kitchen machinery and corners of scrap iron as well as the dwellings occupied by his extended family. He is not aware of anything irrational about this; few habits are more deeply ingrained than those bred over generations in a closed community. Nor is consistency necessarily important to him:

> All the Remblances are big, they look at that packet of biscuits and put a stone on. My Mum was a showman, her dad was Teddo Hopson, they originated from Liverpool and they got generations and generations [of fairpeople behind them]. He [David's maternal grandfather] married a Gypsy, Algigo. They was Spanish. Alfie Green, that was my father-in-law, was well known in Wells. Porki Gizzi, that's [John] Gizzi's father [Edward], he was a friend a me

father's. All our family sold rock like Steven Gray and Gizzi. They was friends together; rock people. We got a photo of my great great granny I think it is with a big hat, selling rock at King's Lynn Mart. I used to manage the Ferris wheel till I was about 16. Went 3 months to one school and 3 months the next but I started my own business on the fairground when I was 11, 12. Wintertime you got to find things to do. I used to chop wood and go round with a barrow. Collect scrap. I call myself an entrepreneur or Jack of all trades. Welder, manufacturer, buy, sell. You name it.

I haven't travelled for thirty odd year an I'm a showman. A Joskin, you'll get one go to work on computers and one go to work on the busses. They'll come home an they'll go an have their meal. They havn' got quite enough in common from the beginning. The family grow up with showmen, they meet and they go together as showmen. And their kids join in as showmen, and they meet showmen. It's like it's one big thing with showmen and when they're separated they stay together. Most of them can't read an write. My mum and dad couldn't read and write, none of us went to school properly. My boy can't read properly. He didn't have an interest in anything like that. It's different these days since they're a bit settled down. We're parted, yes, but the wife lives *there*, I live *here*. We still talk and do, and help one another. We're still friends. Still eat and drink. The daughters are at home, they're courting, the 3 of 'em. Without a doubt they'll marry into the community. Why we are a community and why you're not so lucky as us; I got me sister there, I want me family with me all me life. I got my kids *there*. My boy's ge'in married; he's gonner be *there*. My other girls 'll be *there*; we're all got their separate places, all in Harry's [Road]. I got me brother over the other side. Two brothers, then there's Bradley, me nephew there. One family: where [else] do you get that? My heart and soul is in showmen. They are my life and I want my kids to be part of it. I pray that they stay and marry a showman. Keep the tradition goin' of close families. Because we're a tight knit community, showmen got so much in common.

I can't drink a cuppa tea round anybody's. I don't even like going in a cafe. If I go in a cafe I drink left-handed 'cos I don't like them lips round the other side. I'm not left-handed for anything else. Always clean me knife an fork before I use it. If I see a bit of dirt I walk out. How can people condemn us when we got them morals? They're good morals. Wouldn't dream of washing me hands in the kitchen sink. I've seen people in houses come in with grease and flick it over all the pots and things. All the germs what you gotta eat. We've had enough prejudice against us. 'Gypsy people'. 'Live in caravans'. 'Smelly', we been called everything. '*Them* people.' '*You* people.' Even on the television. In America they call us trailer trash. That's an insult. I'm proud of my heritage as a Gypsy, I got friends who is Gypsies. There's good and bad in all.

In the early '80s, the Remblance land was overrun with Gypsies whom Thurrock Council had been unable to evict. Talks with the council led David to believe that getting rid of them would help him obtain planning permission. His memory doesn't quite tally with that of consultant David Lewis who was working for Thurrock's Planning Department at the time. Lewis thinks a direct arrangement was unlikely. For David Remblance, however, the very scent of arbitration was a call to action he has been dealing with ever since. Mutual respect developed between the two Davids. It did not necessarily result in agreement, but Lewis understood that from the showman's position, the pressure of the outside world felt at times entirely hostile. David Remblance is irritated, for example, by the council's slow provision of street lamps and traffic calming measures. A sense of injury not uncommon among showmen makes it possible to miss his subtle humour, his teasing edge.

My Dad had ten cars at his funeral, photos of it were in *World's Fair*. Right up until he died, he never had a permanent place. The Council said Mr Remblance come 'ere, it was like a bomb exploded and it all went splrkkkkk! I told them [Gypsies] if you beat me, you can stay, if I beat you, you can leave all your horses on here, but you got to go. I fought em with fists. One man wouldn' go ... Their [Thurrock Council] big mistake; they given me 12 months temporary planning permission to stop here. For 15 year the Gypsy's horses wandered up until they started getting over people's fences an the police come an took them away. For years we never done nothink with it. We didn't wanter sell. But then it got so desperate, I sold what's called the Wheatley and they divided it up between em. That's 57 families I put on there. That was about 1998. David Lewis helped us, he's a good man. He's part of a big family and down-to-earth like showmen are.

David Lewis remembers vividly the day he discovered the showmen marking out boundaries on the Wheatley site where they had long since pulled on their trailers and giant lorries. Enforcement notices were duly erected; a procedure to which the showmen were more than equal. Delaying the planning process was in their interests because it is more difficult to dislodge them once they register with doctors, and their children attend local schools. Another ploy was to turn lack of literacy to their advantage. Officers are required to invite potential purchasers to participate in the planning process through events advertised in their local paper. If showmen don't get a newspaper delivered, or claim to be unable to read, the system is foxed. Lewis often felt he had met his match:

> Remblance had acquired the land and it was a matter of creating the plots to sell on. All these fences had gone up, one youngster had a paintbrush in her hand and paint all over her clothes, I said, do you know anything about those fences?" "No, know nothing about them." (Laugh). "OK, can we have a chat." Often their introduction to planning is through conflict. There was an awful lot happening; year after year, enforcement notices would be followed by appeals. They can't read if they don't want to and can't listen either if they don't want to. There's a line of least resistance and in a way the authority gets worn down. Even to issue an enforcement notice necessitates identifying the owner of a particular plot, and where exchange of ownership is sealed informally, though a spit, a shake, and exchange of cash, the deal is not recorded in the land registry. Without records, it becomes difficult for the planner to find out who owns what. The argument that they [showmen] will give you is, all we want is to be able to set up home like anybody else. But what people in houses want is that the same policies that apply to them should apply to the showmen. [ie refusal to allow development on the Green Belt.] Needless to say, this is interpreted by the showmen as total opposition. If you're a soft touch, everybody is drawn from all around, and the councils that deal with a rod of iron have no problems. But it's a bit nimbyism from the authorities, not just residents. You don't always want to be the person who says, get off your land. In land use terms, whether it be showmen designation or Gypsy designation it's still a use of land that's not necessarily compatible with the policies we've got. Neither gets a very good press and the planning system doesn't readily accommodate them. In a way there is greater support through legislation for Gypsies than there is for showmen. For showmen, the system simply encourages us to consult with them when we're doing a local plan.
>
> In planning you try and look at housing *need*. You gauge projections on populations and the needs of the community, you should be doing something similar for the showmen. We tried to do almost a census of how many were there, how many kids, what

schools might they be going to. It was really difficult because again there was a suspicion that if you're from the council they don't want to reveal too much. You might ask whether planning is the right department to deal with it. The current climate has a lot more emphasis on human rights, and all the other agencies that try and look at things more broadly. It's very easy to research something just from one perspective. Had the showmen set up on more valuable land in a higher profile area with more vocal opposition, something more would have been done. Unless you have reason to go down Buckles Lane you wouldn't be familiar with it all.

Part 2 of the Caravan Sites Act 1968 was designed specifically for travellers and Gypsies – transient populations for whom land use doesn't fit into neat categories such as employment, residential or retail. Local authorities were encouraged to make provision in their area but it is easier to respond to the demands of the majority than to designate land for less popular sections of the community. This means making minimal provision for travellers, then passing them on to the next authority. Accepting that something needed doing, officers would grant appeals on a temporary basis of about 3 years. In theory this gave them an opportunity to address the situation but as alternative sites weren't available, nothing was done. The borough planners tried hard to be fair. Lewis felt insufficient options were open to them. They were left handling a situation rather than dealing with the cause.

In his view South Ockendon's residents, too, have been accommodating. In Surrey where he worked for several years, inhabitants were vehemently opposed to integration with travelling communities and good at lobbying. Involvement in the enforcement process led to their buying up land rather than allowing it to be sold to showmen. In South Ockendon, a fair proportion of population came from the East End with its high densities and contingent problems; this gave the town a tradition of tolerance.

Habitually suspicious of established authority, showpeople are ever alert to encroachments of power. This didn't make them easy to bargain with, and theatrical tactics had to be met with the humour they deserved. On one occasion, South Ockendon's showpeople marched from the town hall to the council offices, accompanied by David Remblance with a horse-drawn hearse. Because the population had grown, they were claiming the trailers were too close together, creating a fire hazard. To advance the need for extra space they had set fire to a trailer and taken photographs of it with graphic pictures of children at the windows. Another time, 200 petition-bearers arrived at the offices with dogs and children. Unable to manage the influx, the council had to dismiss the mob, calling instead on a small team of representatives.

By the turn of the century, anyway, some of the families in Buckles Lane had lengthy associations with the area, both personally, and in the fairs they attended. This was the point at which the House of Commons Report on travelling fairs stressed the inadequacy of legislation. Showmen's interests, it insists, were consistently overridden or ignored.[3] Under pressure from the Guild as well as its resident showmen, Thurrock granted and subsequently re-granted temporary planning permission for five years. They also made a sympathetic response to David Remblance's application for a country park and fishing village on the north site. One inhabitant of Buckles Lane, saw that, 'Thurrock has been good to us'.[4]

Not all showmen are happy in Buckles Lane; conspicuously gated yards suggest high levels of mistrust and fear. Questioned about these 'fortifications' the men tended to see them as protective, and show-women mentioned child-molesters. In both cases, fear arises from contact with outsiders rather than the fellow showmen who surround them. North London showman, John Manning made an objective comment:

> It's not a place I'd recommend anyone for a rôle model but there are people up there probably wouldn't have anywhere else to call home. They'd of stayed with someone else. Some of them [plots of land] are being abused to be quite honest. That's their business, it'll all come out in the wash and looking at the large picture, the concept is marvellous. It could be a very good place if they're all made to toe the line.

David's ambitions haven't ended. In 2006 he reapplied to develop the north site with vehicular access from Buckles Lane. Sports pitches, car parks, a café, and the lakes for fishing and boating are what he had in mind. Another of his personal projects is for a restaurant in Thurrock named 'Roses', in memory of his mother. Meanwhile, with European legislation behind him, he is wielding a battle at Parliament level to enable showpeople in general to purchase the land they occupy. To be still a student in the literate world may increase his defensiveness, but it counts for less where it matters most. Having taught himself to read in a rudimentary way, he exaggerates his lack of education to emphasize his success. On his answerphone a sexy voice intones, 'He's a busy boy, he's a very, very busy boy ... When he's done we'll put you through'. It sounded a little threatening. Was he serious? After meeting the man, I knew it was a joke.

---

3   ETR, I: xix: 'All local authorities should ... ensure they consider the needs of travelling showpeople when preparing their development plans'.
4   Swales Elliott.

Got me own property. Not bad for an old boy can't read or write. Rags to riches, I might be daft but I ain't silly. Look! I am just about to build a restaurante. From nothun hardly. Out the back here, there's some beautiful lakes. It's just an empty field at the moment. This would make a beautiful country park. If I'd had education I'd of been stone rich years ago. I'd be a millionaire by now. I missed on not knowing banks, and reading and writing. But I'm happy, I got a few quid. You look on the internet. Put in David Remblance under the Houses of Parliament, my letter comes up and what I'm fighting for. Evry showman got a right. Any minute now it's coming to a head ad I'm going to win. The Government got to find them somewhere in their area.

If you're parked in the yard, you want to watch for your tyres. The things them people do!

CHAPTER FOURTEEN
'HOW TO ACT WITH PEOPLE FROM DIFFERENT WALKS OF LIFE'

Stocks is a prominent name in Suffolk showmen, so it was apt that I should first meet the family at Southwold's Trinity Fair. The show has run on South Green since 1227. It was granted a charter by Henry VII in 1489.[1] Henry Stocks 'Senior' was for many years the fairground organizer, or lessee, and the Stocks were present in force. I found Henry 'Junior' minding his Dodgems; Sally, his wife, coaxed a youngster in a blue poncho onto a motorbike; Bernice, his sister, poured out tea in the Pit Stop Diner,[2] while her daughter, Zoah, sizzled franks at the other end of the stall. My attention was held by her shock of bleached hair. Henry Senior was around, as was Enry – one of the three Henrys, Bernice, informed me, his name spelt without an 'H'. It is not unusual for showpeople to engage in conversation with interested strangers at a fair.

When a car drove right up into the fairground, a showman called out, 'Take the registration number, they know the road is closed.' Zoah, however, bent into the car's window and dealt diplomatically with the intrusion. Two days later, Bernice told me, her daughter would take her final A-level in philosophy and ethics. In July, she would be joining 120 pupils chosen from secondary schools all over Britain to attend a two week course at Eton Summer School. Some weeks after Southwold fair Bernice and her daughter agreed to add to my growing pile of tape recordings. Their contribution opened a new perspective on the fluidity of showmen's culture.

Trinity fair has been well documented over the years, notably by a London stockbroker-cum-artist in 1933 and 34. Today, J. Donan Turner's panoramic water-colour paintings can be seen in the Swan Hotel. Staff are very obliging. Cross the dining room into a hallway in the south wing, and you will be confronted with the delighted engagement of a fairground enthusiast; each of what are known as 'scrolls' 0.5 m high, and all but one of them 2.2m – 2.4m long. Here is the rifle range. Here the pie stall and J. Abbott's Superior Coconut Saloon – every nut minutely depicted in its cup. Turner's sensibility was not without humour, women are washing up outside a smart old living wagon with removable wooden steps to its door. *Herbert Gray's Royal Hunt* seeks

---

[1] Long Melford, the other surviving charter fair in Suffolk, was granted by King John, 1199–1216.

[2] More often referred to as a canteen or kiosk.

customers. *J. Elmer* proclaims provocatively, *Tip the Lady out of Bed to Win a Prize*. Here, not least, a flat trailer with a gaff lad[3] lolling on the long arms of the hitch advertises *B. Stock's Auto-Speed Cars*. The trailer is pulled up in front of a large ride distinguished by scrollwork art designs and smart striped awning hung with flags. Next to it is a showman's engine, its extended chimney puffing smoke.[4] Turner recorded almost as faithfully as a photographer, readily distinguishing between showmen and fair-goers. By listing respective stall-holders beneath the depictions and collecting their autographs, he ensured authenticity.

Off the scrolls, B. Stocks was Bert Sr., the showman who rented from the early 50s, and bought in 1955, two acres in Leiston signposted at the gateway 'Private Prop. Stocks Amusement Depot'. Until 1990, the site was used as a fairground. Then permanent buildings went up – chalets and a bungalow to add to a nest of trailers surrounded by a pile of rubble, the carcass of a spent car, lorries, and the usual scatter of businesses; obsolescent ones as well as those in current use. Notably, Henry Jr.'s Rock City Miami. This is a ride with a massive faceboard painted with suggestively breasty girls, on which a long boat of 16 seats swishes like a pendulum, sideways, up and round.[5] 'It's a typical showman's yard, you accumulate rubbish', said Bert's daughter-in-law, Shirley Stocks, one of thirteen inhabitants from six related families who live there.

The Stocks have travelled in East Anglia since at least 1821 from which time the family have a record of Alfred's birth. Bert Sr. was born in the sail yard at Harleston. Before moving to Leiston, he occupied a yard in Ipswich for ten years, and before that he was based in Bury. Henry Sr. was born in a caravan in the Black Boy pub meadow at Beccles in 1930 and married Shirley, one of the Irvins from Bedfordshire, who travelled with Stanley Thurston.[6] Modernity was creeping into showland by the time Bernice and Henry Jr. were born in Halesworth Maternity Hospital; just one of astonishing changes Henry Sr. and Shirley Stocks have witnessed during their lifetime.

Besides his Dodgems (Auto-Speed Cars), Bert and his sons bought in 1937, a Coronation Speedway – usually referred to as a Noah's Ark. Henry Sr. also had in his time, a Juvenile and a Waltzer. Fifteen when the second World War ended, he was already doing a man's work, helping to build up and pull down the heavy components of a scenery-swirled Noah's Ark with charging wooden horses, chrome-handled and plush-seated; rows of motorbikes, and chariots shaped like a lion's head. From the Rope Walk area of Ipswich they emerged at Easter time

---

[3]   A casual fairground labourer.
[4]   An extra 6–8 foot tube was carried by showmen for extending the chimney when stationary. See chapter 18.
[5]   Similar rides have different names, such as Eliminator.
[6]   The implication is that the Thurstons were the lessees with the rides and the Irvins had stalls.

to move more than 30 times a season, occasionally crossing county borders into Cambridgeshire and Essex. The family's run of rides encompassed Leiston in the Spring; Ipswich at Easter; Great Yarmouth; Bungay May fair; Bardwell May Fair; Hadleigh Show; Framlingham for the end of May Bank Holiday; Southwold Trinity Fair; Kessingland the week before Cambridge; Cambridge for the Midsummer Fair; Christchurch Park Co-op Fête early July; Tiptree Flower Show (Essex); Laxfield and Stradbrook both Suffolk flower shows; Harwich in July; Beccles end of July-August; West Mersea in August; Aldeburgh August; Eye Show for the August bank holiday; Brantham, Bildeston, Finningham, and Kessingland again.[7]

The Stocks' '70s run from Leiston was similar, though Henry no longer went to the last four small villages. By this time he had married Shirley who remembers:

> We used to be here in the spring, before Easter, and again in the back end of the year[8] And if there was a week in between fairs we'd say come on, let's go to Leiston. Ipswich for Christmas used to be London Road where the big Halfords store is. There's a road now where my trailer used to stand.

In 1983, when Bernice was separated and then divorced, she knew of only one other showperson who had been divorced before. With her mother's forthrightness, she acknowledged that her former husband with whom she had long tried to bear a child, fell in love with someone else. Zoah was born eighteen years ago in Leiston yard. Her father is a showman based at Witham with his wife, Zoah's two half-brothers and a half-sister, leaving her effectively an only child. Because she was premature, there was a long spell in intensive care, and the day Bernice brought her home the fair was due to open two hours later. Whatever the circumstances, showpeople turn up, do what needs to be done and fulfill their obligation to an event. They take pride in their ability to cope, and naturally, the baby went along.

Like other fairground children, Zoah mixed with a cross section of the public, providing opportunity for communication across boundaries. The Stocks' yard is relatively isolated from other showpeople, and this too meant that she interacted with the local community. Asked whether she reckoned she was academic she replied unequivocally in the affirmative, and true to her roots, she doesn't shun hard work. Despite a strong family orientation, the time came when she had more in common with school friends than she did with her travelling friends but she has an urge to move outwards, continuing to acknowledge rather

---

7   Henry Stocks Sr with Shirley Stocks.
8   The term showmen use for the Autumn run of fairs.

than dissolve the old bonds, and the Leiston yard gave her an ideal launch.

It was a wonderful place to grow up. There'd be all ages playing together, like being in a little village. I think that's good. You know everyone and everyone knows you. Mum sent me to a Montessori Nursery School where they teach you phonetically. Thanks to them I could read before I went to Primary. Then it was Leiston Middle and Leiston High School. When we pulled in I'd miss my travelling friends but at school I'd see my other friends. I make friends easily, but I have a lot of friends at school who aren't in my year. Some are 5 years younger. Me and my friends have really different views on things, that is interesting. We [fairground people] have a sense of well you've got to get on and do it. Not fluffing about too much. If you've got a problem, find out how you can solve it. It's good to mix with people. At Norwich travellers keep themselves to themselves at school. But the nearest travellers to us are at Bury, by simple matter of circumstances, most of my friends aren't travellers. All my cousins round here went to Leiston Middle School but there's only William at the High School and he's years younger. When I come back from travelling everyone at school was quite jealous. They'd say why aren't you here in the summer? You've had a holiday. I said, no, it's what we do. I've got quite a good work ethic though I do have the teenage laziness too. I worked in a clothes shop in Aldeburgh in the winter. If I sold 3 jumpers and it came to £150.00 it gave me an enthusiasm. I felt a personal interest in seeing business doing well.

I've always liked English literature, but I enjoy history most because I can relate it to how the world is now. I was disappointed with French, we had a slave-driver of a teacher who made the whole thing a chore. I like philosophy because that's something completely new. We had to learn the basics. Plato. Aristotle. You learn an area and then the philosopher related to it. The Cosmological Argument is for the existence of God; so we learned about Thomas Aquinas. Ethics is theories of right and wrong.

It was just announced at School that the Eton scholarship was coming up. It's a charity thing. My teacher said, you're that sort of level. Three other people were taking it and we decided to go for different subjects to increase our chances. I applied for English literature. I did mention that I was a traveller and self-taught 6 months of the year. This was my first complete year at school. It's a little awkward because the last day is one of our Business days at

Stowmarket Carnival but I think I should be able to enter.

People who go the fair at Aldeburgh are middle class. The fairs at Haverhill are different because it's mostly council estates. You learn how to act with people from different walks of life. I won't be going to Cambridge [Midsummer Common fair]. I used to go just to socialize but there's so much to it. What you're going to wear at Cambridge. A day and a night outfit. You must never wear the same outfit twice. There's a travellers' dance here on Friday night but I'm not going. I'm going to the '80s Club. I prefer the music. I like Rock, Indian, and '50s Soul, stuff like fairground music. Most of the girls here would say, Yes, they'll stay with the fair. This is what we do. It isn't what I want to do for the rest of my life. I'd like to do something else first. I may well come back to it. It will always be here for me and definitely, each summer, for the next few years I'll help Mum with the Kiosk.

Although the fairground continued to dictate Zoah's movements until 2007, Bernice and her daughter moved from a trailer to a chalet when she was about 14. This was in readiness for her to study when the rest of the family attended fairs. Bernice also decided to cut the season short so that Zoah missed one term of school p.a, but her daughter has always been very directed and up to a point her academic scheduling was self-propelled. On 8 October 2009, she went up to Murray Edwards College, formally New Hall; the third student to make Oxford or Cambridge from a travelling family, possibly the first who had spent her young summers selling toffee apples and candyfloss.

At Cambridge, many of Zoah's contemporaries were used to being independent, but her friends from Eton Summer School were very supportive. She is convinced of the need to slip between conventional cultures, and has firm family sanction. Her ability to juggle situations in which she finds herself would seem to echo her mother's values. Before updating her daughter's story, Bernice explained the curiosity that led her to cultivate friendships outside the yard:

Me and me three cousins and me brother went to school here with no other showmen [outside the extended family]. Because we're all different ages, we was never in class together. Me cousins mixed at school but they never had friends home. We always did because we're quite outgoing people. The first time I remember going in a house I was about 8. I was friends with a girl called Caroline Geater whom I still know. A very local family. I went round to hers for tea. I don't remember thinking that was the first house I've been in but it was. Having proper good friends out of the business from a very young age, then it's a drip feed.

I remember being on honeymoon in 1978 We went to Lansarotti which was hardly anythink on there. I was 20. We just chose this lovely Canary Island. Anyway, the only other people on this bus was Doris and David Lanscron, Jewish, with their little boy, Justin. He'd got his little cap thing on his head. Because there weren't many people at our hotel, a couple of times we had meals with them. We did get really friendly in 2 wks. Apparently that is a Jewish thing, like us, not to wash your hands in the kitchen sink. We kept in touch with them for years. There's people who wind up Zoah with racist jokes because they know she's so anti-racist. I worked for 5 winters at a restaurant in Yoxford. The owner is Chinese/ Malaysian, the chef is black ... There were often days when I was the only white person there. You start realizing things you take for granted other people don't necessarily do.

Zoah's not a typical fairground teenager. When she was eight, we made her a Lucky Dip to mind. She'd sit on the steps of the kiosk and do her bit. The problem was she knew what she wanted. She wanted the presents for herself. The Travellers' Education people would come about Easter time to make sure that she had sorted everything but basically it was up to her. And because she sort-of wanted to do it – she didn't really did she when she was 12 or 13? (Laugh) – but she kind of knew she should. You have your pack and through the week you do your work, then Thursday morning the Traveller Education teacher [TE Teacher] would arrive, on the Dodgems usually, and all the kids would gather and they'd get their times she was going to come round to their trailer. They're [TE Teachers] from the County Council, so wherever you go, you get different teachers. Sometimes they [traveller children] even have a designated teacher that if they got a problem when they were away, they could phone and she would pass messages on or send it on the computer. The Essex traveller teachers are much more organized because they have a lot more children to deal with. Round here they're more used to the Gypsy children or the New Age Travellers. Zoah and Enry and Ria and Charlee were the only children here.

At the Eton Summer School they were all children like Zoah who come from normal backgrounds but they were bright enough to be Oxbridge candidates. You could only apply if you got As and A stars in GCSEs. It was a fantastic experience. It was like a new world for her because all of a sudden there were people she could talk with on the same level. Two weeks, it give her so much confidence. She met some *lovely* friends there. Zoah's mostly friends with boys. One boy she fell in love with is from the Isle of Wight. They'd all meet up as soon as they had time off from school. In the summer they'd come down loads of times. I let them sleep up the trailer. Half a dozen of these great big 6 foot boys. She is now going to come back to school to make sure that the other children in years below her, apply for it.

She went back to school in September, that's when she done her UCAS statements. The beginning of December is when you go for your interview which was crazy stressful. Her emotions go up and down with the clouds. That's very hard for a mother. From what I can see, when you get to that level of education, no matter how clever you are, you've still got to know that subject. It's whether you can read something and it stays in your brain. They reckon the fifth week [of College] is when you have a proper low and she had the Fresher's 'flue. Mobile phones saved my life 'cos I have been lonely without her but I could just text or phone sometimes 2 or 3 times a day. Thursday night she felt really bad again so I said right, I'm going to come and get you. I can't think of you in your little room, on your own. I was going to take her back on the Monday but by then we were both ill. There'd been quite a big swine flue scare, so they were quite ok with people coming home. She doesn't have to say now. If she can't handle it she can come away; life will just take a different path.

Early in 2010 the usual busyness was in progress in the Stocks' yard. Shirley had walked the 20 yards from her chalet to say hello, and Henry Jr., repainting the back of the Miami, commented that his job never ends; nine to five work would be a lot easier. He was half jesting, half serious. Zoah, home from Cambridge, was tapping out magazine articles on a computer while recovering from a cold. In August she was coping with an insistent public in the Pit Stop Diner at Harwich Fair.

Henry Sr. has been entirely devoted to his business, and unlike the women in his family, he was reluctant to speak with me. There was some softening in his attitude. I guessed that he didn't want altogether to be left out, since he replied courteously to my phone calls and answered from the background, some of the checks to my script about the family that I put to his wife. Henry Jr.'s participation was minimal. I didn't think of asking him for an interview until early in 2012 by which time the whole family were reluctant to participate any more. Henry Jr. was working night and day restoring his Miami, they told me, and this was corroborated by another showman. There was a sense among them that the Channel 5 TV series had served only to confirm their fears: the public were interested in showmen playing the fool, and in their plights, but not in the professional image that is so important to them.

CHAPTER FIFTEEN
'THIRTY-EIGHT YEARS OF BUSINESS AND STILL HERE!'

'Travelling's a *hard life*', Ian Starsmore insisted. Marrying into the Community, he worked with showmen for seventeen years, throughout the summer, at Christmas and at Easter; when ever he could get away from art school teaching. The period came to an end with domestic changes and the death of his great friend Jimmy Bugg but the experience left him with indelible memories. In 1977 he curated an exhibition at the Whitechapel Gallery celebrating fairground apparatus and the people for whom it was made.[1] Starsmore says:

> Having built up the night before, in the cold winter you *have to* be there at nine o'clock in the morning if there's three people around. They call it getting a living and some of the rides can take a lot of money but the pressure is great. The weather is *all-important* and it is precarious. You work hard, you go back to the wagon and count your money and hope you've done well. Then you fry egg sandwiches at 3 a.m. and maybe you have to get off the site before the next day. Everything would have to be pulled down. All the stalls, all the rides. All the wood picked up because if there's a trace of rubbish maybe the council won't ask you to go there next time, so they're very *careful* people in that sense. It's quite an ordered thing. It comes from long experience. Very physically strong people who've been picking up bits of wood since they were five years old.
>
> I didn't have much to do with the Dodgems but two or three times I had to help take one down. Once, on Norwich Hill, it was bitterly cold. It was *hailing*, and those posts – sheets of metal, weigh a huge amount. At four o'clock in the morning you're picking them up when you can barely feel the end of your fingers. I remember Jimmy once lying underneath the Dodgem lorry at Dereham with one other man because there was a problem and they had to get away. So here was Jimmy Bugg lying under that lorry with a major engine thing, it was a *whole night* and that kind of pressure on people is quite intense. On the other hand, the moves are quite well planned, people disperse, it's pleasantly anarchic.

[1] *The Fairground*, Whitechapel Art Gallery, 18 December 1977.

Through the grapevine, I contacted a couple who were proud of the fact that they have worked hard and long. Starting at Easter from Wymondham, Larry and Josie Gray travelled all year with four children, all married, all travelling, *their* children, and four machines. Larry had besides Juveniles, a Dodgems, Miami, Twister, and an Eliminator. In early September, the whole family would be working together at East Runton.

The day I drove from Sheringham, the roadside bore yellow markers advertising FUNFAIR. Up close, you could scarcely miss the long banner flying half a dozen Union Jacks. Arriving early I pulled in to a hazel coppice bordering the fairground, from there you could hear a male voice singing, followed by the kick and cry of ball games. Undaunted by the cough of an electric generator starting up, a pheasant stalked past the bonnet of my car. Not long after Josie was brewing tea for us in her trailer, while Larry finished tinkering with his apparatus. It was mid afternoon and the fair wouldn't start until 6.00 pm.

Josie's father was Billie Abbott of Wellingborough, her mother was not a show-person. Now in her mid-sixties, she is calm and capable; very quick, very direct, and amusing. She could be sharp, and dislikes affectation. A year later, just after her 65th birthday, I found her surrounded by more cards than her years, and flowers, masses of them, in vases and bouquets. She complained of 'lying in hospital like a yellow maggot (the result of bile malfunction caused by pancreatic cancer) and they was weeping and crying all round. I thought I can't have this.'

As a devotee of the electronic revolution, she bought cheaply the large ex-display model TV in the trailer. Then her son bought her a lap top computer to help her with bookwork before she sent it to an accountant. But she didn't get round to using it. Josie told how the past impacts upon the present.

> I live in the past. We've been coming here 31 years, Larry was here as a boy in short trousers. You get this feeling you're being watched, that there's a presence, and then I found out that my grandfather used to bring the fair here before the war; which I never knew because we moved away from Norfolk and travelled in Northamptonshire, but it was comforting to know that this is where my father was when he was young, and I always get this lovely feeling that we're doing what we should be doing, what we're expected to do. I felt like saying that to my dad.
>
> I've been married 43 years, so I've been in East Anglia longer than I've been in Northamptonshire. Once you get to know Norfolk people, if they like you, they like you. Larry was born at Swaffham and he's always been in Norfolk. When we first got married and things were quite hard, we went all over the place trying to make

some sort of route up and every time we'd cross over the A1 he was unbearable to live with. It didn't take me long to discover you're better off to stay where you feel comfortable. In those days we just had a stall, so we said we'd be better travelling on our own [ie not with the extended family]. I come from a small family firm and I didn't really want to do that. It's not the easiest because you've got family round you, which can cause a bit of a problem. I remember my dad saying, whatever you do, my dear, you'll do different to this, surely. You've had it all your life.(Laugh). I said, No Dad, let him [Larry] try, if he doesn't like it at least he's tried. If he doesn't try I should never of asked. Give him a couple of years and he'll realize. This is our 38th year of having the business, before that we were just freelance.

We bought the Dodgems from Walter Underwood who owned this field and they laid in a heap up that corner. Larry spent years and years working on them, we replaced this, replaced that. Me and him [Larry] worked together out in the snow with welly boots on. We worked on them about five years and by then my eldest son was straining at the bit to be big enough and strong enough to help his dad. Then we bought another ride, obviously on hire purchase, because we couldn't see the possibility of paying for it. But in those days things weren't the price they are now. Fortunately I had 3 boys, you just had to keep it [the fairs] going until they were old enough to help. Larry was happy travelling on the road so I let him do it. He's made a good job of it, he's a very good showman and he cares. Everywhere we go they look forward to us coming back, everywhere that's regular. At Pulham Market people come out and welcome us on a village green surrounded by Tudor houses. One lady used to give our children sweets for picking the paper up. She'd say, keeping our green better. You feel like you are providing a service that they want. Because we're very cheap. We work at the moment, a pound each on everything. We work on the assumption that if they can't afford it, they won't come. If they've got £20 in their pocket, the children will get an hour or two. That's the main thing, to keep them coming, because they remember it all their lives. We take it in turns with the Dodgems, he can then look after the generators [while she is minding] and the boys look after the other rides, the Roll-em-in and the Twister, and the Miami – the teenagers like them but I like the nice sedate Dodgems. For each ride we've got, they have their own music set-up. The cassettes I've got in the Dodgems are ... I've got '60s, '70s, '80s popular music.

The boys, they've got the head-banging stuff (Big laugh) which I can't listen to. The kids just love it, they go ump, ump, ump. [Head up and down movements.] The flashing lights and all the modern electrical gadgets that's about now, the lazer beams and the halogen lights and sodium lights that make everything change from blue to pink just by the light that's shining on it. And all the little fairy lights. The lighting gives it a magic to the fairground. In my day there was nothing like that, there was just great big bulbs hanging from a wire. But like with the Pop Shows, the lighting can create it's own illusion. I think it's because of colour television, the videos.

1971 when my father died, the colour televisions had just started. There was no such thing as a video, or a ciné camera, the cam recorders – and all of a sudden, everything – the mobile phones and all these wonderful things especially the mobile phones, I don't know how we managed without them. I should upgrade my phone but they're too technical. I just want a great big button that I can push. I keep it safely in the cupboard so it can't jump out. (Laugh). I'm terrified of it. I'm not ready for change; it'd just give me a headache. These younger generation will bring everything they can into the business, computers and laptops, and a dongle which means you can use the laptop without electricity. You turn it this way and it can get you on the internet. I think the youngsters can spring the fairground into the 21st century. I say to Larry we've got to sit back and let them. We've taught them how to look after people and give good value for money. Everything we've got is tested and safe and properly looked-after. They should now go ahead with the razzmatazz of it. (Big laugh).

Another showman – John Manning – agreed that the gadget which transformed his life had been the mobile phone.

Years ago people used to travel, they'd use the telegram to the lessees. That's how we used to communicate. Mr Sweet have you got room for so many stalls or a ride at so and so, and he would send a reply, paid. You had so many words to reply, and he'd either send back yes, or no room available. When it was pulling-down day, mostly on the Sunday or Monday, you'd see the telegram boy coming. You'd say, don't go. You'd fill that in, and he'd take that back with him. It was 1/6d reply paid. Then I used to have a phone plug in two or three places. Pay for it all the year round, so I was paying more'n once. But the mobile phone come along, done the trick; best thing ever invented for our business.

For the Larry Grays, marriage was not accompanied with a ride for a dowry as is frequently the case in wealthy fairground nuptials. Nor did they inherit dependable sites at fairs. Starting from scratch, building up a run of small fairs has taken intense involvement, close teamwork and what Larry refers to as dedication. The dedication was repaid in 1991, with a move from a tiny yard in Kings Lynn to 6 acres of cedar and willow-hung land behind an enormous iron gate, formerly a farm, on Wymondham's London Road. Yet the combination of effort and struggle behind his calling takes a toll, of this he is fully aware. At 65 he is a bushy-eyebrowed, muscular, ruddy-faced man with an infectious gurgling laugh. His limbs have the specialized tension of a gymnast, animating into theatre when he is elated. Suddenly boyish, his whole body twists and jumps around like a lizard giving a tremendous feel of his pulling at life for all he's worth. As if the emotional spiral of the rides along with the participation of the public produced a longing and excitement, his speech is swift, each statement converted into a rhetorical question. Movements of his hands illuminate his words with improvised drawings.

For twenty years Larry took rides to the May Balls in Cambridge; although not to the west of the A1, which would be stretching his comfort zone, and he is relieved to have passed on the job to others. Twenty five years of comparatively orderly work for the forces suited him better. June 2008 saw the 40th anniversary of cult TV series, Dad's Army, celebrated with a weekend of themed events in the Norfolk town where many of the wartime comedy's outdoor scenes were filmed. In Thetford's local re-enactment, Larry Jr. played the warden who wore the helmet in a film. Since then, the council have written to him, asking if he, as part of Thetford's history, could compile some memories for them. Larry and Josie are delighted that the family is included.

> We've got the Round-up out there, 32 people stand up and that goes up, swings round. We've got the Waltzer which is everybody's favourite, that's the in-thing, it's either a rave or for teenagers. The Dodgems are more of a family ride. They'll never die 'cos everybody want to drive soon as they're 17. My wife, she's very strict on the Dodgems, she won't let them do what they want to do like backwards and all that. They can drive in a proper manner, so she put a lot of people through the [Driving] Test. When they go off our Dodgems, they go back and take your dad's car. The Dodgems'll be here for ever, other rides come and go. They get 2 or 3 good years but they don't last because people want to change. Every 6 or 7 years you get a different generation and that's new to 'em again. Of course the other rides are a lot of money which wouldn't suit us. They've got to be in the big cities where the money

is. We like to keep a family fair, nice and cheap so people can come more than one night. They can tell the neighbour, we had a good night there for a tenner and the children won a prize every time on the stalls. We don't get a lot of money like that but we can keep goin'. Whereas [if] we start trying to charge too much, you won't see em no more. We're going to keep going as long as we can and if we do stop, we won't owe nobody no money. I brought all me children up in the same way of thinking. We go to Newmarket, Bury St Edmunds, Ware Carnival and up to Braintree Carnival, Thetford twice a year. I like Norfolk people cos I'm a Norfolk person meself. I go up the pub the other night and builders and fishermen cuddle me, they treat me like one of their own. That's more important to us than the money part of it. For people to accept you and look on you as friends.

Kings College, Jesus College, Caius College, they was the main three. The last one was, Jesus, it'd be '89. We'd wiggle through these little gates and archways, sometimes we used to have to carry the Dodgems in. On the croquet pitches, anywhere, put boards down and build them up. There'd be perhaps a thousand people and you got one set of Dodgems most of the time, just us, or us and perhaps a big wheel. To be honest, they was so hard work. Whatever you say to the students, they won't take notice of you once they're drunk and there's champers flowing. (Infectious giggle) You couldn't let them go on [the ride] with champagne because that reacts with the aluminium in the floor of the Dodgems and that turn it black instantly, the cars have got wheels underneath, they're brass, and wouldn't go properly. We'd try to keep them off the track, but they'd rush to get on and they'd jump over everything, three of them trying to get in one car, and they'd be in evening dress. Towards the end, it was ridiculous. They're lovely people, but they wasn't paying, the college paid, and you get other colleges come. You'd only need 20 a bit unruly and it just got wild. It used to be all night till six in the morning. Half the time somebody else has got their leg in the car and you ain't got yours out yet! It's a headache really.

I go on RAF Base at Marham for summer balls and I do the Officer's Mess, Sergeant's Mess. They have like 6 hours with the Dodgems. They're in their '50s and probably '60s. I play the proper music for em from the '60s and the '70s. They're all in evening dress and tuxedos and they'll all sing. It's a proper champagne thing. You can give them people good value because they're riding how they should ride. The latest one go on til 3.00 am. They go for breakfast when we have to pull straight down. They can't believe how quick and how professional we are. We sometimes follow the coaches out the main gate. Showmen are basically very good drivers; they say I don't know how you're going to get round there. I say, there's plenty of room, we're used to it. We done Coltishall till that finished and they wanted me to go on there on the last day. Said we're having a party but I had another booking. Once I've booked, I'm booked. Said ever so sorry I'd have loved to come.

Showmen went from London to Yarmouth fair with horses, then [we used] steam engines. Then we went to the First World War, [using] petrol in Tilling Stevens lorries from the War Department, with the diamond rays and the generators in the front. Then came the second World War, [with] the Mack and Diamond Ts. I said [later], 'The railways are finished, the coal mines are finished, but we're still goin'.' It's a hard life; you're never finished. I've never been on holiday in me life, which is ridiculous. My holiday is what I do, I love it. This is what I'm going to do until I'm too old to do it. (Laugh). It's getting a bit close to the time but there you are; it's been a good old life. All the family like it, and if we'd done something else we'd have been working 8.00 till 5.00. There is a lot of showmen settled down and done something else because things got a bit bad, especially now with all the diesel and what we have to go through, the Ministry stuff. Showmen got a bit fed up. No handouts for them. We never ever stop but because our adrenalin's up all the while it keeps you goin. You live on nervous energy. All the Grays have hearts or strokes. Take your pick. But we'd rather work 12–14 hours a day and been happy doing it. When people go off the fairground, we love to see them with a laugh on their face. We've never had people going off saying, what a rip-off. They say, Thank you very much. It was fantastic.

Both partners congratulated travelling showmen in general for a long-term service to the business. Josie adds a personal contribution to their powers of survival:

There was a shop that never would let me put a poster in the window, it was a bit like that (Sniff sniff). Then one day I went past and the shop was closed down, so I put a poster on the front window WE'RE STILL HERE!

CHAPTER SIXTEEN
'MASTER OF ALL TRADES'

Unlike the nine-to-fiver the showman half envies and half despises because the work is, or can be, mind-corroding; he enjoys the variety of expertise that is his boast. It is also an insurance against the unpredictable nature of the business. More than one of those I spoke with described himself as a master of all trades, and John Bugg gave a fairly representative table of personas:

> One day I'm an electrician, the next day I'm inspecting safety certificates, the next day I'm a heavy good vehicle driver, the next I'm a surveyor.

Larry Gray simultaneously enlarges on the work's extended repertoire, and eyes the benefits of the settled man's apportioned hours:

> We do everything that's humanly possible to do ourselves, and if we can't do that, we'll get another showman to do it. That's how we work, it's an inner circle, we all help each other. They're good welders, good painters, they're good carpenters, so when they settle down a lot of 'em realize how easy it is, weekends off, finishing at five.

The public don't fully appreciate the multiplicity of skills required thinks Peterborough-based Frank Sedgewick. In his youth his family kept a travelling menagerie; when he came home for tea his mother would say 'Come and see the lions'. Caring for exotic animals required another set of proficiencies. When the fairground went through a bad spell in their area, Frank and his wife, Margaret, took 17 years out to run a catering business in Wellingborough. This they continued until health troubles intervened, whereupon they returned to travelling 'in a reduced manner'. Throughout the Wellingborough years, he also took on welding repairs and 'manufacturing' for other showmen. At 82, he is prevented from exercising his abilities by lack of space and deteriorating eyesight but what he minds most is not being able to drive a car.

> The showman does the complete bag of tricks. Riding master or a lessee will liaise with the Council – most fairs are council-controlled today,[1] signs a contract for 2, 3, 4 fairs a year, does his own

---

[1] Council control is largely due to the fact that the councils either own the land (such as parks) where fairs are held, or have succeeded to the ownership of the fair charters.

advertising, then he does all the paperwork – the regulations, then he goes on the ground and physically sets out hundreds of tons of equipment, erected, tested, tried and electrically lit up, everything ready for the public.

There is a lot of routine involved in some of the tasks the showman tirelessly performs, the most obvious ones being building up and pulling down the rides. Each occasion varies with the weather, the venue, with regulations introduced, but the procedure is in essence the same each time. The biggest change over the years concerns transport which is to some showmen almost as important as their rides. Gallopers, for example, arrive in a specially-built lorry or a box trailer with two decks.

Once the trailer has been parked over a position that marks the centre of the ride and lifted a few inches from the ground with hydraulic rams, the centre pole is erected to give the full height. When a steam engine is to be stationed inside the ride, the top part of the chimney is secured at this stage, so that smoke can escape through the hole in the middle. After the preliminary operations, round after round of equipment is moved from the trailer, building up the overhead parts first with 20 foot wooden swifts, separating them with quarterings, and securing the framework with cranks to form an umbrella-like skeleton before a cover, the top tilt, and rounding boards are fitted on. The key to the job is not to handle things twice, a showman explained. The ground might well be muddy; to rest parts down and pick them up later, just increases the workload. A central paybox and shutters go in next, shutters being the painted boards rather like screens that fit around the centre truck to conceal the underworks. Then come fitted brass horse-rods on which the horses and other creatures hang in mid air. Platform rods precede the platform itself, after which a series of other rods known as stabbers and stabilizers, secure different sections together, synchronising the speed of the top and the base. With four men on the job and no coffee break, the whole thing can be accomplished in four and a half

At Hereford, for example, the May Fair granted in 1121 to the Bishop of Hereford, was transferred to the city's Corporation by an Act of Parliament in the 1830s. Although many borough councils used to run their own fairs, after the Local Government Reform Act of 1974 they were unable to continue in this role because of their considerably reduced status and staff. The newly-created, larger authorities were also reluctant to take on the job. Instead, agreements were entered into either with individual showmen or the local Section of the Guild to take over the organization of the fair under licence from the council. A few authorities have maintained their direct control over the running of (mainly) chartered fairs. Such is the case with Cambridge Midsummer Fair, Oxford St Giles Fair, Nottingham Goose Fair, Hull Fair and Loughborough November Pleasure Fair.

hours. A more elaborate set of Gallopers with an organ, steam engine and perhaps chariots, takes most of a day.

The showman takes pride in his work which is different from being proud. Pride from the Old English *pryte or pryde* is, according to the Oxford Dictionary, an '(unduly) high opinion of one's own qualities'. For him, this wouldn't be right. Pass on to a 'proper sense of what befits one's position', or a 'feeling of elation and pleasure due to action or circumstance that does one credit' and you have him to a 'T'. The showman is able to live fully in the present. Only a limited amount of worry for the future is allowed to interfere with his involvement in the work, which is why he tells you he enjoys it. He takes pride in the shininess of his machine, the cleanliness of his kitchen, the pleasure he provides. A sense of identity surfaces in show-people's speech. They are what they are, the point is made with phrases such as 'We do what we do', 'With us it's a way of life'. 'That's showmen.' They are all-of-a-piece and proud of it.

Perhaps winter is the period when the showman's flexibility has been most useful to him, says Victor Harris.

> In the winter when you used to go for a job, you daren't tell them you were a showman because they didn't want yer but once you had a job, they wanter know when you coming back because they know you pull your weight.

A popular option for males in the second half of the twentieth century was carting coal, a job in which employers soon recognized the showman's aptitude for physical labour. Josie Gray remembered her husband's discipline; how he would be more competitive than anyone else. Larry says there was another reason for his approach:

> Peace-work. I'm here to earn the money, not to sit about. You either like it or you don't and you don't get a second chance. It's a long winter. You just got to tighten yer belt a bit more. We're not lavish people, we don't go out and spend what we don't have.

Two other one-time coal men, John Manning and Kenny Gray, report on their work respectively:

> The winter's the hardest part, you're a lot of time closed. In theory you take enough in the summer to allow you to live through it and concentrate on your repairs. It don't work now, there's not enough money in the game but I was a coal man for years, took me lorry to work in the winter.

Me and Carl [Kenny's brother] got, I think when I first went, £6 a week delivering coal. Then of course we loaded it – one of the best jobs. Showmen done it all over the country until that become smokeless coal and you subcontracted to Charrington which we did at Norwich. Two Irish boys here tried the coal but it was too hard for them. Women could always dig pertaters. We used to just load the lorries because it was harder work, but easier than bending over, doing the picking.

Various types of land work, fitted round the busy fairground season, might occupy the whole family. Cutting down trees, for instance, suited the Irvin clan. Shirley Stocks has strong impressions of her parents. Her mother at her happiest performing tasks her father regarded as the male prerogative.

Dad used to do logging in the winter at a little place called Hatch near Sandy, and at one time he had 2 lorries. One going down the woods for sawing it up, and one bringing it back. He had this big saw in the yard and another huge big saw with a platform he used to drag along to make the pit props for the mines. Used to cut the whole length of the tree into big boards. I can see this saw now, hear the noise it used to make. And the butchers used to come for the sawdust. I've been out on the lorry! They used to fill the skips up with logs. People would buy them, two bob a skip. Dad didn't let me go very often but I used to like to get on the back of the lorry with me scarf and gloves on when we took em round. Mum used to love to be out if she could, out in the yard working that saw.

Collecting scrap iron has been a popular standby, though not necessarily restricted to winter, and not one that could be managed without a permanent yard. It is unpopular with local councils because piles of metal are unsightly and nowadays metal theft exposes the scrap merchant to the risk of inadvertently receiving stolen metal. Once again, Shirley Irvins's father was readily assisted by his wife, Violet. Their daughter said:

Grandad used to do scrapping and one of her jobs used to be breaking up batteries. She loved it. Days I wasn't at school I had to learn to do the inside work, cos she was sorting the iron and stuff like that. [I] Soon learned how to cook.

Today's options for the younger generation include driving articulated lorries, and employment in the Christmas market. This might be growing fir trees, organizing festive lights, hiring empty shops over the Christmas period in which to sell decorations, or donning fancy dress to serve in a grotto. A 'grotto' being an extensive windowless room in a garden centre that gets stocked with inexpensive seasonal baubles. There are many options open for market-orientated retail work. As John Manning says, the object is to keep 'little bits and pieces coming in'.

CHAPTER SEVENTEEN
'HE LIKES ADVENTURE'
FOREIGN TRAVEL

Most showmen enjoy driving, they're good at it, and it's all in the course of business. If they are on the road they can't be doing much else, so travel becomes the space that keeps them going between physical labour and the incessant need to make decisions. King's Lynn-dwelling Nipper Appleton, who has a fondness for the West Country, covers a fair number of miles in a year. But some showmen have taken extraordinary trips overseas despite the cost and inconvenience of shipping the rides. Ian Starsmore noted the precision that they need for such undertakings:

> Everything has to slot in like the military. Everything has to work efficiently, and some of the equipment they use *is* ex-military.

A precedent had long since been set. George Sanger claimed to have carried his tents to every European country except Russia by the end of the nineteenth century,[1] and the Thurstons visited 14 different counties in the UK with traction engines in the first decades of the twentieth century:

> With a great steam engine and 3 big loads weighing 30-40 tons, they could only average 7 or 8 mph. The rides were much bigger then and the roads weren't tarred and were full of pot holes. The iron wheels would spin like hell on granite. In hilly parts of the country, they'd winch up the loads and lower them slowly the other side of the hill, running the back wheels of the trailer on skids and blocks. Yet nothing seemed to get damaged.[2]

Overall the showman's luck in foreign countries has been mixed. John Manning offers a less than enthusiastic view:

> A lot of them go abroad, not always successfully. If I couldn't get a living in this country, I'd pack it up. I mean some of 'em've been to Russia! John Nichols did, just when the empire broke [in the 1990s]. Must be mad! John Bugg's going this winter to South of

---

[1] 'Lord' George Sanger, *Seventy Years a Showman* (MacGibbon & Kee, 1966), p. 14.
[2] George Cushing with Ian Starsmore, *Steam at Thursford* (David & Charles, 1982), p. 37.

France. A lot of them go to the big festival in Dubai. All the equipment's packed on the boat. The boat sails. They give it so long to get there, then they fly out by plane. They've got an agent over there who handles it. A lot of them got out there, done very bad and couldn't get their equipment back. Them that went to the Far East done very well. Stevens went out 10 or 12 years ago and stayed out; gathered together some big amusements into a theme park. He was in Hong Kong and then travelled to different places. He's still there now. They originated out of Gloucester. They used to call his father Black Billy.

The epic journeys a few have made in pursuit of foreign venues suggest that some just like pushing boundaries. By the mid-1990s, for the new generations, the earth had seemed to shrink. It was then that a small group of North West showmen made a tour, tales of which filled Victor Gray with awe:

My daughter in law and her father travelled all over Africa, it must of paid because he did it 3 years running. He's written a book about it advertised in *World's Fair* every week.[3] In my day if I got to London I thought I was doing something marvellous. Went to Majorca on my honeymoon but I've never been anywhere else. Our eldest son, Victor Junior has been operating his fairground equipment in Iceland, on the wharf there, at Reykjavik. Did that for 3 years. Took it down to the docks and then ship it all out, it's pretty expensive. Last year and the year before, two of them drove to Gibraltar, all the way through France, Spain, cross the border and opened for about 6 weeks. What an adventure to drive all the way! Thank goodness my children are doing now what I'd like to have done. If somebody said, we're going to open on the Moon, they'd be gone.

If ever there was a tribute to showmen's spirit of adventure and opportunism, it has to be the record of the two Davids' (Wallis and Taylor) family trips to South Africa, men and women and youngsters, trailing a Twist, Miami, Meteorite, Dodgems and a Kiosk among their equipment. Three lorries and a Toyota jeep to move with. They left home aware there was an element of risk to their travels. There were, Wallis admitted in retrospect, 'some hairy moments'. He 'gambled a lot of equipment' and wasn't sure, afterwards, that he would have made the journey had he been fully aware of what they would encounter. At the same time, he had no regrets.[3] Words like 'plucky' and 'courageous' are inadequate to describe the humour in adversity that prevailed

---

[3] David Wallis, *David Wallis' African Adventure* (New Era Publications, 2000).

while travelling thousands of miles in unknown territory. The initial run was from Durban to Harare, and back via Bulawayo where they had ground booked at a Trade Fair. Leaving sufficient time to explore, they stopped and opened up in sites that looked favourable on the way.

Shipping from Teeside to Durban had its own surprise in stowaways who broke into some of the trailers. This might have prepared the travellers for what was to come. In practice, each part of the journeys had its obstacles. White ants and termites were soon eating through the base of plywood containers, and snakes lodged in the loads. Inevitably, lorries broke down and the trailers came off the road. There were punctures, broken machines to mend, a small fire, the rainy season and incredible heat to contend with. Despite meeting agents from time to time, they encountered stealing, obstreperous traffic police, border guards and customs officials, all of whom, on occasion wanted bribes before the showmen could make their way. In Mozambique, money devalued so fast, the takings diminished each week. Largely undaunted, they returned several times, staying in South Africa for months at a time. There was time out to go white water rafting, and time to visit David Livingstone's Memorial at Victoria Falls, but for the most part, it is their relations with the indigenous showmen and others met in the course of business that colour the story of *David Wallis' African Adventure*. For an outsider, the overall impression is of just how much the showman remains true to himself.

Another pioneer, Eastern Counties showman, John Bugg can not resist the chance of a businesslike proposition. He has tried his luck, he told me, in Jersey, Guernsey, Eire, Cyprus, Hong-Kong, Dubai, Singapore and Malaysia:

> We've got wheels, so we'll travel and go. At the moment I'm working on a project in Lisbon. That's the area I'll be working in December and January with a couple of small rides. We'll be in Campera, that's owned by the Freeport Company – you know the shopping outlets. We've taken our rides to Hong-Kong Winter Carnival, Summer Festival and the Kai Tak airport [Hong Kong], and to the Malaysian border of Singapore, Kuala Lupur, Dubai. We had the rides inside the World Trade Centre at Abu Dhabi.

Financial incentive is not the only reason for his journeys, John's mother says. It is the lure of travel itself; the sheer exhilaration of discovering new places that has taken him so often to foreign climes. Margaret Bugg should know; in 2007 she joined her son for a week at an inland park near the French Riviera they had patronized for ten week periods over five successive years. For her the trip was an unforgettable holiday.

He likes adventure you see. He said on a mobile, Guess where I am? He was in a lorry with an Arab, they were leading the way with all the loads behind in the Abu Dhabi Desert. He said, all I can see everywhere Mum is sand, and he *laughed*. He said, it's *so hot*. He was out there for several months. It's blisteringly hot outside, so he opened in one of these big brash shopping malls. They open at night until 2.00 am in the morning with all this air conditioning. He opened in Ireland for six weeks, but he didn't like that.

In France it was a beautiful place, palm trees and flowers. It's a permanent thing, owned by a French family. They let people in for so many years, then they like to have a change of equipment. John had a big aerial ride called Oblivion, so knowing him, he'll change his ride [in order to return with something different]. Sarah [John's wife] had the American trailer out there. John said I'll introduce you to everybody; there was German, Italian, French, Swedish. They're lovely people, John and Sarah don't speak French or any other language, but they made them understand. They could only charge a set price and Sarah said it's quite easy with the euros. She had tickets up in French as well. She learned how to give change, she done it all her life.

Robert and Kim Thurston began married life gently and became more venturesome. In his mid-forties, Robert took the plunge.

We went to Gibraltar in August 2007 and 2008. We only took one ride [A Super-Bob]. There was at least another 50 English showmen all drove across France and right through Madrid. This gentleman David Taylor, who comes from Cumbria, he's been all over the world with fairs. It was him organized it so we went along, me and Kim, my son and daughter and a member of staff. We was open at West Mersey for the regatta on the boat yard car park, and we went from there to Portsmouth; across to Le Havre, then we drove right across France, round by Bordeaux and up thro 'Gibe' where we done 2 weeks. It was called Gibraltar Week; they do a ceremony in the middle of the square where the Guards come in. Then we took it all down and came all the way back. The first year it was worth it, they hadn't done an English fair there for years, they'd always had the Spanish in there.

Starsmore reflected on the environmental aspect of travel:

One thinks of all the terrible pieces of machinery that are being manoeuvered around the world in pursuit of god-knows-what, and here on the other hand is this wonderful piece of magical, primitive, theatre, which is using the same kind of engineering language. I'd much rather people transported fairground equipment to the Middle East than the disgusting things people are doing at the moment. This is an ancient, primal thing that's going on.

Early in 2012 I caught up with John Bugg. It was two years since we had exchanged notes, an interval that had seen him take an exploratory trip to Norway, and back to two or three places in Europe, most recently, Antibes in the South of France, where, a single ride was manned for three months by his son. John Sr. was circumspect about future prospects for foreign travel, nor is it his nature to throw caution to the wind, the way the North West showmen did some sixteen years ago:

I won't say far-away travel is a thing of the past but you got to be particularly careful the kind of deal that you put together. Money's tight at the moment and there's been such a huge progression in the leisure business as far as rides are concerned. For example, when we went out to Hong-Kong there was no Disneyland there, when we went to Dubai, they'd only seen street entertainers. Now there's one of the largest operators in the world, – Frije Entertainment, that's operating perhaps eighty plus amusement rides in the Middle East. They've got their own, so it's not a sound proposition for a UK showman.

If you were to take the average two metre RO RO, roll on, roll off trailer [in which the heavy load drives on to the shipping vessel instead of being craned on board], one way, you'd be looking at about fifteen thousand pounds to take it to Dubai, and that would be three weeks travelling. The return fair is always slightly cheaper because there are ships running around the Mediterranean for the return freight. You can't do that for one week's business, you've got to make that a six months operation to generate that kind of money to repay your costs. Operating UK rides in Europe is not so expensive, and the road system is fantastic. You'd pay a standard ferry charge whether you cross with P&O or some other shipping company. That would be per linear metre, I'd think roundabout the three thousand pounds mark for a return trip. But you've still got to be there long enough to generate your shipping costs, your road-fuel costs, your staff costs, your electricity costs, before you get into profit. There are the odd one or two showmen that will take a chance at this kind of thing. Not too many now. I don't have to explain to you. In all businesses money's tight, you got to be cautious. It's no different to running an ASDA supermarket. If they keep increasing fuel costs, the food's going to cost more. I still have that enthusiasm but it's no good entering into a financial agreement blind. And of course we're not doing it for the fun of it, we're doing it to earn money and pay your repayments, so you've got to analyse the deal. Then you got to be confident that you feel safe with the people that you're dealing with. If we were going to ship from Ipswich to Hong Kong, you got three weeks travelling time so you're missing three weeks business. Then you got a week setting up and a week going through all the stringent testing procedures in Asia. After which you open and hope that what you're presenting is popular. There is no guarantee with that either. So trying to play all the ace cards is a little bit like Russian roulette.

CHAPTER EIGHTEEN
'THE ENTHUSIASTS' – INDEPENDENT SHOWMEN

'The Independent showman is one who doesn't belong to the Guild', Kim Thurston said:

> There is quite a few. We call them non-runners which we shouldn't really. They're enthusiasts who bought old equipment. There's Perrots from Saffron Waldon, there's also Michael Rule there, he's got a set of steam gallopers and Jamie Bloomfield based at Claydon, he do Suffolk and all round there. They tend to stick to the old-time fairs at steam engine rallies and small villages. They do now go to the charter fairs too, it isn't such a closed shop as it used to be because of the European law.

Although Martin Loades and Jamie Bloomfield were brought up with houses to retire to when they weren't travelling, both had paternal forbears who built and exhibited model rides, both were attracted by showland at an early age, and both work like a traditional showman, teamed with their families. Not to join the Guild has been a conscious decision; Jamie is markedly independent, and Martin has a streak of anarchism, but to think of them as less competitive than its members would be a mistake. There could hardly be two showmen more dedicated to the art of spinning a livelihood from their businesses.

The most obvious difference between their lifestyles today is that Martin and Tiffany live with a small daughter in a modern house in Ipswich while Jamie and Charleen live in one of the classic Sipson trailers[1] from the '70s in a yard at Needham Market. Martin (born in 1976) has ready humour, it could be a hereditary trait; his grandfather, Fred Loades's vast model fairground, constructed between 1929 and 1977, featured midget pantechnicons bearing such legends as 'Loades of Fun, Fun On Tour'. You pressed the time-switch; the lights went on, and everything clicked into motion. Jamie, seven years younger than Martin, can't yet afford much relaxation.

Jamie's father, Colin Bloomfield, led a double life, incorporating the romance he still felt for his travelling days in mini fairground replicas when he wasn't driving lorries. His obsession so affected the son that it fixed his future. Basically, Jamie is a mechanical engineer, with the usual detailed love and knowledge of his apparatus. While his business was developing, he took a conventional job. It was through needing a set of Chairoplanes that he met

---

[1]   After which the Sipson firm went out of business.

Michael Starmar and his daughter from Chelmsford. Two years later, in 2008, he married Charleen, pretty and shy, from an established fairground family. She does the paperwork and paints the signs they display before each event. As the lessee, Jamie travels to small towns and small villages, equipping each fair accordingly. Once a member of the Association of Independent Showmen (AIS), he no longer is. Without belonging to the Guild either, he relies on a fervent dedication, and trial and error; building up relationships with communities as he goes along.

I met Jamie Blomfield in mid-April 2010, showing in the heart of Suffolk's countryside, already his twelfth consecutive year at Thurston's New Green. Three rides were set up with painted pay boxes in the arc of a bank of flowering cherries which happened to harmonise with the pink of his Twister and Swinging Gyms. Three trailers housed Bloomfields and the Tommy Bonds who regularly travel with them as tenants. The sun came out fitfully on what could hardly have been a prettier picture.

> I've gained the interest from as young as I could walk and talk from me dad telling me about fairground ways of life. He went away with Charlie and Amelia Bugg when he was about 8 yrs old. He worked for John Bugg till he got married, then he come away from the business and never returned to it. Monday to Friday me dad was a lorry-driver; the late 1980s he started making these fantastic little models of all what he used to travel with. He built this show of how he remembered it. It was so real life. He made an Ark – a Coronation Speedway, an Octopus, a Cakewalk a Twister and hooplas. I took quite a fancy to the Twister model which had all the associated side joints. They used to come to pieces, all packed in their little lorries and trucks, exactly the same as the real thing. We started showing those models at rallies, in an awning at the side of a little trailer. It got bigger and bigger to the stage it was taking us about 9 hours to set them all up for a weekend show so we bought an old-fashioned Thames trailer lorry from Tommy Bond which had stood in the yard near Bradfield for years, and restored it. All our models stayed in the back of this lorry, the floors folded down and the ceilings went up, and a cloth tilt went all the way round, and it was a walk-in show.
>
> Taking the models around was in my early teens, in and out of school. In 1998 we bought the Swinging Gyms, that was the first ride. Sixteen onwards I done an electrical apprenticeship and got qualified. When I started having me own fairground stuff, I organized myself a few places such as what we're on now. I was

commuting backwards and forwards to work in Needham Market, with Mondays and Fridays off so I could conduct me own business, but that got a bit difficult when I bought the Twister, so I give the job up in 2004. That Twister was made in 1978, imported from America. Unlike modern Twisters, everything lifts off and has to be put together. There is other ones up and down the country but not round here, and a lot have been trailer-mounted. They look exactly the same, you take the cars off; but ours, you start with the centre pole and everything pins, nuts and bolts on. Nothing folds, it's a day's work to put together. The Swinging Gyms is 1958, they were made by a firm called Lusse in Blackpool but I think that company has folded. Our particular set was made as a Park model.

I organize all me own fairs. It does make it harder work because not only have you got to get all your equipment there on time, and get it set up safely, you've also got to sort next week out. They expect the grass to be left how we find it and that's what we expect to do, but if we've had a week of rain it can involve me cancelling the next place. I can't move on for damaging the ground. There's two heavy goods drivers, meself and me father, cos I've got three loads. We do one each then I have to fetch a lorry back for me living trailer. I can come back at a more respectable time (Laugh) so Charleen ain't got to be up all through the night. We have different tenants; in about three weeks time we'll have a set a Dodgems joining us. It depends on the places, I found out it doesn't pay to have a lot of equipment in small villages because there's basically only so many slices out the cake.

Every venue in the annual round is documented in Jamie's meticulously updated appointment book. This means on average, some 36 planned and recorded moves in a year, a few of them to repeat venues.[2] Occasionally he is prevented from leaving a site because his contract stipulates that the ground is left in good condition; and owing to rain, the very act of moving would damage the grass.

The year started at Easter, we was open at Shotley; last week we was at Sonham Barns; then here at Thurston. Next week we go to Glemsford near Long Melford; Glemham Hall for the country show; our home town of Needham Market where we'll be open on Crowley Park. From there we go to Stanton; Kedington near Haverhill; Billesdon; Hopton; Ixworth; Mendlesham; Rougham Airfield for a wings, wheels and steam rally – we're now into the later part of June. Then Helmingham Hall where I do 2 or 3 events a year at cart shows and horse shows. Heveningham Hall, like a big stately home, for another show they call a Country Craft show, they have classic cars, steam engines and a lot a livestock there. Then we go to Wickham Market; on to Stradbrook; back to Helmingham Hall; Bacton flower show at the start of August; again Rougham Airfield for the air show; Woolpit; then Quy in Cambridgeshire- another 2-day event for the August bank holiday; then we start our back-end run, a lot of these are second visits. Shotley [Suffolk]; Saxmundham; Glemsford; and towards the end of September, Thurston again; October the last event at Rougham Airfield; Eye; finishing up in Hopton; that takes us through to the middle of October, we pull in then. We've got our own yard, about three-quarter acres outside Needham Market, just us; all the maintenance takes place in some sheds up there. By the time you get to the back end it is nice to look forward to a rest but we ain't in five minutes then we got to get ready for the bonfires. We do six, one after the other, just take the Swinging Gyms because the Twister is too much hard work for one night.

The day I spoke with Martin Loades, he looked exhausted; it was the end of what he described as a bit of an odd week. He and his father were moving the Gallopers to new storage when the transport broke down on the outside lane of a dual carriageway and they spent 3 hours sitting on the edge 2 miles short of their destination. That it made for an interesting life was a comment of dogged acceptance. He knows what he wants; and bit by bit, he tends to achieve it. After all, he waited 30 years for his Gallopers. One of about 50 travelling sets in country, they were made in 1885 and take four people six hours to assemble. From the moment of purchase, he went into action. In February 2010 he took part in a fair run by the Showmen's Guild on the outskirts of Ipswich. Rulings exist to keep non-Guild members out of Guild fairs although the twenty-first century is seeing a relaxation of established etiquette:

I was probably 4 months old when I was travelling, right up until I was about 6 when we stopped because fuel got so expensive. I've always enjoyed watching showmen build up and pull down and move, I'm fascinated by the mechanics of it all. We used to do about 8,000 miles every summer, round agricultural shows and steam rallies with the miniature fair. My grandfather started building that; *his* father was a florist and his grandfather worked for Burrells at Deptford making traction engines. My grandfather did an apprenticeship at Garretts – the traction engine builders at Leiston that had their own railway to move the components round the yard. That took a lot of Leiston up but now it's been flattened for houses. The Long Shop Museum exhibits some of Garretts' stuff. While he was there he built models – he started out with cardboard and pins, then he went into the Ministry of Defense and worked on the first radar for the Wellington bombers. He came out of there at the end of the war and moved to Westerfield where the family home is now and bought the village store, but he was still building models for Christmas displays and the model fair. We've got a Dragon Scenic which is fantastic; that's 4 ft in diameter and stands about 18 ins high. When we stopped travelling they went to Pleasurewood Hills [a theme park near Lowestoft] for about 9 years – had a permanent exhibition there. That was in a purpose-built exhibition trailer where people would pay to walk round. They'd been out on the road with that three to four years before I was born. When we left Lowestoft I was 12 or 13, we did a bit of a run-up round Ipswich at school fêtes and carnivals with a Bouncy Castle and a set of swing boats. We'd go out to rallies and things on a Thursday or Friday and come back home on a Monday. I was at school then – and we [that's me dad and his dad and mother] gradually bought another trailer-mounted roundabout, and another roundabout. We've got four, a set of swing boats, two candyfloss kiosks, an inflatable slide, two bouncy castles and an inflatable adventure playground. And now a set of gallopers to add to the complications. (Laugh). The love of Gallopers came from when I was about three. For the summer we went to a place called Billing Aquadrome, a static caravan park near Northampton. Where our major caravan was parked, at night, out of the window, I used to look at a set of Gallopers before I went to sleep every night. I've always had a hankering to have a set.

There's something about the Gallopers that clicks with people, or it doesn't. Now Henry [Stocks Jr.], Gallopers don't fuss him at all. He'd never be interested in owning a set; anyway, there's a lot of work involved. We're been looking for about 5 years, several weren't what we wanted, they needed a lot of work doing to them or they were too big, so we went ironically, back to Billing Aquadrome, near enough to the spot where I first saw them. This was through knowing engineers at Boston who manufacture new ones. A very plain set from this firm, Rundles, start at just over £200,000. If you want something that's nice you have to spend £250,000. They'd be quite lavish. If you hire a set like mine for a summer season, it'd cost you £25,000, so you might as well be buying your own. We paid £140,000 it was the cheapest we could find. We looked at them in August [2009] and took possession of them in November. If you're a Theme Park and want a permanent thing, you're better off to buy a new set because there's less upkeep, it's probably galvanized steel frame, an aluminium framed platform, and everything else is fiberglass, so nothing rots. Ours is all good quality soft wood. They are a particularly gold set; they don't all look that gold, it just depends who's painted them up I suppose. It's stained but you have to keep replacing things. I do that myself, I enjoy it sometimes. (Laugh). You find with a lot a showmen they're handy because you can't afford to be paying people. I'm going to talk to my friend at Rundles to see if there's anything I can do, but I have a feeling that the centre's going to have to go up to Boston next winter, that's all the gearing in the middle. I can see it's going to be a bit of an expensive winter. There's another company in Boston we should be buying some chariots off to replace six horses, to give a wider family appeal. If the child's too young to go on a horse, Grandma can sit with him in a chariot because she remembers them when she was young. There's a lot in static sites; Butlins own 4 or 5 sets, there's 2 at Great Yarmouth, Walton on the Naze have got a brand-new set on the pier, Brighton have got 1 or 2. The sets that John Bugg's got are all trailer-mounted. Personally I don't like the proportions, I think they're too high. There's 2 manufacturers in this country, Matthews, and John H. Rundle Ltd. If you want to know anything about an old set, Rundles are the authority. They copy the old sets and upgrade them to modern technology. Fortunately Rundles don't build them very quickly so they're not putting too many of us out of business.

The first place we went to was Sutton Hoo at Woodbridge for a Christmas Gift weekend, that was a nice low key appearance, secure place with plenty of time to build up, give us a chance to get to know them. A month later we went up to Stamford for their one-day Christmas market, which was a long way for one day and was hard work in the end. The plan was to build up Friday night, open on Saturday, then Sunday was the event. I had a lad come up with me on the Friday and another 2 lads come up on the Sunday which was supposed to be a busy day. Then I had 4 of us there to help pack up. In the end we never built up until Saturday night, Sunday wasn't very good so we packed up and came home. We got to bed about half past three on Monday morning. But we hadn't got to bed until three o'clock Sunday morning either. The next place was Ipswich town centre, four days between Christmas and New Year. We've opened in there anyway for a month with our children's roundabout for 28 years but it was the first time a set of Gallopers had been there and we were very pleased with that. My wife said if we'd had the Gallopers at our wedding, she would have had them there. I said then I'd have had to pull them down before we went away on honeymoon, I'd have been up all night! We've done a couple of wedding fairs. The bride can sit in the chariot with her dress all laid out to have her pictures taken. One of the venues rang up yesterday to see if we can liaise with them. I've got to go and see the access. People plan their weddings so far in advance that one I've got penciled in for next July [17 months ahead]. At Christmas they're very sought after, there aren't enough sets in the country to fill the need. You can open them in places you wouldn't get another ride in, like the shopping centre in Bury St Edmunds. They wouldn't want Dodgems or a Waltzer or these massive thrill rides.

It's difficult trying to put a run together. Some of the places, someone else with Gallopers beat me to it or they don't want a fairground ride at their event. But we're going to Felixtowe for Easter Bank Holiday weekend, then probably back there for the first May Bank Holiday. Towards the end of May we're going to Christchurch Park in Ipswich, then we're going to the new shopping centre in Bury St Edmunds for 8 days for Whitsun week. July's looking reasonably busy. You have to pick your places because it's labour-intensive and costs a lot to move them about. Travelling the world isn't something I'd want to do. We try to stay Suffolk-based to keep the expenses down. We don't get too much out of Suffolk though we've got to look further afield. Like we go to Yarmouth for the horse-racing, and we went to Stamford. It was strange to be asked to go to the Valentine's Fair because theoretically they shouldn't ask a non-Guild person but John Bugg [the lessee] was prepared to sidestep the rules. That was carefully worded in *World's Fair* that I was asked at the last minute due to the fact that his Gallopers hadn't finished being re-sprayed. And it *was* last minute. We're [only] allowed to open a recognized time before a Guild Fair comes to a town, the idea is to protect historical registered fairs. But organizers don't always like it because it means they can't make changes if they want to. They have to go for so many years without a Guild fair until all the rides have lapsed, [in order to change] then they can start again. We don't have any restrictions on where we can go or when we can go, but if you're in the Guild you get more support so it works both ways. We have a very good relationship with the councils round here and work very hard to try and keep everybody happy. We're the lessees for some of the best events in Ipswich. And some of the [Guild] showmen come and open with us as well. Theoretically, when Henry Stocks Junior comes with me, he can be fined by the Guild for opening with a non-Guild person but that rule is not often enforced now because everybody needs to earn a living. Most of the showmen are good friends and will speak with me whoever they're with. There's just one or two who won't, in company – because I'm not in the Guild and haven't been born into it. It's funny. I don't think you're frowned upon quite so much as you used to be. I am a member of SIRPS.[2] I have to be to get my transit lorry insured. You could say SIRPS and the AIS are alternatives to the Guild which you have to get voted in, then abide by their rules. SIRPS has no rules, and it's only for showmen with old-time equipment. AIS takes showmen with old and modern sets. In the country there's an awful lot of independent ride operators but they're mostly Midland based.

Two years after the long interview, Martin's Gallopers were in an aircraft hanger. It was, he said, an expensive time; he was spending £15,000 on a new platform and horse cranks, a job he reckoned would cost another £10,000 were he not working on it full time himself. It would be finished by Easter. Prior to Christmas, he'd spent three months erecting Christmas lights, in December he had been with his Gallopers. Then he'd taken the lights down before the present renovations to the ride. From Easter he'd be moving into a busy season, its climax the Jubilee weekend when every Galloper set in the country was in high demand. He had a few overnight moves at the end of June, with one booking following hard after the next – this included some corporate work for British Telecom. He and five men with him were anticipating what he called 'a total tear-about'. As the years pass, he works less and less in big fairs, 'Gallopers do best when they're on their own'.

<hr>

[2]   SIRP is the official acronym for the Society of Independent Roundabout Proprietors; members tend to add an unnecessary 'S'.

CHAPTER NINETEEN
'A BIT OF A LOVE FOR IT'

During the First World War the showman was in demand for his equestrine husbandry, during the second, for his vehicular expertise. Always he has been obsessed with the tools of his trade. Attentiveness to detail is long established, and this covers making, adapting, and improvisation. Fiona Gray is familiar with an ability to improvise that increasingly embraces new technology:

> They have to repair things all the time so they're very practical and they like inventions. Kenny's dad had one of the first televisions with a 3-scaffold pole high aerial tied to the wagon to get it [reception] from London. Kenny's been the same, making things. When we got married he made a children's roundabout, 5 sets of Dodgems and a trailer with a pull-out. A lot of people bought them new but we didn't have as much money so we made ours. He got a set of horses, what we call Dobbies, he'd make spare bits for that as well.

Arthur Morrison explained how a young would-be showman's inventiveness extended to the creation of the hole or 'frog' in a brick. This meant that less clay was required, and the perforated brick was actually stronger.[1] After his unorthodox start, Henry Thurston (1847–1917) invested his creative energy in the machines that founded the extensive Thurston family amusement enterprise:

> Henry Thurston, a young brick maker worked in a yard in Cambridge. He got a large sum of money for his invention, and retired from the trade. With his money he purchased some play-rides and vehicles and travelled to fairs round the country. We called him Froggy Thurston.

It is hard now to imagine the impact of a fair's visit in small villages of the late-nineteenth and early twentieth centuries. When, out of a rural landscape emerged these exuberant vehicles propelling carved monsters and swinging chairs, their mechanics painted and polished to represent the power, the speed and the mysteries of the experience. Cinema had its beginnings in travelling

[1] See Peter Sneddon (ed.), *Brickmaking in Sprowston* (Sprowston Heritage Publication, 2006).

bioscopes or cinematographs. Many of the earliest films were made by showmen in their home towns starring native lads and lasses.[2] From 1896, up to a thousand viewers could watch at a time. A few were still touring when war broke out. Fairs brought electricity when rural communities had only gas; to the uninitiated, it was like opening up the solar system. Before the wireless, new tunes were banged out on the showman's organ; before air travel became commonplace, people's first experience of something like flight could be on the fairground.

A close look at an old photograph of a bioscope may reveal the wheels or a chimney of an engine behind the decoration. Steam engines had been part of the agricultural scene from the mid–nineteenth century, and collaborating closely with showmen, engineers like Charles Burrell in Thetford and Frederick Savage in King's Lynn worked over the ensuing decades to produce their celebrated engines specifically for the fairground. Full-length canopies with twisted brass supports, gaily painted bodywork and tall chimneys to carry the smoke away from the public, made them a familiar part of the scene.[3] By the early decades of the twentieth century, steam traction engines were hauling dismantled rides from fair to fair, while smaller steam engines drove each ride. But steam power wasn't to reign for long.

Showmen had been using electricity for their lights instead of gas and naptha or 'flare lamps' since the last years of the nineteenth-century, when carbon-arc lamps appeared on the shows and on some of the rides. Invented in 1830, flare lamps were commonly hung from the swifts of Gallopers, a somewhat alarming habit in retrospect. Arc lamps, used before the Great War, were powered by dynamos for showmen's engines that generated 55 volts. Dynamos that could manage 110 volts were able to power a filament light bulb. This development took place after the war. The changeover was a gradual process; naptha-fuelled flare lamps were still being used on the stalls in the 1920s. By this time, rides which had been driven by small steam engines could be driven by electricity generated by a central steam traction engine instead.

---

[2] George Cushing with Ian Starsmore, Steam at Thursford (David & Charles, 1982), p. 147.

[3] Burrell made his first heavy-duty steam road haulage engine in 1856. Of over 4,000 traction engines the firm built, 207 were designed for showmen, the first in 1889. Even at the turn of the century, Burrell was exporting all over the world engines which were basically unchanged since the early days. When the firm went into liquidation, Garretts of Leiston assembled the old company's spare parts. Savages, best known of all fairground engineers, constructed their first steam-driven ride in 1865. Savage & Co. closed in the 1970s. They hadn't done fairground work for years but the wooden patterns were still there and so were the craftsmen who had the skills. Cushing says, it is often forgotten that the stuff in the Kings Lynn museum once belonged to and originated with showmen (Cushing with Starsmore, pp. 144–5, 172).

The showman always wants his equipment to be a modern wonder, but he is aware that fashions change. With permanent quarters, he can hold on to outmoded gear, at least for a time. But where a replacement is also more efficient in terms of labour, this might appear unnecessary. If fashion then takes a backward step, he can reclaim, resurrect, or even reproduce equipment to satisfy a popular nostalgia. This was his dilemma when road locomotives were supplanted by internal combustion lorries and tractors. By the '40s, the equipment he had treated like a favourite animal was either left to rust or sold at a knock-down price to be acquired by steam enthusiasts. All over the country, they were scrapped in their thousands. Who was to know that their value would eventually escalate?

George Cushing saw what was happening, understood the showmen's dilemma, and stepped in to rescue some of their engines at a critical moment. First a haulage contractor and road maker, George began his career by buying a steam roller and converting it to a tractor. He was in thrall to the showmen's machines so that when they came up for sale in breakers' yards, it was to him as though the crown jewels were on offer. One by one, he acquired four big showmen's engines that had belonged to the Thurston family,[4] not primarily as an investment, but because he couldn't bear to see them destroyed. The museum he founded to share what began as intelligent romanticism, would celebrate his debt to showmen:

> With the old engines, the arc lights, the carved work all the gold and the organs, fairs were like nothing on earth … I've seen men and women ten or twenty deep round a set of gallopers or standing looking at the showman's engine with the dynamo humming away, and all the electric lights … When they'd done a long journey and were weary and tired, they'd rub the old engine down, look up and say "Old girl, you've done your job well."
> … There was the smell of the engines' smoke, the smell of the oil; the smell of the engines on the roundabouts which were driven by steam. The atmosphere was marvellous …[5]

Ian Starsmore who wrote a book about Cushing, also points to his support for showmen.

> He is one of the most famous collectors. I think he was born in 1904 and he died maybe two years ago [2003] at the age of 99. He knew the Grays and the Buggs and had *enormous* respect for them.

---

4   Cushing with Starsmore, pp. 10 and 42.
5   Cushing with Starsmore, p. 146.

George was the son of a labourer, but he built up a huge business, the Fakenham laundry from almost nothing. He saw the engines when he was a young child at Walsingham fair and bought them when they came up for scrap. They were 40 quid each and now they're worth a fortune. The same went for his organs, showmen had been scrapping them. They even set fire to them. Thursford is probably one of the best museums of its kind in the world. The point I'm making is that George was a very shrewd businessman, and he *adored* the fair.

Some feel it is regrettable that commercialism should have changed the experience of Cushing's museum, but steam has become a crowd-gathering spectacle. Smaller rallies manage to retain a local flavour, otherwise, the materialism of the last decades has rather taken the reins. The bonus for the showman is that old-fashioned rides have flourished on the wings of nostalgia, and they get as much pleasure from steam fairs as anyone else. Today the Great Dorset Steam Fair covers over 600 acres – one of the largest outdoor events in Europe, attracting several hundred steam engines among its displays of vintage transport and over 200,000 visitors in 2010. Showmen like to take five days off work to congregate in their living trailers, with plenty to see in daytime and a night life in various beer tents. The rally was visited regularly by one of Victor Harris' sons:

> He goes to Blandford Forum for a big engine rally. We call it Stourpaine.[6] It's absolutely *massive*, you can't do it in one day, there's so many things to walk round and see. There's a craft tent, Christmas puddings, you'd never taste anything like it. And sausages that all break open, what you used to get years ago. It's set out in a horseshoe, all the old rides at the front of the fair, the Gallopers and that, and in the front of that there's a row of steam engines. Must be fifteen, it's fantastic if you like that sort a thing.

UK showmen own less than 15 steam run rides, all of them Gallopers said 42-year-old David Downs, an ingenuous, likable man with a marked Essex idiom. We met at Braintree's Meadowside where the Downs were present in force; David's wife, two sons, a brother and an uncle. His daughter was taking her GCSE exam, he explained, proudly inclusive. He hopes that his children will benefit from a better education than his skimpy one and still want to uphold the fairground tradition. Seventeen-year old John and a younger brother were setting up one of two Juveniles. Of three adult rides, one was a Big Wheel, another a set of ornate steam Gallopers built in 1895, and bought by the family in 1948 with

6   After the village where it was first held in 1969.

an 89-key Gavioli organ. Building up had taken the whole of the previous day. The ride was put to bed under tarpaulin, and the engine further wrapped. David removed the inner wrapping to display the name *John Bull,* painted above the makers' insignia 'works number 638, F. Savage & Co engineers, Kings Lynn, 1895'. Beside the engine stood one of Anselme Gavioli's eponymously named 'paper' or 'book' organs in which a strip of cardboard sheets is passed through the key frame then refolded like a concertina.[7]

Starting from the yard in Witham, the Downs move about 20 times a year, to a different place each weekend between May Day and the end of September. Where the Gallopers operate for more than a single night, additional elaborations are made to an already highly decorated ride in the form of hanging panels with an extra 120 swiveling mirrors. They make it like some fairytale palace. The central engine starts to steam up, the organ rings out tinny music, mirrors flash and vibrate to rows of circling horses and the odd cockerel, and the observer begins to understand the lure. Round and round the gilded horses go. Horses with their barley-sugar stick supports to cling to, scarlet nostrils, golden manes, and feet that never touch the ground, making a sound that could be a bronchitic wheeze. 'Does this machine take the crown once carried by Noyce's, of the best-presented Gallopers in England?' a reporter asked.

This could have been the end of my conversation with the Downs but wasn't, at least, on my side. Often I'd follow up a visit with a telephone call to check something I couldn't quite hear or to clarify a point a showperson had made. David said this would be fine, after Braintree they were heading for Cambridge fair. Maybe for him my visit was overly stressful. At all events, no one answered the phone. After several tries I left it a few weeks and tried again. It's possible I was just unlucky, but showmen usually have gadgets to let them know who is trying to call, and the same thing happened. I heard later that David had taken part in a BBC recording about fairground music, his subject was organs and he spoke well. He had seemed obliging; I would like to have kept the door open. 'That's all bluff; he's very shy' a friend of his tried to resolve the riddle. 'It's the showman coming out in him', a showman I knew better said, as if *that* explained David's sudden reluctance to fill me in. As much as any showmen I'd met, he struck me as an original. A round peg in a round but possibly vanishing hole, and someone with important things to say:

[7]   Fairground organs of the period varied from barrel organs at small shows to the Marenghi or Gavioli, the organs used most frequently on the Bioscope. Gavioli invented the cardboard system in Paris in 1892. The peak of development was about 1910 when Gavioli organs came with Louis XV figures and Marenghi organs with highly decorated prosceniums. Charles Marenghi worked for Gavioli until the early 1900s.

I left school at 14, obviously doing a shift working beside me dad, learning the trade. I can read, but if I have to write and spell things, I'm not very good. I look back now and do regret some things. At the time me dad wasn't a very well person, he had bad legs and things, so by me leaving school I was helping the family. All 3 kids we made them stay and do their exams, my John the eldest one, the teacher was really pleased with him. He can spell better'n my wife but he's keen in this business as well. Someone got to take it all up han't they? It be a shame to see it sold off, it been in the family this long.

I been coming here all me life since I was born. We only missed one year, we had a field job to do over a two week period and it clashed. Me grandad took off, he originated from Gestingthorpe near Sudbury. He got the Big Wheel and the first set of Gallopers. Me wife's mother is a Townsend, they go back a long way. They're down in Dorset. They was quite a big firm. Because we come here before, we got measurements off the path, we got writ down. Other places sometimes you start to level, you see where the hole is from previous years. You near enough mark it with the same cross year after year if you got the same equipment. If it works it works. Here we just measure down from the pavement and up from the brick wall. It [building up] takes a day, if we're pushed we can go faster. To get up steam take 40 minutes before you can start running the ride. We use coal like they used to. It doesn't drive a generator, it's mechanical. John Bull that's what me dad called it. I'll tell you why, John Bull's a short fat man with short legs. He stand for England and beer-drinking and that. It come off a ride with 4 horses in each layer, the first set of Gallopers which me grandad bought. But I won't be running off steam this weekend, I 'ave got an electric motor. Believe it or not, I 'ave got to in some places, it's in the contract, not allowed to run steam ... air pollution.

Originally the engine would drive the organ. That work off a cam shaft, but we now got an electric motor with a blower on it. This [organ] was made in Antwerp, I think that's in Holland. They got one very similar to this in the Steam Museum [at Thursford]. Snare drum one end of the pipes, base drum other end. It's cardboard music, you know the name, *Songs for Keeler?*[8] Each one of them holes represents a note on the organ. That's definitely the base drum [large oblong hole]. You get someone who knows, they can

[8]   Christine Keeler was the subject for songs by Dusty Springfield and Pet Shop Boys.

go all the way through the music. There's about 40 books in there, some are selections. There's no problem getting new songs, that's [cardboard music book] only 5 year old. Verbeeck's a really old one, they had a branch at Islington.[9] The organ pushes into a box and goes on the one trailer when we get on the road.

After this [Braintree] the Gallopers is shut for a week cos we got a couple of private places with the Big Wheel, then the Cambridge Midsummer Fair. From there we're going to the Hollowell Steam Rally which is near Northampton, it'll be steam there. From there we're going to Chichester. Then back to Peldon in Essex for a wedding. From there, we're across to Tewkesbury. Pretty much the same each year but it can vary if you do weddings. Christmas time we go into Bath City centre right in front of the Pump Room for three weeks. That look really nice in there because of the architecture and the buildings. We got 30 horses and 6 cockerels. We can put the organ in but we're not allowed to play it cos it's amongst the shops and they say it's too noisy, so we leave that at home. In Barleylands near Basildon I am the lessee there. Go to Woolpit [steam rally] in Suffolk. We do a lot of steam engine rallies. There's steam yachts owned by Saunders from Stockfold in Bedfordshire – they're breakdown specialists for the motor services, not Guild. There's the Gondolas at Thursford [Steam Museum] which they don't run on steam no more. In the Guild what run commercially there's about three of us, me, James Horton from Chichester, and Bimbo Biston but he's got a modern steam engine built for him which is only about 6-year old, made similar to mine by a man Northampton way. [Among] What we call non-runners, there's another 10. The majority [have] got organs. There's a lot of people with them like contracting firms, people with a bit of wealth use them as a toy but we're running week in week out. We have to rely on what we take for our living. You got to have a bit of a love for it.

---

[9] 'Jimmy' Verbeeck was a refugee from Belgium who set up as an organ builder, first in Birmingham and then in Islington during the 1920s.

CHAPTER TWENTY
'GOOD TIMES, BAD TIMES'

It's an interesting life; very good times, very bad times. You might go to a place, like Felixtowe this weekend. It rained all day Saturday – that's Carnival Day. Oh it's cost me this, it's cost me that. Then when you get home, 'Hey! You remember Felixtowe, we got all that rain!' You do laugh about it. They say there's no business like show business; they smile when they are low, and that's completely true. Lots of low times, lots of high times. The high times is when we're getting a few bob and everyone's so friendly. If you have a row with your next-door neighbour, next week they're gone or you're gone.

Stoicism touched with humour is a quality you often find in showmen. Victor Harris uses 'interesting' synonymously with 'ever-changing'. He is so used to the ups and downs that he's relaxed about them. Not feeling good means he's not feeling bad, and may even lead to his feeling exhilarated. Others adjust to bewildering fluctuations provided they receive some encouragement. Two of them expand on their experience in this chapter.

Page 44 of the Manning Family Chronicle[1] shows a photograph of John Manning with his brother-in-law outside Alexandra Palace in 1988. They are discussing, he says, the poor state of the business. The back cover pictures the family Coat of Arms devised by Fred Fowle for the paybox of the late Albert Manning's Autodrome. The motto beneath the shield make mindfulness and courage twin goals; *Memor et Fortis*. Twenty years after the photograph was taken, 74-year old John Manning, ex Chairman of the London Section of the Showmen's Guild, is once again, outside Alexandra Palace, a location he has long regarded as his home. He is a genial patriarchal figure with willingness to see what he calls the larger picture:

I'm not particularly East Anglian, you know. I'm Essex-based more or less, but this is my main place. I was born down the bottom of this hill in Tottenham. Born in a caravan, in a yard behind the Plough Public House. I drove by there yesterday with my boy, they pulled it down; it shocked me. So, not far from home now, am I? I suppose everything has revolved round Alexandra Palace over the

[1.] *Mannings Amusements: Chronicle of a Hertfordshire Family* by Herbert Haines, n.d.

years. This used to be the greyhounds' court, in 1911. Uncle Sam took it over and me dad left his father and come to help him. Dad was here quite a while, then me. So me mum and dad got married up here. Mum left this Palace, a bride in a car, and went to the church down the hill. Her dad wasn't fairground but *her* mum was. Got married 1934. I was born 1936 just as the war broke out. It's ridiculous really, everyone name their eldest child after their father, it's just a tradition. Except I wasn't named after my father [Samual Thomas] cos Mum didn't like the name. I was named after me Uncle John.

I'm here for Easter, two weeks; Whitsun for two weeks; May Day Bank holiday for a weekend. Then I come up here in the middle of July with the family and other tenants for a couple of Bank Holiday fairs. From July 26 I think we're open every Saturday till 6 o'clock, I'm the lessee. Then we have Stevenage three times a year, and the fireworks here in November. Welland Valley have a big fair there in the spring. We go to Dagenham and Alton Cross, twice a year. The greatest pleasures are when you're young and in your teens in't they? (Laugh). Cos you didn't have your responsibility. Hard work but we used to travel all over. Villages, towns, I used to love it; lots of fun. Years ago, young people, when they see the fair come, especially in a village, they'd turn out, it'd be an event but there's *so much* entertainment going on now they can get it without going out their room. People ought to bring their children out. *Away*. Come up here, have a day out up the Palace, go on their boats, do whatever they do. Get away from television if you like. It's a different life. I think the biggest mistake for children is television. As you get older, you got more responsibility. Ups and downs. You're never settled. *I'll* never settle, I'm too old, but I wouldn't do anything else. Sandsneakers, like you got at the seaside; they're settled. So that's it, I just like travelling. When it's raining and it's blowing, I say what am I doing here? (Laugh). It's all part and parcel.

One or two of John's comments were interchangeable with those of Lawrence II, usually known as Nipper Appleton; but although at 66, Appleton was the younger by 6 years, his nostalgia for the past was the more pronounced. Appleton's Yard, Rope Walk, Kings Lynn was where we met, a street so-named because rope was once twisted there for fishing boats. The family bought the four-acre site 20 years ago, and now inhabit some 15 trailers lined on either side, separated only by a matter of feet and in constant communication through mobile phones. Several showmen have mentioned the benefits of the mobile to their lives, and here were people industriously engaging with them. Between calls, Nipper told how the past meant the shows, a type of entertainment in which his family claimed a notable niche.

A few years ago he lost a cherished wife to cancer. They had married young, making a complementary duo for 44 years. As head of the family, he bears responsibility for an ailing mother; and each season he moves out on his run of fairs but without Sandra his life has lost its central pivot; this could help to make the past seem more alive to him than the present. It is worth remembering too, how quick the demise of shows has been. In 1934 Mitcham fair covered 17 acres: there were 35 riding machines, 168 hooplas, ten circuses, 50 dart stalls, 14 coconut shies, 59 refreshment stalls, palmists, ices, the fattest lady, the biggest rat, boxing booths, performing fleas and Wild West shows. Roll up! Roll up! These were heroic days. The postwar period brought the menace of flick knives and Teddy-boys; candy-floss, peppermint rock and toffee-apples, because none of these things were covered by sweet coupons, but much of the show traditions had gone. Background music for the Appleton's performances was produced from 45-r.p.m. records on a turntable. Nipper's son, Lawrence III, remembers his grandfather buying the electrical parts in London to build his own amplifiers and speaker boxes as well as supplying other showmen.

Despite the cold outside, Nipper Appleton was wearing only a string vest in his heated wagon. His face wore a disciplined sadness.

> It's an interesting life: I wouldn't change it. You get a lot of flak in the fair but there is good times. When things is going good you got your freedom, you go where you want when you want. Everywhere I've got friends in the local communities I can get on with, and talk to, and visit. We've been associated with King's Lynn for many many years. Two of me sons are in here and some of me grandchildren. Me son-in-law's here and me daughter. I like the West Country an awful lot but the pride and joy for me is the King's Lynn Mart, Feb 14, because I live 'ere and know a lot of local people in the town. The Civic Officer and her husband, Henry Bellingham the MP, and past mayors and councillors are all friends of mine. They come every year down the West Country and see me. I go right down to Lands End, Cornwall, Devon, Dorset, Somerset, London, Midlands. Torquay that's a lovely place, I'm there for a month on the seafront, then I move to Lands' End, Newquay and all that area. We will go to Cambridge because we are people that try to maintain old traditions but that is deteriorating dramatically over the last ten years. Sunday I'm off to Milton Keynes to be with

my brother.

Sandra and me married young, she wasn't out of this industry. She was from London and her people was shopkeepers over by Peckham. What it was, they come on the fairground looking for a job, and we got friendly. She did the life adapting quite well to it. She done all the bookwork and everything. I 'aven't got a brilliant education but Sandra was quite well educated.

Back as far as 1805 Randall Williams [from Nipper's maternal grandmother's family] came to the Mart with the Bioscope Shows.[2] Me grandmother was a fine showlady back in the 1920s. She would dress up as Mae West and talk the talk, and walk the walk, and got such a reputation she was known as Mae West of Show Business. Lots of showmen's families operate different equipment, but all of my family and my grandmother and their family – the Williams side, and me dad's family were all showmen. We operated the novelty side shows, the boxing booths, the dancing girls, the giants, the midgets, all these type of things, and in the old days, they was the main part of fairground. That's where you got all the free entertainment. When we had these dancing girls, 1940s, '50s, showmen had to attend all major events, fireworks, carnivals, where you got volumes of people, so at every major fair like the Nottingham Goose Fair, Mitcham Common, Cambridge Midsummer, there was always lots of side shows. We used to travel all Wales; Carmarthen, Brecon, Abergavenny, Aberystwyth. We've refrained from going to Scotland because of the distance but I don't stay in the East Anglia area now. Since 1975 with the change of

2   Nipper Appleton's tale of his illustrious ancestor is a little 'romantic'. Randall Williams wasn't born until 1846, so he couldn't have attended King's Lynn Mart in 1805, though he did present shows at the Mart, probably from the 1860s. He didn't present a Bioscope show until late 1896 – moving pictures were first demonstrated only the year before – and he could have attended the Mart with such a show only a couple of times before his death in 1898. Randall Williams has long been credited as being the first showman to present moving pictures on a fairground, but new material suggests that he may have been pipped to the post by a matter of months. Ironically, the new claimant to the title is one George Williams (no relation), who began his working life as a sign-writer at King's Lynn where he may have done work for Frederick Savage. He was a versatile man who turned to the life of a travelling showman, exhibiting lantern slides and a cinematograph for a few brief years. He later moved to Birmingham where he worked as a photographer, eventually running his own business. His effects have recently been found to include a print of a film by Birt Acres dating from 1895 that is unique, and a copy of Edison's catalogue of films that even the National Library of Congress doesn't have a copy of (note by Graham Downie).

laws and things changing dramatically in our industry, all the side shows is faded away so the dancing girls and the dancing dolls are no longer prevalent on British fairgrounds which is a sad thing because it was a magic part of a funfair. There's just one boxing booth [left] but it only goes once a year to one fair. We had shows in the family such as *Rhona the Rat Girl* – a girl in a pit of rats, a fantastic jungle show known as *Tianga the Jungle Girl*, that was a girl caged alive with giant pythons and boa constrictors and prehistoric iguanas. My dad's brother bought that show from America in the war. Had them shipped over here. He had Frankenstien's monster shows, Spotted Lady; anythink that was a novelty. Dad painted all the scenery hisself. Me father would do sword-swallowing, fire-eating, eating razor-blades. He invented new lights, he could letter and paint figures, and used to mend engines. When we'd break down he'd strip the engines and rebuild them. Plus he was a good showman. Whatever he done he would present hisself as a part of it. He would have the Mechanical Man with him.[3]

I keep on referring to me Daddy, his name was Lord Lawrence Maxwell Appleton and he was always doing [new] things. Like he created a show called The Mexican Twist. Me and me brother we was two Mexicans. I was 9 when I first started going on. I did enjoy it because me dad used to dress me up on that King's Lynn Tuesday Marketplace. He used to dress as a Chinaman, I was suited up as the drummer boy, and when he put the record on, you used to play the big drum. We used to have the big drum and what was called the snare drum – the kettle drum, because you use like wire snare sticks. They give a more softer sound, ch-ch-ch like, me dad would beat that. I started doing it [the show] with me father and progressed to doing it on me own with the girls. Light entertainment on the Front stopped '76, '75. Me [old] things are in the museum at Spalding.

I just come from Barnstable in North Devon and done a speech for them. Barnstable's a lovely little place but the recession is not so good. The Mart did show out [takings were good] but after Easter time it took a nosedive and it never really recovered all the way through what we call our back end – what I do in Cornwall and Devon and Dorset. The major fairs did pick up a bit but lots a

---

3 The Mechanical Man sometimes called 'Mad Max' had a white-painted face, and moved and spoke like a robot, as do some of today's street actors. He worked for the Appletons.

people have found it a struggle to make ends meet. They been just looking and not patronising the industry because they ain't got the money. We're no different to anybody else, plus we only have a short season; I finish in November than we start again in February so you got a lot of dead time.

Good times are not heaven, bad times are not hell. Using their ingenuity, together with big measures of the Manning family ideals – courage and mindfulness, showmen make the best of the situations they find themselves in. The picture does contradict a tediously repeated media image of insouciance.

CHAPTER TWENTY-ONE
THE THURSTON CLAN

The status of the Thurston clan is legendary, as Arthur Morrison says:

> They've got huge fairgrounds; in the Norwich area it's the late John
> Thurston; in Cambridgeshire, Stan Thurston; in Northamptonshire
> it's William Thurston. They're all descendents of this one man.

The one man had already made a name for himself before he moved into
show business by designing the recessed brick. Henry Thurston, sometimes
alluded to as 'Froggy' after his first creative flair, merely changed tack when he
married into show business. Re-inventing his in-law's equipment, he was to
develop a series of rides that supported five generations of showmen.

There was a fair chance that his dynamism would surface in his heirs, and
it did. Henry had two wives, four daughters and more importantly, three sons.
The custom for families to pass down the male Christian name, together with
early child-bearing, the regularity with which showpeople intermarry, and the
small size of the Community, make their genealogy confusing. The Thurston's
are no exception. Henry, John, Charles, William, Stanley, the names crop up
over and again.

Henry Thurston's eldest boy, Charles, also found the builders' yard a
useful alternative to the fairground during winter months. In Harwich he is fêted
as the creator of their much loved Electric Palace Cinema, now one of the five
oldest purpose-built cinemas in the country, complete with silent screen, original
projection room and an ornamental frontage. Charles didn't waste time over the
commission. The task was completed in 18 weeks to the imaginative design of
Harold Hooper. Its doors were flung open on November 29, in 1911, to show
The Battle of Trafalgar and The Death of Nelson to an admiring house. The cost
was £1,500.[1]

Charles, had two sons of whom the younger, generally referred to as
Charles W. R., served with distinction as a flight lieutenant during the Second

---

[1]   The cinema closed in 1956 after 45 years interrupted only by the 1953 floods and
was listed as a building of sociological interest in 1972. It is now a grade II* listed
building. As such it reopened in 1981, since when it has opened every weekend, a
community cinema showing films.Other features include an open plan entrance
lobby with paybox, and a small stage with dressing rooms, though the latter are now
unusable. There is also a former gas-powered generator engine with a 7 foot fly wheel
situated in the basement.

World War and later became President of the Showmen's Guild, the youngest to have held the office. 'Old Charlie' as Charles W. R. is referred to by friends[2] was by all accounts a perfectionist with his machines; a good angling friend and a lovable man. The photograph of him in the *Guild Year Book* shows a benign face with a dimpled chin.[3] Another of Henry's grandsons was the charismatic and sartorial Stanley (1898–1981), lessee at the Cambridge Midsummer Fair where he owned what was known for its remunerative value as the golden row of shows and rides. Stanley had a house not far from the common in Gilbert Road. From it, he left for work each morning in a suit and bowler hat. The first showman to provide fairground amusements for American Forces stationed in East Anglia during the Second World War, he had a resolute strain that made him an inspiring showman; notwithstanding, he was charitably disposed towards the less able.

With a grandfather like Stanley, it is not surprising that John Thurston often weighs up the achievement behind him, especially when he is engaged in the old run of fairs. A handsome man with an aquiline nose and a mane of gray hair, John has his great uncle, Charles C. W.'s dimpled chin, but it is the ghost of bowler-hatted Stanley who most inspires his showmanship. One of John's regrets is that he didn't buy his grandfather's house in Cambridge when his aunt died.

John's diplomacy makes him a respected committee man. A family tradition of service prompted him to become chairman of the Showman's Guild Eastern Counties Section for five years, then vice chair for two years before he was chair again. Born in Bedford, he married Gina Whyatt who gave him four dishy daughters, and they provided him with some wonderful son-in-laws. The family yard is in Kempston. The day we met, he spoke with the weariness of someone older than 52. It could have been a bad day, or that his continual ploys to engage the public are, if successful, wearying. He speaks fast but in a pleasant manner, respectful of his role as a custodian of a culture that places great value on loyalty, the elderly, women, children and disabled people. Charity can do more for the showman than support human welfare; it can complement consultation with local councils. Where occasion demands, John mediates unconventionally.

In Luton his grandfather equipped children's playgrounds and installed bench seats in a garden for the blind. But Stanley Thurston's successes were made in a very different climate. If his benefactions eased the course financially for some of his descendents, each showman has had to adapt to enormous changes. Luton has the biggest Carnival in the area after Notting Hill, yet efforts to integrate with showmen haven't been entirely successful. Every year John visits

---

2   Cushing refers to Charles W. R. repeatedly as 'Old Charlie'. George Cushing with Ian Starsmore, *Steam at Thursford* (David & Charles, 1982), p. 37 *et al.*

3   *Guild Year Book 2010–2011*, p. 39.

Wardown Park, a pleasant location on the outskirts of the city with a river running through it, as well as several sites near the city centre. Rowdy behaviour has been a problem on some of them, and elsewhere, middle-class venues have their own disadvantages. Although John's tale appeared to be one of diminishing custom except for the reliable if modestly remunerative corporate events, not all his comments squared with a picture of endless disappointment:

> When you've got a problem that's when you need to call on someone. At Dover now, the main Town Clerk is a personal friend; I said to him when we come down here, we want to put something back in. We made a few donations to local charities and they know that you're genuine. The first time, we had all the disabled schools. About 2 busloads turned up. They were riding for free and we put drinks on for the staff, and sandwiches and tea and coffee, candy floss for the kids. One woman over at Deal said, my boy's disabled. She said what you done now that's fantastic. You don' 'ave to do it; that is really appreciated. So I said we always did it. Me grandad used to do it; my dad used to say that's why we were respected. We have one big fair at Cambridge and we do it there. I said the kids can come in, they get on and off safely, we can look after em be'er. The rewards are the letters you get back. The painting of the fair. I've had stacks and stacks. A big folder come, I can't throw them away. It's gone from crayoning, now they draw the stuff up on a computer. It breaks your heart sometimes. I've seen em with tears in their eyes and there but for the grace of God go I. We're rich really aren't we? You don't know how lucky you are. And they think [know] at least we're not just coming in here, because most people think you pull in, you're a load of Gypsies, you don't pay no rent. I said the difference is we're business people, we're living like this because it's easier. You've got to introduce yourself.
>
> We had trouble with the residents at Dover, about the noise and one thing and another. So let's have a resident meeting. I give them my mobile number, then if they got a problem, rather than ringing the council, they ring me up and I can deal with it straight away. I did the same in Cambridge. Once I got to know the residents, they come down, walk the dog in the morning, say that was lovely last night. One woman there was always complaining and I said, any problem ring me up. We have a laugh and a joke. I said, I'll send you out for a meal to discuss all the problems you had. She said, you're bribing me. I said yes if that's what you want to call it. I said a friend of mine sent a couple away on holiday. She said, that

sounds better. I said as you're open to bribery, how much am I going to spend on you? (Laugh). She said we'll talk about it next year. But where she was an old nark, she's like a good friend now. Went round the council office, [where they] said old Mrs .. she's always complaining; I said, she's all right with me! So it works, this talking to people, sometimes.

Usually Luton's our first place [in the annual run of fairs]. We open in Manor Road which used to be on top of Vauxhall [car factory]. It used to be all terraced houses then when Vauxhall came, the staff cross the park if they had a union meeting, there was always activity. Now there's like factory units down there, it's an industrial estate, so you don't see many people. Whilst the war was on, me grandfather opened on the Moor [Park] which is just before you go under the bridge into the town. They had the blackout fairs on the Moor and they actually put a bridge in to get the [showmen's] engines over the little ditch. Me grandfather paid for that. Then he paid for all the parks, roundabouts and slides. I think me grandfather started here [Wardown Park] in the penny days after the war. [Subsequently] It used to be Irish, then there was a big black population, I know quite a few of them [Asians]. One, I've known him since he was a kid, he'll come up and have a beer. He want to buy £200 worth of tokens for the Dodgems and he'll share them out with his mates and ride all night. They feel safe down in this park. We used to take a lot of money over the Bank Holidays. It was unbelievable. Used to open ten o'clock in the morning until ten oclock at night and it'd be absolutely packed all day long. You couldn't get away from the stalls. People would take their tea out with them, take their dinners out. There used to be a fish and chip man out the front and people'd be sitting out on the grass, it was a big event. On the Dodgems it used to be tupence, it was unbelievable. We charge a pound a ride now. There was a lot of people last night but not fighting like they used to be to get on the rides. We used to come in the Park here for Whitsun, then they had the Carnival so they moved us out, up the top end of the town. Last year they [the council] had 3 rides in the Carnival, but you got to get your money out of one day where you had a weekend. The first thing they ask you when you roll up is when's the cheap day? Our cheap nights are better now than a Saturday. That took off really the last day, everybody said, it's a good fair. I said but we're finished now, we're off. So I think next time we'll have the cheap day on the first night. We used to go to Lucy Farm which is down

Leagraves end of Luton. Get the Dodgems down and the kids would be all over 'em. Hundreds of kids jumping about everywhere, pushing the cars round when you was getting set up. It was torture. You know the Tilt Bang, it's like a big ball, when we come out in the morning, where they all jumped on it, having a game, it was just flat like a pancake on the floor. We had to tie the rides down to stop them moving 'em. Had to be out there all the time. You couldn't say, we'll be closed Sunday.

We used to open at 2 o'clock. Half one [o'clock] there was so many people out there you had to open. Now if you see 3 kids on the ground, when you're setting up, it's a rarity. It was nice when you got people queuing up waiting for you to open. They're not really interested. They got the computers, got the phones, they got mates. When the lottery started, Saturday nights were completely dead because people were staying in to watch the result of the lottery. Think they're going to win a million. We were told when it started in Germany, it took 6 or 7 years before people give up staying in to watch the television. It did take a while to come back. They say it takes one generation to build something and one to hold it and one to lose it; and that's what happening. Like this year [October 2008], it's been fragmented; we're losing places. It's no good just turning up. The only way I've kept going is paid events and moving about, you got to change your agenda. Spend a bit more on the advertising and try and keep kids coming down. We do a lot of fairs in London. Colchester was ok with the Dodgems but everybody wait for the cheap night. At Bedford, we have 2 weeks at the beginning of the year, that's not too bad but the second visit's not worth going, you're struggling most a the time. We tried Hitchin and it was ok. The problem was with one of the staff on the Council. They was on a case; every time I come away I got to keep going back to try and smooth things over. But it's a good fair and the people down there are completely different. They like the fair. They're pleased to see you like it used to be. I been to Windsor 3 weekends this year, on the Brocas, along the river. It belongs to Eton School, to get to it you got to go into the College. You get a few Asians down from Slough but most of them there are tourists. There's some lovely little places me son travels round London but the upper class places you've got so much competition. You got Legoland, Chessington, Thorpe Park and when they open at Richmond for Easter, there's about five fairs in a four or five mile radius. You've got Hampton Court on at the same time, Hayes not far away.

We're running quite a few novelty rides; the faster, the higher, the better. We had a traditional English caravan built about 18, 20, year ago with all the pull-out sides on, we sold that to buy this ride. We paid £240,000 pounds for that Topstar down there, it's worth about £300,000. To have one made, £340,000. Then we've just bought a set of Dodgems, they were meant to be £220,000, that's without the cars, generators, pay-box, anything. With the euro going up strong against the pound, it cost me another 50,000 pound. So all the money's out there. The charge is £10 some places for the Booster and people are paying it. A friend of mine a couple of years ago had 50 pence fairs, trying to get people back out. He said it's like the '70s and '80s, when you go out to open, it works! But then, when he went back up to a pound, it just dwindled off. He's been struggling for a couple of years.

We don't spent a lot of time at base now. We've been open up to the end of November, then we have a week in the yard. Me cousin Stanley's got a chalet. To be honest with you, I don't really want one at the minute, 'cos I'm not happy where we are. As the family grow up they go their separate ways. I got one girl down at Ockingham, one of her family's down at Chertsey. I like Chertsey, so I don't want to go and get a chalet in Bedford, then I'm stuck. There's a lot of memories in Cambridge. My grandfather was very enterprising, good at advertising and good with the councils. When he was 20 odd, he bought out his brothers. He bought everything off them; the Dodgems, Gallopers, Ben Hur, the Skid. Then me Dad and his brother bought the Twist Ride and their sister had a Big Wheel when she got married. We bought this caravan as a stop-gap, it's got everythink in it. We've just had all the grand-children here pulling everything to bits. You know they're not very strong [trailers]. I think next year we'll have a look around, see if we can find something a little bit be'er but [only] for the two of us. I got 4 girls, 3 of them are married into the business, one at home, she's 27. The youngest one [Stacey] married James Manning. I get on well with James, and most of the time they travel with us. We started up a few fresh fairs together, did Colchester and Durham between us, and he's looking at buying a few fairs [placements at fairs]. Where I've got in a bit of a rut, he's pushed me and pushed me. Seeing as we've got no sons, it's been handy too now I've got bad hips. It takes a lot of stress off you. We do work really well together, the kids are always down here. If they want anything I'll lend them money. Even the three sons-in-law, they'll help one another out. It's more like Italian, you look after your parents. It's funny, when I go round different fairs, they call me Uncle John. Sometimes you feel a bit embarrassed. There's probably ten years [age difference] and you call them uncle. I say like, call me John. One of them, he don't like to, he don't know what to call me. (Laugh). He'll say Donna's Dad. It is about respect in the family.

In December we've gone into corporate events through an agent. It's a couple of hundred pounds a night. Not a lot, but there'll be different parties [clients] each night; one might be for Access or Nat West Bank. You'd have 6 or 700 people turn up and you open the Dodgems for and hour or so. We do a lot under a marquee. There's security on the door; they charge; we go on their generator so it's easy. February time I been getting out to Crystal Palace. Last time I went up there, they had a stabbing outside the ground, it was nothing to do with us but the police were concerned with these little gangs, so they asked them to shut the fair about 7 o'clock time. Obviously if you've got a novelty ride, you want the teenagers at night, so to close at 7.00 pm, it's not acceptable. Problem is with us, nearly everybody's been on here too long. They've grown up together. It gets complacent, and you need sometimes a kick up the arse to get things going. I had a row with someone the other day and he come back and apologise. He said someone come round and wound me up. He was on about being too tired on the ride, and he said you was right what you said. I said, well I appreciate it you come round. Some people are so stubborn. When everything's going smoothly, I enjoy to be doing something different all the time. You're taking something and you're getting by and paying your bills. Sometimes you think you had enough because it has been hard these last few years. But I make good money, you don't complain and when it's working well, you can't get a better life. You just about had enough of somewhere and you go somewhere else. We had 3 weeks at Windsor. It's beautiful, you look out and see the Castle every day. Like if you was in a hotel it'd probably cost you £300 pound a night. Meeting different people all the time. Find as I've got older, moving round East Anglia, I've met a lot more people.

CHAPTER TWENTY-TWO
'A MODERN SHOWMAN'

Everyone had something to say about the Eastern Counties showman John Bugg who dubs himself on his website as one of the global pioneers of the industry.

> He's all over the place. He's had a ball this year [2008].
> John Manning

> I know he goes to France with the Dodgems.
> Cilla Morrison

> He's a very good showman. Spent a bomb advertising a skating rink at Peterborough which cost a quarter million pound.
> John Thurston

> He's really good at presenting himself to councils. And the way he presents a fair, he's nice, clean, tidy, you know.
> David Downs

> He promotes a fair and all his transport looks fantastic, consequently he gets invited to a lot of things. John's never idle; he's always trying to find new places. For all his faults, you can't knock him for how he carries himself and his presentation is absolutely first-class.
> Martin Loades

> John have to keep going, he's an organizer and a perfectionist.
> Margaret Bugg

> He's what you'd call a modern showman.
> Arthur Morrison

John's far-flung industriousness made him difficult to catch up with but we eventually met on the River Embankment adjacent to Peterborough's Key Theatre. Here, when we had talked, he led me on a guided tour that would have done credit to the owner of an eighteenth-century country house. It was the morning before the fair in Bridge Park opened, and all the rides and stalls were in place. They included some smart Dodgems that had recently won a prize in Paris, and a pendulum ride known as an Oblivion[1] with cars at the end of a

---

[1]   A name applied by this particular showman to his white-knuckle ride, generically known as an Afterburner.

swinging spinning arm. An attention-grabbing notice John wrote on the Oblivion paybox at a fair in Antibes, read 'The Oblivion is fast moving, and is not suitable for people with back or neck injuries, expectant mums, the faint-hearted or whimps. If in doubt do not ride.' It was designed simultaneously to satisfy health and safety regulations and whet the anticipation of a prospective rider. At Bridge Park, vehicles were orderly, trailers tucked away, cables dug beneath soil level to prevent tripping.

In an age when image is everything and the showman likely to be pushed into less congenial corners, there is no room for disorganization that might lay the industry open to criticism. The problem with the outskirts of a town or village, adjacent to its games field, is that it's not where the general public necessarily congregate. This means that showland must do all it can to be accessible, i.e. consumable, and that means presenting itself in essentially competitive terms.

Born in 1956, John Bugg grew up with the usual family closeness. His great grandfather, William Freeman Bidell, played the music for a bioscope. Brother William is another showman and both he and William married, as they say, into the business. Circumstances that set the immediate family apart were his father's poor health. Chronic diabetes gave John Bugg Sr. blackouts and comas. For years before he died he was confined to a wheel chair. John and William had to grow up quickly.

At 18 he was running his own show, starting with a side stall, knocking cans off a shelf, then he bought a ride known as the Rib Tickler. Once bitten, there was no going back. A couple of years later news of a more innovative ride called a Rockerplane took his fancy. Building himself up from scratch was 'not in the circumstances an easy task'. The Buggs were careful people. His mother, Margaret, endlessly reconfiguring her chalet, was full of concern for some of the risks he took, yet John continued to increase his fairground investment. Business came first until he married Sarah Thurston in a partnership that has been pivotal. With a twenty year-old son, they have a house on the outskirts of Peterborough.

Margaret knew Sarah from the day she was born. But how was her son's single-mindedness instilled?

> Right from being a little boy he had got the ambition to better himself. Meccano and Lego was the thing. He'd sit for hours ever so quiet and he'd build rides out of Lego bricks. He'd got it in his mind that that's what he wanted. He could have got on a lot better doing something else but he love what he's doing. He's a bit of a fuss-pot about cleanliness and polishing. I suppose I'm like that, I mean I was; I'm 80 odd now so I haven't got the energy, but honestly, every time he gets to a place he says, right now, wash everythink down. My dad was like that, see, he was an army man.

I always say to John, I know where you get the changing from, because he's always changing something. I get bored and swap the furniture round. I'll even change ornaments. I'll go months then I think, where am I going to move that settee? I like to see things nice but I couldn't with my husband because he was ill. We only had little stuff; that's all we could manage. When the boys became 18, they said, is it all right if we go out on our own? Broke my heart though. John went first, he got a little trailer and a lorry, he started with nothing. Couple of years later, William done the same. They did leave home but not really, they was backwards and forwards. William's younger, 17 months between them. He does catering and his wife has got fairground equipment. He married Gay Remblance; they've now got one of these big chalets. His daughter is getting married next month in Croatia which is just off of Italy; we're all going, she's married [marrying] a showman. Two years ago her brother, my grandson, got married in Italy.

We were here in Hooper Lane when John said, I'm going to buy a ride from America, I said, what d'you mean, you haven't got any money. He said, I can go, I've got enough for a deposit, and that's what he did. I didn't believe it because he went one day, he was back the next. He threw some peanuts on the table, said, that's the proof that I've been on a plane! In England you work for yourself more-or-less. Tampa airport he went to, and they was there to meet him. In America its different from here, they've got concessions: one person owns the lot and people work for them. This man was in charge of a theme park called Six Flags which is famous in America. I said, what is it you bought? He said a Rockerplane, it's a sky thing with big egg shaped cages on it. It worried me to death. How you going to pay for it? He said, I'll pay for it Mum, and he has. That was brought across by boat and delivered here, Dad was alive then and they went up the top. Built it up; I couldn't even go and look, it worried me that much. I said, you'll never do it. He said, yes I will. He never ever had a car for ages, wasn't married until he was 28, his business come first. I was there, mid-summers day at Cambridge fair when Sarah was born, never thought she was going to be my daughter-in-law. She knows about mechanics and everything; three years running she went to France with one of these big main rides, and she looked after that alone. I've known both of my daughter-in-laws for ever! John's very ambitious. He wanted to get on and make something of hisself. It's been hard, and he've had his ups and downs.

Emboldened by his success and self-belief, John Bugg continued to take risks. He was already making a lively contribution to the fair business when he bought shares in John Thurston & Son Ltd. around 1990; it was a big commitment at the time. The less obvious trait for a risk-taker is his marked need to be in control, an exactitude he admits can be demanding. In practice, a penchant for order makes sense financially because the fairs for which he is the lessee have seldom been docked, and well-maintained apparatus can more easily be resold. Presentation is his first care in an absorption with image that extends to his personal appearance. He is on the short side of medium height, his roundish head fashionably bald, a short moustache, and a beard clipped to an immaculate triangle. For a fourth generation showman it is all part of the business he constructs his life around. To his mind it is the parades and banners of ceremony that give the Bridge Fair in Peterborough its *raison d'être*, so his remarks about the past need context. What does not interest him is nostalgia for the past that excludes the present. In his own words:

> There's always someone to show you photographs of years gone by, but the younger generation are not too over keen on years gone by. After all, years gone by are years gone; lets talk about the present. There are 86 families here and I need to give it my full attention because whatever project I'm working on, I try to give it my best shot. It's more than a job, it's a way of life. I can be difficult to work for because I'm particular on how things look. Particular over the markings. When you arrive at the fair, the stuff need to be laid out so there's no blind corners people won't walk in to, so it's not like a poor business area. I try to make it so there's a flow, people walk around easily and everyone has a fair chance. The lorries, I don't want one back and one forward. The transport, the trailers … when it's moving along the road, people say to me, John I saw your lorries on the M25. Not that they're all new, but they're well maintained. I take a pride in what I do because you are supposed to be entertaining people. But I can't see the point in owning expensive equipment and having it laid up, so I try my best to keep everything working all the time and I prefer to buy something new, try to keep it looking that way. Most of the equipment we've bought has been built in Europe, on the never-never. When it's time to sell, we advertise it on the web and people recognise the manufacturers' names so it shouldn't take too long to change hands. Safety is another major aspect in all amusement arts, so you need to comply. You need to have first-aiders around. At times you need security companies to avoid

gangs building up. There's a lot of work involved because I honestly think that people expect value for money.

At this fair last year, if you walked on to the site, every single piece of equipment whether it's a ride or a stall, was all planned to comply with the HSE [Health and Safety Executive]. People like the local mayor will open the fair. It's the biggest civic procession because there are 24 mayors invited and all are attending. They parade from the Town Hall, then the Marine Band plays in front, then the mayor and her husband followed by deputies, councilors, then the mayor from next nearest town which will be Wisbech, and so on. A huge procession comes in by the lido and marches into the middle of the fairground. You can see it's not an obstacle course, there's a large avenue all the way down. I like it so it looks good when you stand in front of that fair on opening night. So we are keeping up the tradition here. The fair dates back to the 14th century. The charter belongs to the citizens of Peterborough, the city council are the overseers and I am the licensee. There are 4000 shop posters out for this fair, 250 large boards. We advertise it on the web, so a huge amount of advertising. At the same time as we're doing this [Bridge Fair] we've got a fair in Lisbon; you can see I've quite a lot on. Just hoping for some fine weather and a good turn-out.

The rights to all the fairs in Peterborough lay with Charles Thurston and we've bought the shares of the company. Before that we were travelling all over the UK and slowly moving into Europe. This got curtailed a little bit whilst I was getting used to running the new fairs. It's difficult to keep control of work in England when you're in and out of the country, and I had one year to learn the ropes. The Bridge Fair was the biggest fair with Charles Thurston. It's a little bit bigger now than when he was around but he was a great teacher, I admired him very much. I stuck with his pattern for a while, then I wanted to alter the layout. So I've added our component here as well as taking part in projects overseas, some that have been in my control, others where I've been sub-tenant for another lessee. December each year our Dodgem ride is inside the SECC [Scottish Exhibition and Conference Centre] in Glasgow. We don't stick to one area, we go and get the money. To maintain the interest of the general public, that's what count; there's so many other things they could spend their money on. It's about advertising because even the top-brand names are always on TV. Holding people's attention with the radio, and putting stuff on websites. I did something with radio for this particular [Bridge] fair called the Hook-a-Duck, where you rang in, answered some questions, got a number, they raised the duck from the water and you received a prize. My prize was a golden wrist band for a family of four, so they could enjoy unlimited rides throughout the evening. We have promotional days, reduced price days, and I always try to alter the layout a little, moving the rides around so it looks a little bit different. Fetching in rides from other areas. You've got to keep the fairgrounds traditional but they must include innovative stuff. It is all about change and some people don't like the changes. It was a difficult task writing letters to people prior to a fair opening, but now when it's late at night or when I get 5 minutes, I'm able to start emailing, so we mastered that anyway. I'm not saying every decision I make is right or everything I do is right but changes need to be made.

I'm not a guy that's walking through life and not looking at anything other than the fairground. I'm always trying to move forward and keep my options open. Caravans, the bigger they get the more expensive they become, especially them that are purpose-built in the UK. You cannot just get anyone to come in and wallpaper, it's a completely different ball-game. With a house, a painter or a plumber haven't got to climb into boxes underneath the trailers, they can work with standard parts. To be honest, the house is my retreat; some time out from looking at fairground. OK you have to have 2 teapots, two of everything, but even in the present climate it's not losing any money because we've got a mortgage and it's something I can fall back on, a kind of a pension I suppose. We are steering John (Jr.) in that direction. I enjoy what I do but sometimes the regular showmen that attend the fairs just don't understand how much work goes in. Since we've been running fairs there was only one occasion where they decided to cut one, that was Lowestoft. When they closed the Rotunda in Folkstone I rented the Amusement Park and we ran our own fair within the existing park. It's not always smooth running; in some of the street fairs you can get away with rain, others, you're wasting your time. When it rains I'm worried because I know all those families are relying on that fair for that week. That's why I try to change things. Conversations with people who are not in the fairground business, who've attempted to become successful at something, and failed, and never tried again; that's not a good way to work. My theory is that every member of the Showmen's Guild should be the lessee for one week then they might appreciate what's involved.

When we're working, I can work as good as the next man but I tend to work with gloves when I'm taking down the rides and moving because the people in the local authority know me. They call me up on the phone, say can they come down. It's fine for them to see the everyday running of the fair, but in general there should be a director sitting in the office. When somebody's coming, if you represent the fair, you need to present yourself well because that's what they expect. I have excellent relations with the [Peterborough] Council. It's blowing my own trumpet but I think they consider I do a good job. When I call them up, there is always someone to listen. I prefer to be in control of everything myself, not passing a job on to someone else but this year I've negotiated with the city council to include the Great Eastern Run, the last Sunday of the Bridge Fair. It's a charity run that starts in the city and finishes up on the Embankment. It's taken me 8 years to persuade them that I can combine the two. In the evening time I've arranged a big firework display which will be the first one before Halloween.

My grandfather on my mother's side [William Capon] was not a showman but he married my grandmother and became an excellent one. He retired and lived in Wellingborough where I was born, the eldest of 2 sons. Then he moved to Norwich and became the caretaker of the site in Hooper Lane, because he liked to be around the showmen. We lived there in the winter months. I would not be as successful if I never had my wife. The fairground business is hands-on, not just for the men, for the ladies too. Sarah is a very hand-on person, a good manager, an excellent driver and a good home-maker. She can see a light bulb missing from about 300 yards. So I'm lucky. Sarah thought we should get into ice-skating. Jonathan Gray has an ice rink in Norwich, I went to see him to get a few tips. What I wanted was to set up the world's first portable ice-rink during the winter months. The company Adesko in Belgium built it for us – that's a 24m by 14m ice pad with its own sound system. We opened November, 2007. We have our alpine lodges and Golden Horse Carousel[2] so we can create our own winter wonderland. At the moment our Carousel is in Regent's Park Zoo, we're just deciding on the location for Christmas. We keep all of our options open really because the seasons in the UK are poor.

[2]   The correct term is Gallopers.

The last time we met, I was waiting for John Bugg outside a McDonalds near Ipswich. Home from ten days with his wife in Thailand, he was brown, beardless, and full of plans. They'd not had a holiday for two years, he said; they'd felt the need for a break and a little bit of sun. His son, John Jr. had been in Hyde Park with a ski-jump ride over Christmas, and John Sr. had been 'doing the winter wonderland' with his portable ice rink on the Norfolk Broads. Each year the ice rink is set up in a different location– Liverpool, Ipswich, and Cambridge – where celebrity Linda Lusardi had performed with them. Ever alert to change in the entertainment industry, and an excellent publicist for his enterprise, John brought along a flattering letter from Liverpool county council about the impact of the ice rink in the city. Despite snow on the ground and sub-zero temperatures, his fair was on site in Bury Road, Ipswich, preparing to start up at 2.00 pm.

CHAPTER TWENTY-THREE
THE FUTURE

There will always be fairs, believes the Showmen's Guild General Secretary, Keith Miller, whose chief evidence lies in the group's dedication to its survival.

> After about five years in this job, I realised it is the sort of industry that will go on for ever in different ways. It's in the nature of the people. Because it's such a hard life, it's moulded a sort of character and it gives them strength. Some of the new rides are computer-controlled, they've developed with the age. I feel they'll change to make sure what the industry provides is always wanted. They're very shrewd businessmen; I've noticed that some of the immigrant communities and specifically the Asian ones, absolutely love funfairs.

While showmen lament that it gets harder all the time to stay solvent, none I spoke with could conceive of fairs disappearing, if occasionally it seemed as if their insistence helped to bolster themselves. It is over a decade since they roundly rejected the view that travelling fairs had had their day.[1] Nipper Appleton had a conservative bearing on the argument:

> I often get this question asked to me, d'you think you'll still be here in ten or twenty years time? The answer is yes, it's still a major event in places. People of King's Lynn look forward to their Mart, it's nearly a thousand years old. There's small private events do collapse. A lessee may take a field and go and put a fair on; they're just trials. The major events will continue in one way or another. It's important to have sons to keep your name going. I'm not saying anything about the young ladies but I've got two girls three boys, all married, all got their own businesses. We meet up because they've got rights to a site at a particular event.

Victor Harris had his own logic:

> I think fairs will go on and on because all the while there's [showmen's] children being born. Some of the little village fairs has gone, but the bigger fairs still go [continue]. It's a struggle because

---

[1] Environment, Transport and Regional Affairs Committee, *House of Commons Ninth Report on Travelling Fairs*, 2000 [ETR], I: xii, 12.

the bigger fair, the council want their slice of the cake, they want the rent which keep going up. There's lot of money going in when they buy these big rides, thousand of pounds, then people come down the fair say, Two pound for a ride? My answer to that is, have you been to the garrige lately? Do you drink? Do you smoke? Packet of fags is nearly six pounds. Tesco put their prices up, but you're denying a child her ride on a roundabout. One fifty at most fairs, but the big rides are £2.00; got to do it.

Like Victor, Swales Elliott's reaction to the possibility of extinction is to dwell on the effect rather than the cause. It is difficult for him to imagine an alternative future for his heirs when they seem born to lead a particular life. He would not want an outsider's life anyway. What is most precious to him arises from being community-based.

I worry about the kids because it's getting harder and harder all the time. They're all feeling the pinch. Got to try and ride it. It's hard for em to do something else, when you're born into it. When you only done one thing. It ain't just work, this is your life. A nine to five job is very hard to do [imagine] when you never watched the clock, because we don't watch clocks, it's not in your nature. What's to be done gets done whether it's 12 o'clock at night or 6 o'clock in the morning. Like today, we're moving now, be about ten o'clock tonight they get there [from South Ockendon to Strood in Kent]. Bonfire night: it's a busy time.

Another uncertainty relates to the Community. Placing emphasis on those who leave obscures the fact that there has always been an ebb and flow between the fairground and the society it serves. The settled contingent of former fair people at Wells-next-the-Sea have five daughters between them; one married a traveller although the marriage didn't last, another – the elder of two sisters – is engaged to a traveller. The father of the youngest pair doesn't think they will marry into showland and reverse the change, but he can't be sure. Another showperson (Cilla Morrison) suggests, it will be with their children that the future rests:

I would think if you talk to the younger generation you'd get a lot different outlook to what we're telling you. They're are quite a few what don't want to be carrying on with the fair ground business. We've got John Green and his family, now, he's got two young boys, one of them says he want to carry on, the other says he's going to college. Not everybody stays in the business.

CHAPTER TWENTY-THREE – THE FUTURE

In the meantime, a trend less perceptible to those involved than to an outsider is for showmen to standardize their habits. Victor Gray admitted:

> I stopped living in a trailer 6 or 7 years ago. I probably wouldn't have bought the chalet, [but] I got 3 children, they're all married and they put their money together. I'm more than pleased to be in it, I wouldn't want to go back to a caravan, not if I could help it. For a couple of nights but not to live in. We had one of the big ones, about 35 ft long, made in this country. It was the well-known people made it [Sipson], very very expensive. My children have American trailers, they've all got them now because they press a button and the side goes out so you've got more room. They've got every convenience, washing machines inside, and my poor sisters had a rubbing board and a dolly peg keep the stuff spinning round.

Expectation about the future was enlarged upon by a member of the Community with ground at a number of big Eastern fairs. I first met Theodore Whyatt with his cousin, John Thurston, trying his luck at Luton's Wardown Park. In King's Lynn, the following year, it was wet, cold, and at 6.30 pm the fair in Tuesday Marketplace had just about opened one eye. People were coming in in dribs and drabs; there was Theodore high in a transparent-sided paybox beside his giant Jumping Frog. The music danced, the ride's arms gyrated up and down, all the seats were empty and he sat, smiling, detached, king of his tiny kingdom. Not long after, at Yarmouth Easter Street Show he had a prime position and the Frog was full to capacity.

Theodore's mother is a Thurston, making him, like, John, a grandson of the exuberant Stanley Sr. In 1979 he married Gay Summers, a quiet attractive brunette, and another showman's daughter. A mixture of rationality and romanticism infuse his view of a newcomer's joining the Community:

> Years ago if you had a bit of property you were considered a wealthy family. People want to have an easier life now. Buy land and go out with a little touring caravan for weekends is a lot more appealing than dragging the old-time caravans around and having to go on a muddy field. You need planning permission for showmen's yards a lot more now, but once you got somewhere as a base you tend to travel from that base and perhaps have a chalet or a bungalow. We got land at Kempston which has been 60 years in the family. It was probably on the outskirts when me grandfather bought it, you wouldn't want a yard in the middle of the town. But he had three children and they're growing up and had their children, we're outgrowing the premises. My youngest brother,

about 5 years ago, he bought a piece of land – he died in a car crash, that happen to ease the pressure in our premises a bit. I'll be looking for somewhere for my son to stay, we're probably be buying a house.

What would I say if someone wanted to marry into the business? I think if they love that person (Laugh), like you say to anybody – Gay's a lovely person, put it like that – but if they don't know the running of the fair it could be a bit daunting for them. Most showmen [he corrected himself] – *show-women* are very hardworking. But to be honest with you, it's not the best business to be in. It's a hard business, 'specially if you're not used to it. If you're getting on a bit, if you're 50, like I am, uprooting once a week or once a fortnight, move your home to 50, 100 miles down the road, it's very stressful. I've been in a family business all my life, so you carry on doing what your father is doing if you're that way inclined. But I would say you have to be prepared for it. Not so much the rules and regulations; there's so much competition. Costs are getting dearer and there's a lot more equipment about, people's chasing the same pound. When my grandfather was in charge, we'd book our fairs from the beginning of March to end of November, you knew exactly where you was going and nobody else'd be stepping on your toes. Nowadays if you're trying to argue with the councils about the state of the site or something, nine times outer ten it's take it or leave it. Even in the big fairs now, say you ride up on a site, there's probably ten people with the same type of ride. What it boils down to that your bargaining power's not as strong as it used to be. We go to places where we hate being.

Historically, competition has increased and decreased with the value of remuneration. It follows that the recession will be responsible for untimely infighting until the Community shrinks. David Remblance made a similar point:

It seem to be a bit more of a rat-race now. If that man was getting a living with coconut, there'd be coconut, coconut, coconut all the way round. They're all on the bandwagon, an he'd say I gotter think of something else to do. Travelling fairs is not what it was; some people go out, they can't afford to feed themselves; other people, they're doing all right. It's better up the North, London isn't so good. They've not got as many principles as they had years ago, I'd trust more a Joskin than I would a showman. I think the big man will win, eventually they'll be all carnies [monopolies].

CHAPTER TWENTY-THREE – THE FUTURE

In the footsteps of German counterparts who run shops and crane firms, young UK showmen taking over the business from their fathers began finding new outlets to supplement their fairground interests in the seventies. John Manning spoke of enterprise in his family that makes him feel a survivor from a different era.

> Fairgrounds will always be here, the format's changing, mind. My nephew, Joe, he runs a completely different system. He's got a big fence all the way round with a big gate on the front and you pay to come in, get a roll of tickets, then when you go inside you get so much knocked off of each ride. He goes into rough areas. It started off as security but that's the way he operates now. He's also got a Farm just off the M25 on the A12 at Brentwood. Old MacDonald's Farm. That's permanent, an educational place, he's got animal lovers come in there. That was a farm years ago, he's took it over and transformed the place. All domesticated animals. Proper animal man, knows where to get them, how to look after them, specialist vet and all that. He's got one cart horse, sheep, an emu, ostriches, beautiful owls in compounds, rabbits, goats. He's got like a bridge over a road, and a little device where sheep go up over the bridge to feed, his wife looks after that, they got good staff. The fairground stuff is up there just for the children. They got a cafe in there, it's worth a visit. Me other cousin, David, he's got a place in Broxbourne, Paradise Park; he's retired from the road and he concentrates on the amusements in there. A lot of them [fairpeople] went into different things like catering, they come back to this at the end of the day, but it's hard to get a living out of it. They're all settled, I'm the only one going, really.

Three showmen spoke of the contributions to the amusement industry made by their children. In Nipper Appleton's family, Lawrence III and Charmaine run the Silver Sands pub on a sea-front caravan site at Heacham. It is a stylish presentation, the walls hidden behind enlarged black and white photographs of '50s and '60s film stars. Theodore Whyatt's eldest daughter runs a candyfloss store and a juvenile ride in the centre of Bedford, despite being settled there, she travels with her parents from time to time. One of Kenny Gray's daughters and her partner hire out trampolines to fêtes and galas. Kenny described booking up with individuals rather than working through a system of lessee and client, as 'modern-day travelling'; that would be omitting the fair.

It is an axiom that institutions suited to their environment are those that survive. King's Lynn's St Valentine's Day Mart and Peterborough's Bridge Fair are in reasonable health. There, well-built Mace-bearers parade between the

Dodgems and a pressing public, make appropriate prayers and 'Oh yeas', read charters and lead the singing of national anthems, continuing hundreds of years of ceremony. Without a doubt it is the value councils put upon these fairs that ensures their future. Other fairs tell a different story. Norwich's Good Friday Fair is lost, despite the Minister for Planning's clear stipulation that no large community should be without a central focus designed for public entertainment;[2] a typical victim of city centres torn up by repressive development and redesigned for the car – acts which now seem shortsighted. The May Bank Holiday Reach Fair in Newmarket, the oldest in England, is a ghost of what it once was. The Easter Fair on Hampstead Heath contends with lack of parking as well as the usual competition from other entertainments and the risk of untimely weather. Sometimes barely a handful of pleasure-seekers brave the trail. Stourbridge was held sporadically from 1933 but despite a twenty-first-century revival, its future remains precarious.

The Midsummer Fair in Cambridge is the lone survivor of the city's four medieval inheritances. Held on its original space in beautiful willow-fringed meadows along the River Cam, it was within living memory the height of fashion among eastern venues. Stripped of atmosphere by physical reorganization to zealous standards of health and safety, an event with huge competition became annually less inviting. Recognition of the problem hasn't helped. Thanks to insistent pressure from the Guild the fair was allowed to take place in 2010, but Cambridge has dreadful congestion problems and the event takes a huge toll in time and energy to run. Unless it attracted sufficient numbers, the council was none too anxious to carry what had become a burden of hospitality to the fair's 800th anniversary in 2011.

It is not as if the struggle goes unnoticed; Vanessa Toulmin of Sheffield University's National Fairground Archive said the question most frequently put to her is how long fairs will last. The majority of showmen say they will continue, and fight valiantly to make this happen, but the thumping soundtrack of a 90s Miami or the reiteration of statistics to prove vitality do not disguise the fact that many are pushed into uncongenial suburbs and poorly attended. Showmen compete with one another on an overcrowded raft, with permanent attractions like Alton Towers, Disneyland, and with all the solitary, sedentary pastimes offered by the computer and multi-channel television. Showpeople have been skilled improvisers, and improvisation on popular themes is something that their admirers insist on seeing and hearing. At Ipswich Guild fair on St Valentines Day 2010, where world-wandering showman John Bugg was the lessee, a little calculation revealed that almost two-thirds of his new rides were made abroad.[3]

---

[2] ETR, I: xiv, 23.

[3] John Bugg's *UK-built Rides*: Gallopers, Savage, Norfolk, 1885; Daredevil, Nottingham UK Ltd.; Extreme, Tivoli Enterprises, Canterbury, UK; Twist, Stevens, UK;

Dependence on foreign rides limits the showman's control of the industry, and sticking to what has proved reliable results in less individuality among exhibits and rides. At the same time, showman/reporter, Mike Willis' figures show a healthy number of rides and shows in circulation at present in the UK. He calculates some 230 Fun Houses, c65 Ghost Trains, 41 Round Up's, 30 Paratroopers and 16 Tagada's travelling. While rides include about 155 Dodgems, 127 Waltzers, 114 Twists, 95 Miamis, 41 Gallopers – 15 of them steam propelled, 30 Jump & Smiles, 28 Big Wheesl 26 Orbiters; 22 Matterhorns, 17 Super Bobs, 14 Freak Outs and 13 Boosters, and other rides in only single figures.[4]

Red tape remains frustrating. Bureaucracy is cramping for everyone but while responding wholeheartedly to safety measures, showmen feel they are on the receiving end of continuous new Government directives. On top of this, they have no insurance against hostility, infirmity, or the weather, and the recession is biting hard. Sandscratchers go into shops selling comestibles, run cafés, clubs, bowling-alleys, hotels and permanently-based amusements such pleasure parks or the Golden Nugget gambling Arcade set up by a branch of the Thurston family along Great Yarmouth's Marine Parade. As a rule, investors have more security than their travelling brothers.[5] They may use some of the same equipment to the showmen who fill Yarmouth's town centre over Easter but from an aesthetic point of view, the two are not comparable.

What is a fun fair for? Is it a kind of adventure, essentially physical that doesn't involve the conscience or the intellect? While an af-fair might also qualify as adventure, the fair is more straightforward. The fairground pushes boundaries. It may be terrifying, may be exciting. It asks the fairgoer to accept a world where, in Dannie Abse's words 'the stars below us / the cerebellum disordered / we juggle on the edge of the earth / one foot on earth / one foot over the abyss.'[6] Falling, spinning, whizzing, swooping, bouncing, screaming and playing games with vertigo, the fairgoer is invited to make a visceral assault upon the senses; briefly and without responsibility, to stretch endurance to its limits. The fair costs something but is remarkably cheap. Good, clean, fun and by

Waltzer, Maxwells, Musselburgh, Scotland. *Foreign rides:* Booster, made by Fabri, Italy; Thriller, Sobema, Belgium; Oblivion, KMG, Holland; Big Apple, Dal, Turkey; Junion – Formula, Saragossa, Spain; Super Bob, Sobina, Belgium; Dodgems, Adesko, Belgium; Move It, KMG, Holland.

[4] From personal email from Mike Willis, giving a fairground enthusiast's list of fairground rides in the UK, January 4th, 2011.

[5] The Golden Nugget Arcade closed during the recession in 2010.

[6] Dannie Abse, *Funland*, Brynmor Press, Swansea for Portland University Library, 1971, has more surreal connotations than a funfair, but the imagery fits. By permission of Oxford University Press, Inc.

definition harmless because the risks are make-believe; any real risk is transferred to the muscular man, or the attractive girl who take control.

Showmen have long been innovators. Think of the 'Booster' at King's Lynn Mart on St Valentine's Day where youngsters could fly on two 130 foot high-rise, skywise arms. To reflect the brash noise and speed, the colour and sensation of their predecessors, contemporary fairs keep reinventing themselves, renewing the bid to be 'unpretentious, uninhibited and exciting'.[7] A certain familiarity conveys a sense of dependability, vulgarity is an extra: together they trick the mindset out of the mundane. Introduce magic.

The fair's traditional enterprise is continually usurped, as happened in the Waveney Valley towards the end of the twentieth-century. The first Barsham Faire, held in August 1971, was born from a casual meeting of a few friends who had moved from London and decided to hold a medieval fair. Some were living in communes, developing ways of sustaining themselves; an enterprising hippie element was supported by the Lowestoft Theatre Centre. Printed circulars such as the *Waveney Clarion* promoted the fairs, and the money they raised was used to run music, theatre, and childrens' acivities, art shows and a travelling cinema. There weren't really big acts so much as acoustic sets and theatre, but immediately popular, Barsham flourished for six years, when plans were laid to introduce such events as the 'Insect Circus', the 'Can Can Girls', and 'Reg Rabbit and the Fast Breeders' to other localities. The Albion Fair was formed in 1977, and another five years saw more than thirty such East Anglian fairs, while other groups created their own variants elsewhere in the country. No one was paid, or paid only nominally for their contribution, and ten thousand people are said to have flocked in.[8] By 1893 the leaders had found the responsibility too much for them to continue.

More recently, it is art galleries that have purloined the showman's repertoire. The twenty-first century visitor is no more likely to be robbed at a fair than she or he would be in a gallery, so it is bad luck for showpeople that the bid to attract the public finds galleries offering shock, horror, sleaze and lunacy along with everything else. Damien Hirst courted his public with a pickled shark, and a pickled bear you can walk right through the middle of. Anish Kapoor asked people to gaze at distorting mirrors. Mungo Thomson's custom-fabricated bouncehouse in the Tate Modern's Turbine Hall in the late spring of 2010 could have been straight out of the fairground, and Mark Wallinger won a Turner Prize for dressing up as a bear, while the 2009 winner Richard Wright painted a gold

---

[7] *All the Fun of the Fair*, Graham Downie, The Showmen's Guild Publication, 1986, page number.

[8] 'Diss Can Hall Celebrates Albion Fairs History', *Eastern Daily Press* (September 8, 2011).

leaf wall fresco of marvellous baroque sunrays and angle wings that, like the travelling fair itself, was shortly to disappear. All these art forms come close to fairground prerogatives. Moreover, the experiences can be enjoyed without getting muddy shoes or chancing rain and wind. Perhaps the Great Dorset Steam Fair at Blandford, a relative newcomer, is the showmen's equivalent to the Tate Modern. While showmen cast round for novelty and new outlets in a virtual world, basically they are traditionalists battling to marry old and new.

> forgive me:
> I still can't resist
> the sound of a fair in the distance
>
> the new crushed grass
>
> those sixties songs
>
> the heat of the machines
>
> John Burnside

APPENDIX 1
GLOSSARY OF SHOWMEN'S LANGUAGE

Some specialist words were gathered in an interview with David Smith on January 2, 2011. These definitions, quoted verbatim, are marked '(DS)' Graham Downie has also helped with explanations of words in this list.

Afterburner: a pendulum-based ride. Riders sit in a cluster of seats arranged around the bob of the pendulum, which is swung beneath an A-frame. A secondary motion is achieved by rotating the cluster.

Arcade: a sidestall enclosing coin-operated machines.

Astroglide: a slide with multiple, parallel chutes.

Autodrome: a circular switchback ride with dummy cars mounted on steel girders that also serve as axles. It was introduced in the late 1930s.

Auto-Speed Cars: see Dodgems.

Back-End Run: the autumn sequence of fairs running from early September until mid-November.

Big Wheel: a ride consisting of a large, vertical wheel fitted with suspended cars.

Bioscope: the generic name for the shows in which moving pictures were first exhibited on the fairground.

Booster: a propeller-based ride. A group of four seats is attached to both ends of a propeller mounted on a high, vertical steel pillar.

Booth: temporary canvas shelter.

Bridge Fair, or Brigge Fair: the famous Peterborough fair established in 1439 by Henry VI.

Bucket and Chuck It: sewage disposal prior to flush lavatories.

Build Up: the process of erecting amusements on a fairground.

Burster: a day of exceptional business at a fair. 'That's taking tons of money' (DS).

Cakewalk: an amusement first introduced in 1907. Riders walk along two narrow, parallel platforms mounted on cranks that cause the platforms to rise and fall. Named after a dance that had originated among slaves on the Florida plantations in the nineteenth century.

Can-Can Girls: high-kicking dancers once popular in fairground shows.

Candyfloss: machine spun 'cotton candy' invented 1897 and introduced to a wide audience at the 1904 World's Fair. Made by machine since the 1970s.

Carnie: David Smith used this word to mean a monoply, or (as Carnies) those showmen who enjoyed the monopoly; another showman said "I have never heard this word used in the UK. In the USA it is a word derived from 'carnival' and means anyone associated with a travelling funfair".

Carousel: a type of roundabout derived from a device used to train cavalrymen in parts of eighteenth-century Europe. It is peculiar to the continent and North America, where the ride was taken by nineteenth-century emigrés from Germany and Italy. The name is often mistakenly used to refer to British Gallopers, which differ from their continental counterparts in several respects.

Chair-o-Plane: a roundabout consisting of rows of individual seats suspended on chains from a spinning frame; it was introduced from Germany in the early 1920s.

Chalet: bungalow dwelling that passes as a mobile home with planning authorities.

Chav, Chavy: 'A child' (DS) or childish. The Romany word has becoming increasingly popular and mainstream to describe directionless youths who congregate in public wearing the latest fashions in sportswear.

Cock Peg: the fitting at the top of the central pole of a round stall into which the rafters are slotted.

Coconut Shy: a throwing game usually enclosed within a simple frame covered with canvas. The targets are coconuts (or 'duds') mounted on wooden pegs.

Coffin: metal end plate for the Dodgems.

Coronation Speedway: a version of the Noah's Ark ride, introduced during the coronation year of 1937. Much grander in scale and decoration than earlier versions and fitted with dummy motorcycles.

Cushti: 'Worth having, good' (DS); the Romany word is the origin of the mainstream word 'cushy'.

Dobbies: a roundabout fitted with carved wooden horses as mounts which simply move outwards under centrifugal force as the ride rotates. Gallopers have an additional rise-and-fall motion created by the cranked rods from which they are suspended.

Dodgems: the most popular ride on a fairground and generally regarded as a staple component of a fair. First introduced from the USA in the early 1920s, this is the only ride on a fairground in which the rider takes control over his or her direction.

Dropped Dart: used by David Smith for an ostentatious showman; a pejorative term with an imprecise meaning.

Eliminator: a Miami that has been given this name to reflect its decorative theme: it is peculiar to that one machine only.

Ferris Wheel: see Big Wheel.

Fiddling: a term implying a steady and acceptable level of business on the fairground. 'It isn't something wrong for a showman. It's when he's open, and he's taking a nice few shillings' (DS).

Flattie (or Joskin): a showman's term for someone outside the business. Said to have originated among those working on the canals in the nineteenth century.

Flea Circus: a side-show in which fleas which appear to be attached to miniature carts are encouraged to perform tricks.

Freak Out: an Afterburner that has been given a particular name to distinguish it from its competitors.

Fun House: a self-contained amusement, usually trailer-mounted, that incorporates various devices such as slides, moving walkways and rotating tunnels.

Gadge: A Romany word for an outsider.

Gaff Lad: someone employed by showmen to erect, operate and dismantle equipment, usually the larger rides, a term derived from 'gaffer's lad' or boss's boy.

Gallopers: the classic British roundabout, perfected by the nineteenth-century King's Lynn engineer Frederick Savage, consisting of rows of carved wooden horses (or other animals) suspended from a spinning frame, to which a galloping motion is imparted by overhead cranks as the ride rotates. The ride always rotates in a clockwise fashion, a direction dictated by the long established convention of mounting a horse from the left-hand side.

Gammy: bad day, or just 'bad' ('It's Romany, that could be rotten meat, or rock that's got wet and you try to sell it again' (DS)).

Geldy: The word is Hindi for 'haste' or 'hurry'. It is usually transcribed *jaldī*. So, it can mean 'go faster' (for more fun on a ride) or 'come away quickly' (if there is danger).

Gavioli Organ: an organ made by a company founded in 1806 by Giacomo Gavioli. He patented the use of book music.

Ghost Train: a small railway operating within a portable, totally enclosed structure. Often referred to as 'a dark ride' or 'a ghost ride'. Owes its name to the famous 1923 play by Arnold Ridley, *The Ghost Train.*

Gipsy / Gipsies: member of the wandering people known as Romany, who are ultimately of Hindu origin, though the word 'Gipsy' is a short form of 'Egyptian', based on the false belief that they came from Egypt. In fairground communities Gipsy and Romany are interchangeable.

Gondola: the elaborately decorated, gondola-like carriage fitted to the steam-driven switchback roundabouts built in the late nineteenth century.

Hiring Fair: a fair at which servants, mainly farmworkers, were hired for the following 12 months. Originally held by statute, these fairs are known in some parts of the Midlands as 'Mop fairs', a term that derives from the practice of those seeking work wearing some form of emblem to denote their particular skill. A shepherd, for example, would wear a tuft – or mop – of wool.

Hook-a-Duck: a game in which customers catch a plastic duck on a tub of water to find prize-winning numbers printed on the underside.

Hoopla: a round stall enclosing a variety of games, usually dependent on manual skills.

Insect Circus: a variant on a flea circus, a Victorian exhibit which used flies, wasps and beetles.

Jollity Farm: see Noah's Ark.

Joskin: a term used by travelling showmen to describe someone outside the fairground business (see also 'flattie'). Originally, it was a term prevalent in Norfolk to refer, perhaps disparagingly, to someone from rural parts. (Similar in application to 'country bumkin'.)

Jump and Smile / Jumper: see Jumping Frog.

Jumping Frog: A ride that consists of eight arms that rotate around the centre. When in motion the arms are raised and lowered hydraulically to give a jumping action. The cars are mounted on the ends of the arms.

Juvenile: a collective term for a children's ride.

Kecka: an instruction to children to 'Leave it alone or be quiet' (DS).

King's Lynn Mart: a fair granted by a charter of Henry VIII. Opening on 14 February in the town's Tuesday Market Place, it marks the start of the annual round of fairs.

Matterhorn: A modern version of the Mont Blanc, which is, in turn, a form of switchback ride. The name is derived from the scenic backflash, usually painted with Alpine scenes.

Lessee: one who negotiates the lease of the ground from the authorities and organizes a particular fairground event.

Living Wagon: the showman's mobile home.

Machine, see Ride.

Marenghi Organs: very ornate organs made by Charles Marenghi of Paris, previously forman at the Gavioli workshop. He set up in competition in 1902.

Mechanical Man: a showman who moved and spoke like a robot as do some of today's street actors.

Merry-go-Round: a roundabout.

Miami: The first such machine, for which the correct generic name is Trapeze or Acrobat, came into this country from Holland in the early 1990s. Its existing décor bore the title 'Miami Trip'. Henceforth every (British) version was known (and still is) as 'a Miami'. The ride consists of a bench seat on which the passengers sit, swung backwards and forwards before achieving a full circle.

Mickey Mouse Circus: a type of show in which mice are exhibited in a cage containing various devices on which they can play.

Mingra: 'A policeman or [police-]woman' (DS).

Mop Fair: see Hiring Fair.

Mort: 'that's killing somebody, the French for dead. You could say I'm going to *mort* him if you're getting unfriendly' (DS).

Mozzy: 'a loose woman' (DS).

Noah's Ark: a type of switchback ride introduced from Germany in 1929. The name derives from the early models with flat-sided mounts shaped like various animals. For the same reason, these rides were sometimes known as 'Jollity Farm' (the title of a song popular at the time). Later versions were fitted with dummy motorcycles (see Coronation Speedway).

Non-Runner: a travelling showman who is not a member of the Showmen's Guild.

Oblivion: Yet another Afterburner that has been given a particular, and unique theme.

Octopus: an eight-armed novelty ride on which the cars are fixed at the ends of the arms. As the ride rotates the arms rise and fall and the cars spin round.

Omy: means a man – from the Latin 'homo'. More common in circus parlance than on the fairground.

One-Armed Bandit: a slot machine.

Orbiter: novelty ride first produced by the engineer and former showman Richard Woolls in 1976. It has six articulated arms on a rotating axis, each supporting a cluster of three cars. Both the central axis and each cluster of cars rotate.

Parader: a performer (usually female) on the front of a show, employed to encourage customers in.

Paratrooper: is a specific form of aerial ride, which come in two versions: (1) The Upright Paratrooper consists of a spinning frame. Cars are attached to the frame fixed at an angle to an upright metal column. Because of this configuration they can only be loaded one at a time. (2) The more modern Lifting Paratrooper has a spinning frame which starts off in a horizontal position at platform level. This enables all of the cars to be loaded at the same time. The frame is mounted to a substantial boom which rises at an angle to the platform as the frame starts to spin. It then, more or less, operates in the same fashion as the upright version. The frame is lowered to ground level at the end of the ride cycle.

Parney, parny or parni: 'rainy'; another variant form is in the expression 'It's panying' (David Smith). However, the word has a double meaning, urinating, as in 'I'm off for a parney', so it is considered vulgar when used for rain (exactly the same as with the mainstream expression 'pissing down').

Pick-a-Straw: stall where straws are chosen without being able to see their length.

Platform Rod: a rod connecting the platform to the spinning frame on a set of Gallopers.

Pooving: 'Means find a field with plenty of grass, steal it if you like. That was used years ago when we had horses' (DS).

Puccarikush (pronounced poo-carry-kush): 'It's Hindi, cush is a cosh or a stick. A signpost' (DS).

Pull Down: the process of dismantling fairground equipment.

Quartering: a component in the framework of a ride or hoopla. Quarterings fit between the swifts and stick out like the spokes of an umbrella.

Rackler: a woman. The word derives from the Romany 'rakli', a girl; 'A woman, not a show-women unless you didn't like them a lot. It's what travellers call a Joskin if they're a bit hoity-toity' (DS).

Rawni: 'Top quality, that could be a diamond or a man.' (DS)

Rib-Tickler: a form of amusement consisting of a bench seat suspended from the axle of a box-like structure which totally encloses the seating. The seat is swung backwards and forwards as the box is revolved, so the riders think they are being inverted.

Ride: fairground apparatus that literally takes its customer for a 'ride', generally in a circular or swinging motion. Also referred to by showmen as a machine.

Riding Master: the owner of one or more rides.

Rock 'n' Roll: a Cakewalk rebranded to match the musical tastes of the late 1950s.

Rokker Romany: a phrase travellers use to describe speech derived from Romany.

Rock-o-plane (or rockerplane): A ride that derived from flight simulators developed in the USA (and made by the same firm that built the simulators). It consists of egg-shaped cars mounted on the spokes of a vertical wheel. The cars are pivoted, allowing them to sway as the wheel rotates.

Roll-Up: stall where the fairgoer rolls balls to achieve certain numbers.

Roma / Romany: see Gipsy / Gipsies.

Round-Up: A ride with a large circular cage. The riders are strapped standing to the inside of the cage, which is at first rotated horizontally. By means of a hydraulic ram the cage is gradually elevated to an almost vertical position. This American ride was introduced to the UK around 1960.

Rounding Boards: the upper circle of decorative boards fitted to most rides.

Run: succession of fairs through a season or a year.

Rye-Buck: 'A gentleman, not a showman' (DS).

Sandscratchers, -sneakers, -dancers: showmen who have given up the travelling life, often to operate amusements during the summer months at seaside resorts. The phrase has been attributed to Fred Warren ("they don't travel any more, they just dance on the sand").

Satellite: An American ride also known as a Trabant. A rotating platform, fitted with seats around its circumference is raised into the air by means of a hydraulic ram mounted on a turntable, which adds a further apparent motion to the ride.

Scarp / Scarper: 'If you're thieving something and liable to get caught, you scarper. That's Italian, *escapare* [to escape]. If you're in a fight and you're going to get beaten. Scarper!' (DS).

Showmen's Guild of Great Britain: the trade association for travelling showmen. It was founded in 1889 as the United Kingdom Van Dwellers' Protection Association to resist the Moveable Dwellings Bill then being proposed by the evangelist George Smith. It was subsequently decided to maintain the organisation as a means of promoting and defending the interests of travelling showmen.

Show Row: a phrase used in fairs where shows are positioned in a line, with stalls and rides occupying the rest of the ground.

Shyster: 'That's slang, it mean not worth bothering with; it could be shit, or a person or an object. A car or a horse' (DS).

Sideground: The perimeters of the fairground, usually occupied by sidestalls or any other amusements (such as the Miami) which can operate on restricted space.

Sideshows: a show positioned on side ground.

SIRPS: Society of Independent Roundabout Proprietors.

Sizzler (Twist or Twister): a novelty ride in which long arms rotate seats or 'cars' connected to a beam above them. The seats are spun in the opposite direction from the ride as a whole, creating the sensation that they will crash into each other.

Sleepers: wooden beams that form the base of rides such as Dodgems and Arks, the same word is used in railway sleepers.

Spewpan: see Tagada.

Spieler: a showman who entices custom with patter. German for player.

Steam Fair: a relatively modern term to describe a fair where some of the rides are steam-powered.

Steam Swings: a conventional row of swinging boats powered by steam.

Steam Yachts: a pair of large swinging boats powered by steam.

Stretchers: a component part of the base of a Dodgem track.

Super-bob: another modern variant of the Autodrome switchback ride of the 1930s.

Swagman: a wholesale supplier of prizes and other goods for fairground use.

Swifts: the main spokes of the spinning frame on a set of Gallopers.

Swinging Gyms: A row of (usually no more than four) rectangular cages suspended beneath an elongated A frame. The cages are swung backwards and forwards through the effort of the riders.

Switchback Roundabout: A circular ride consisting of a plurality of cars driven round an undulating track. The original switchback roundabouts had two hills and two valleys, although later variants, such as the Waltzer, could have as many as five hills.

Tagada: A ride that resembles a metal bowl. The riders are strapped into seats around the inner circumference of the bowl, which is spun round and shaken up and down. This is a modern version of a ride that first appeared in the early twentieth century nicknamed 'The Spewpan' because of its characteristic shape – and the effect on its riders.

Teacups: a rotating Juvenile ride which has seats fashioned in the shape of tea cups.

Tilt: a canvas covering to a ride, stall or any other form of fairground equipment.

Tilt Bag: the bag in which the tilt (the canvas roof covering) is stored between fairs.

Tip-Top: A type of ride that first appeared in 1980. Like the Orbiter of the 1970s, it consisted of a spinning frame of four or five arms from which cars containing the riders were suspended. When in motion the frame would be raised into the air and tilted.

Tober: 'The ground that you open on' (DS).

Toberman: 'The manager. Clerk to the market he's called in Norwich' (DS).

Travellers: any itinerant group.

Twist: see Sizzler.

Twister: see Sizzler.

Two-Year Rule: the rule of the Showmen's Guild under which any member who has occupied a particular position at a fair for two years in succession is deemed to have 'established rights' on that position, and is entitled to occupy it to the exclusion of all other members in the following years.

Wagon: see Living Wagon.

Wafty: a term denoting something (or somebody) that is useless or not fit for purpose; 'Bad. Say you go to hire some ground and the man you're paying is on the take, asking for £50. You'd say he was a wafty omy' (DS).

Waltzer: an established ride on which tub-like cars mounted on a revolving, undulating platform rotate freely on their own axles.

Wheel-em-in: stall in which pennies are rolled down a chute.

White-Knuckle Ride: a term for any ride, usually modern, which operates in a manner designed to create extreme experiences.

Winter quarters: showmen's yards.

Yard: a pitch or base, where showmen live, usually in extended family groups.

APPENDIX 2
LIST OF INTERVIEWS

Name	Place	Date
Appleton, Lawrence, Snr. (Nipper)	Kings Lynn	24.10.2010
Bloomfield, Jamie	Thurston, Suffolk	16.04.2010
Bugg, John	Peterborough	02.10.2008; 14.02.2010
Bugg, Margaret	Norwich	14.08.2008; 07.08.2010
Bugg, Pat	Norwich	08.08.2008
Downs, David	Braintree	10.06.2010
Elliott, Beverley	South Ockenden	29.10.2009
Elliott, Swales	South Ockenden	29.10.2009
Gelder, Kay (née Gray)	Wells-next-the-Sea	20.11.2007
Gizzi, John	Wells-next-the-Sea	02.12.2007
Gray, Jac	Norwich	26.07.2010
Gray, Kenny	Sheringham	18.12.2007
Gray, Fiona	Sheringham	18.12.2007
Gray, Josie (née Abbott)	East Runton; Wymondham	04.09.2008; 05.09.2010
Gray, Larry	East Runton	04.09.2008
Gray, Victor,	Wilburton, Cambs.	12.08.2008
Harris, Victor	Wilburton, Cambs.	12.08.2008
Hedges-Stocks, Zoah	Leiston, Suffolk	30.05.2008
Loades, Martin	Ipswich	09.03.2010
Lewis, David	Basildon	09.03.2010
Manning, John	Tottenham	30.07.2008
Miller, Keith	Staines	19.05.2010
Morrison, Arthur	Norwich	12.12.2007
Morrison, Cilla	Norwich	26.07.2008
Sedgewick, Frank	Peterborough	03.11.2009
Smith, David	Syderstone, Norfolk	20.07.2007; 22.01.2010; 02.01.2011
Starsmore, Ian	Wood Dalling, Norfolk	26.12.2007
Stocks, Bernice	Leiston, Suffolk	30.05.2008;

		06.11.2009
Stocks, Henry Sr.	Leiston, Suffolk	06.11.2009
Stocks, Shirley (née Irvin)	Leiston, Suffolk	06.11.2009
Thurston, John	Luton	29.08.2008
Thurston, Kim (née Irvin)	Wyton, Cambs	15.01.2010
Thurston, Robert	Wyton, Cambs	15.01.2010
Underwood, Perry	Wells-next-the-Sea	06.07.2007
Whyatt, Theodore	Luton	29.08.2008

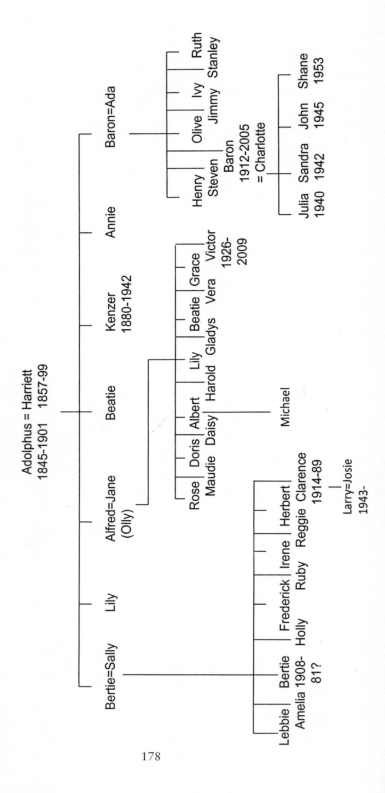

Gray Family Tree I

178

Gray Family Tree II

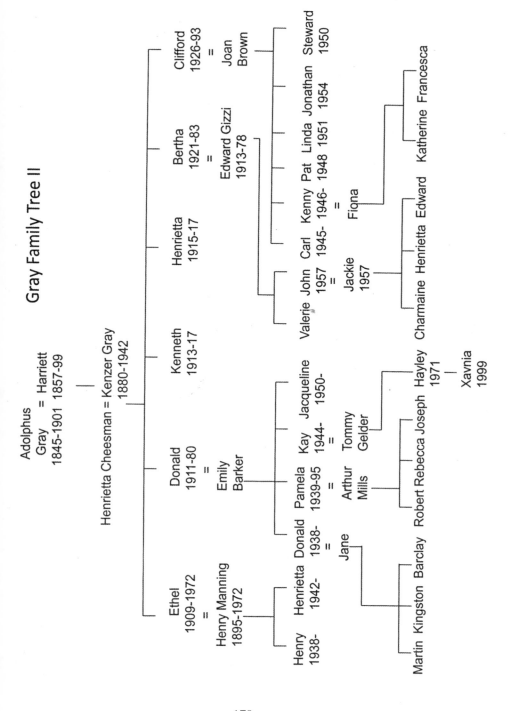

Thurston Family Tree

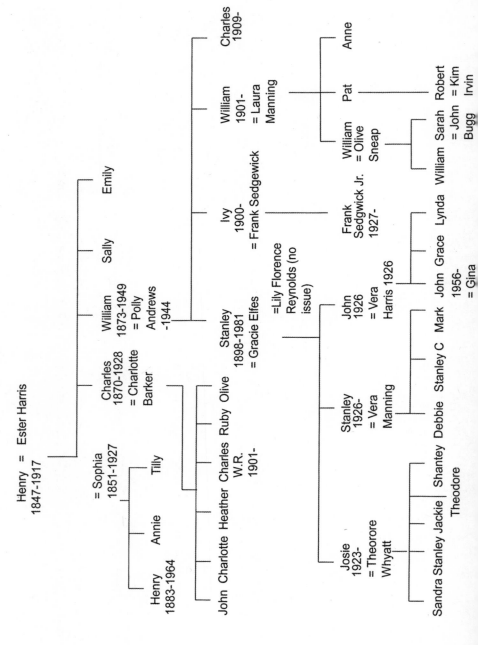

Underwood & Smith Family Tree

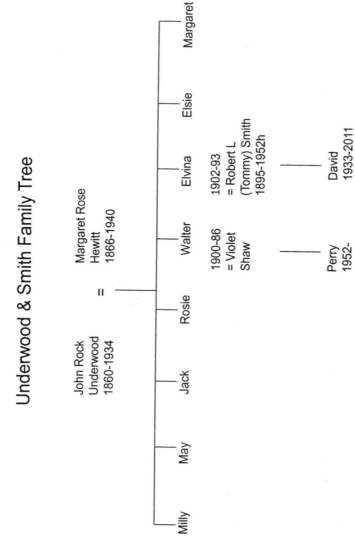

John Rock
Underwood
1860-1934

=

Margaret Rose
Hewitt
1866-1940

Milly

May

Jack

Rosie

Walter
1900-86
= Violet
Shaw

Elvina
1902-93
= Robert L
(Tommy) Smith
1895-1952h

Elsie

Margaret

Perry
1952-

David
1933-2011

INDEX

1. Here today and gone tomorrow: trailers in Wardown Park, Luton, 2008.

2. David Smith, Syderstone 2008, with his brother's encampment in the background.

3. Perry Underwood as a school boy.

4. Perry Underwood's amusement empire, Wells, 2011.

5. Jacqueline Gray above her Wells Shop, top centre, 2008.

6. John Gizzi's Shop on Wells waterfront, 2008.

7. Kay Gelder in 2008.

8. Gravestone of Adolphus and Harriett Gray, St Mary's, Watton.

The inscription reads 'In Loving Memory | of | Adolphus Gray | interred Sep^br 12th 1901 | aged 56 years | Also of | Harriett Gray | his beloved wife | interred Sep^br 23rd 1899 | aged 42 years | Not gone from memory, not gone from love | but gone to our Father's home above | erected by their sons & daughters'.

9. Kay Gray in the pay box, Wells Arcade, 1967.

10. Pamela Gray's wedding, against Donald Gray's Gavioli organ, c.1960. *From left to right*: Donald Jr., Arthur Mills, Pamela, Kay, Jacqueline, Emily, Donald Sr., John Gizzi.

11. Gray fishing expedition, Blakeney, 1940.
From left to right: Kay, Julia, Pamela, Carl, Donald Jr., Kenny.

12. Fiona at her marriage to Kenny Gray,
Norwich Trinity Church, 1979.

13. Fiona and Kenny Gray in the paybox,
Sheringham Amusement Arcade, 2010.

14. Cilla Morrison in Hooper Lane Yard, 2008.

15. Larry Gray with his grandchildren, Darcey and Morgan at East Runton, 2008.

16. Imogen and Eden, daughters of Adam Bond at Southwold Fair, 2008.

17. Swales Elliott, Guild Education
Officer, at South Ockendon, 2009.

18. Grace Howard
with Gangster, 2011.

19. Margaret and Pat Bugg in Hooper Lane Yard 2009.

20. Pat at the time of her marriage to Jimmy Bugg.

21. Eastern Guild Football team at Kings Lynn 1962. *Back row*: Kenny Gray, Tommy Gelder, Steven Summers, Richard Harvey, Jimmy Norman, John Remblance. *Front row*: Richard Hart, David Harvey, Michael Gray, Michael Abbott, Arthur Morrison.

22. Arthur Morrison, Hooper Lane yard 2008.

23. Robert Thurston, 2010.

24. Kim Thurston, 2010.

25. Kim Thurston's wedding in 1985, outside Northill church. *Left to right:* Victor Gray, Robert Thurston, Marshall Tattam, Henry Stocks, Daren Irvin. *Page boys:* Bradley Thurston, Scott Gray, Patrick Phillips.

26. Marriage of Victor Gray and Ann Thurston in Cambridge, 1963.

27. Pulling Larry Gray's Waltzer in 1990. *Left-to-right:* Trevor Watts, Sheldon Gray, Renny Gray, Arthur Morrison, ?, Marshall Tattam, Bill Abbott, Gary Saunders, Robert Tattam, Leslie Carey, Larry Gray, and Larry William in the lorry.

28. Larry and Josie Gray, East Runton Fair, 2008.

29. Victor Harris, with his son, Frankie and grandson, Junior, Kimbolton Street Fair 2003.

30. Harry Remblance at Barking Carnival fair, 1973, with his grandsons Levi Willis and the late Russell Willis in the pram.
Courtesy Margarett Carter.

31–34. Four of the paintings by J. D. Turner, made 1933–4 as murals at the Swan
Hotel, Southwold. *This page, top:* Bert Stocks' Dodgems; *below:* Southwold
Green, with caravans. *Opposite page, top:* J. Elmer's 'Tip the Lady out of Bed';
below: R. Day's Latest Games.
Courtesy of the Swan Hotel, Southwold.

THE FAIR'S LITTLE (TRACTION ENGINE ABOUT) TWELVE YEARS OLD
ESTABLISHED 1875

DUKE OF YORK'S CAMPING GROUND
SOUTHWOLD COMMON SUFFOLK
FRIDAY AUGUST 13TH 1926

35. Bernice Stocks in the Pit Stop Diner, Southwold Trinity Fair, 2008.

36. Zoah Hedges-Stocks, Southwold Trinity Fair, 2008.

37. Stocks' Dodgems, Bardwell fair 1977 with *left-to-right:* Charlie Smith, Willia Abbott, Henry Stocks Jr., Charles Stocks, Michael Abbott, Jimmy Hale, John Jones, Paul Hedges, / Roberta Stocks, Bernice Stocks, Jane Hale, Hazel Smith, Eva Bugg, Charlotte Stocks, Dougie Day, Florrie Hale, John Stokes, / Tommy Bond, Ada Bond, Victoria Smith below, Deborah Smith, Beryl Bond, Jackie Day, Tracy Stokes, / Emma Hale, Charlotte Smith, Adam Bond, Heidi Bond, Bert Bond, Lee Abbott, Sally Day, Carl Jones, Joseph Stokes, Mark Hedges, Thomas Bond.

38. Stocks leaving Haverhill May Fair, 1983. *Left-to-right:* Hired hand, Tommy Bond, Henry Stocks Jr., pushing lorry, towing Henry Thomas Stocks in Jimmy Day's wagon.

39. Charlee and Ria Stocks about to leave for Hadleigh Bonfire night, 2009.

40. Henry Stocks Jr. painting the Rock City Miami, Leiston, 2009.

41. Girl on a
Sally Stocks
Juvenile at
Southwold fair
2008.

42. Frank Sedgewick,
Peterborough, 2009.

43. Jamie Bloomfield with his Swinging Gyms
on Thurston Green, Easter 2009.

44. Fair Poster by Charleen Bloomfield.

45. Martin Loades on his Gallopers, Ipswich Valentine Fair, 2010.

46. David Downs under a red awning on his steam-driven Gallopers, Braintree, June 2010.

47. George Cushing with the Burrell Showman's Locomotive, 1984.

48. Nipper Appleton in the family yard, Kings Lynn, 2009.

49. One of the Appleton family side shows, 'a magic part of a funfair' remembers Nipper.

50. John Manning as chairman of the London and Home Counties Section
of the Showmen's Guild, 1997–2000. Courtesy of the Showmen's Guild of Great Britain.

51. John Thurston in Luton's Wardown Park, 2008.

52. John W.
Bugg and John
Bugg against
their Dodgems,
Peterborough,
c.2005.

53. Detail of a
gilded horse
from a historic
ride in the
Thursford
Museum, taken
in 2011.

NOTICE

THE SAFETY RESTRAINTS ON THIS RIDE MAY NOT ACCOMODATE PASSENGERS WITH CERTAIN BODY DIMENSIONS

We apologise for any inconvenience

54. Health-and-safety concerns, which put showmen in a difficult position, Southwold Fair, 2008.

55. Detail of a ride under cover at East Runton, August 2008.

56. John Bugg's
Rock o Plane,
Cambridge Fair,
c. 1979. Copyright
Roy Campbell,
Milton Keynes.

57. Newspaper cutting of John
Bugg giving rides in the Tahiti
Express to handicapped
children, mid 1980s.

□ John Bugg, Jnr., with a group of mentally and physically handicapped children on the second morning of the fair. The showmen give the deprived youngsters free rides and refreshments. They are pictured on the new Tahiti Express owned by John Bugg.

58. Theodore Jr. and Theodore Whyatt with Robert Summers. Courtesy of Keith Hamilton.

59. Meteorite at Witham Fair, October 2009, courtesy of Paul Hodges.

60. Paris Whyatt attending a bouncy slide,
Great Yarmouth Street Fair, 2010.